An Introduction to Interpersonal Communication

James C. McCroskey
Illinois State University

Carl E. Larson
University of Denver

Mark L. Knapp
Purdue University

Prentice-Hall, Inc., *Englewood Cliffs, New Jersey*

13-485425-X

Library of Congress Catalog Card Number: 71–126966

Printed in the
United States of America.

Current printing (last number):

10 9 8 7 6 5 4 3 2 1

Prentice-Hall International, Inc.,
London
Prentice-Hall of Australia, Pty. Ltd.,
Sydney
Prentice-Hall of Canada, Ltd., *Toronto*
Prentice-Hall of India Private Limited,
New Delhi
Prentice-Hall of Japan, Inc., *Tokyo*

Preface

A wise old sage is alleged to have said "A book should never be written by three authors." An examination of a few three-authored books will indicate that the old sage had an essentially good thought. Therefore, it was with more than a few qualms that we decided to prepare this volume. Our decision to embark upon such threatening waters was based on two considerations: We felt there was a major need in the field of communication for a work of this type, and we felt that with our diverse backgrounds we could write a better book collectively than any one of us could alone. Whether the results of our combined efforts are worthy is a matter for your judgment.

This book is divided into four sections. The first attempts to define and describe the communication process as we see it. Several models are presented which should help you visualize this complex phenomonon. The second section focuses on the primary outcomes of interpersonal communication: information acquisition, attraction, and influence. While we recognize that these outcomes are not separable in actual communication transactions, we have separated them in this section so that we could examine each in more detail, in what we hope is a less confusing context.

The third section concentrates on the three most important variables in interpersonal communication: the source, the receiver, and the messages —both verbal and nonverbal. The limitations each imposes on interpersonal communication transactions are considered and the related research is summarized and interpreted. After having dissected interpersonal communication and looked at its constituent parts, we attempt to put it back together again in Section IV by considering interpersonal communication in its three most common contexts: in marriage, on the job, and as a part of the mass communication process. Research and theory relating to each of these contexts is summarized and an attempt is made to indicate the implications of this material for everyday use.

The approach employed in this book is descriptive. We have attempted to avoid platitudinous prescription. Where we have made suggestions for practice, the suggestions have been based on our interpretation of the results of behavioral research. Thus, this is not a "how-to-do-it" book. For that, we offer no apology.

It is difficult for a single author to acknowledge all of the people who have influenced his thinking. For three authors, it is impossible. We would, however, like to acknowledge the contributions of several groups of people: our former professors and graduate student colleagues at Pennsylvania State University and the University of Kansas; our former colleagues at Michigan State University and the University of Wisconsin-Milwaukee; and our present colleagues at Illinois State University, the University of Denver, and Purdue University.

It is customary to acknowledge the assistance of one's spouse in the preface of a book. This is a fine tradition. We gratefully acknowledge the assistance of the three charming ladies who are the spice in our lives. We trust they will read Chapter 9.

J.C.M. / C.E.L. / M.L.K.

Contents

An Introduction to Interpersonal Communication

Introduction

Chapter 1

The Interpersonal Communication Process

Man is a communicating animal. What we call "civilization" has been achieved by man through communication and is dependent on communication for its continuance. Our daily lives are filled with one communication experience after another. From the moment we arise in the morning until we go to sleep at night we are immersed in a sea of communication. Our very existence, to say nothing of our happiness and professional success, depends on communication.

All right, let's grant that communication is important. Just what does "communication" mean? Like any other word, it means whatever people say it means. Also, like other words, not all people have the same thing in mind when they use the word "communication." The purpose of this chapter is to examine some of the different interpretations people give the word so that we will have arrived at a common meaning for the term as we proceed through later chapters.

The Dimensions of Communication

Transmission vs. Stimulation

One of the main distinctions between the ways people look at communication is in terms of whether it is a process concerned with the transmission and reception of messages or with the effect of messages on people. The transmission approach to communication is represented by such industries as the telephone and telegraph companies. Their concern is with taking a message from one place and reproducing it in another. Human beings, of course, are involved. But the significant element in transmission-oriented communication is the process of conducting the message that people create. And we can say that communication is successful, from the transmission vantage point, if it is technically possible to pick out a message in one locality, carry it across the air or wires to another locality, and recreate a semblance of that message. The telephone industry has succeeded as a communication medium if John can pick up the telephone and say "hello," and Mary can pick up a different telephone and hear him say it. Whether the "hello" means different things to John and Mary is not relevant. The only thing that *is* relevant is whether or not the message per se, "hello," is transmitted and received.

This book approaches human communication from the aspect of stimulation. Our concern is not merely whether another person receives our message; we are concerned also with what that message means to the other person. When we say "good morning," we have a desire to convey some type of thought to the other person. Communication, then, from the stimulation point of view, can be considered successful only when our words evoke in the other person's mind a thought somewhat similar to the one we had when we said "good morning." The important thing to remember here is that messages do not contain meaning. Meanings are in people, not in messages. That this is so, we will attempt to show in this chapter. We will try to establish a shared meaning for the term "communication" as it applies to us, the authors, and to you, our readers. Our publisher, Prentice-Hall, is functioning as a transmitter of the authors' messages to the potential receivers, namely our readers. The publisher's concern is accurate technical transmission of the message. The authors' primary concern, however, is to develop for their readers shared meanings for the messages contained in the book. It is important that you remember the distinction between transmission and stimulation while reading this book. Whenever we refer to interpersonal communication, we will be referring to the process of one individual stimulating meaning in the mind of another individual by means of some kind of message.

Purposeful vs. Accidental Communication

The second extremely important distinction between the way people use the term "communication" is whether or not it refers to a purposeful transaction. Although we communicate with other people throughout our lives, we are often totally unaware that we are doing so. At other times we are very much aware that we are communicating and are consciously controlling our emission of messages in order to determine what kind of communication will result. Accidental communication is not unlike purposeful communication in its essential process. Both types of communication occur as a result of a source transmitting certain messages that stimulate meanings in the minds of receivers. Accidental communication, however, often can interfere with what we would *like* to communicate to another individual. Hall, in his book *The Silent Language* (1959), gives an example of this when he discusses what can happen in interpersonal communication between Latin and North Americans. Latin Americans and North Americans have a cultural difference that manifests itself in how closely they stand opposite one another in everyday conversation. The Latin American tends to stand closer to the other person than does the North American. Thus, when people from these two different cultures or backgrounds stand and talk with one another it is not uncommon to see the North American continuously backing away from the Latin American, and the Latin American continuously moving toward the North American. Each is unconsciously trying to establish what he considers the appropriate distance for conversation. While doing so, however, each may accidentally communicate certain feelings to the other person. The Latin American may perceive the North American as being distant and aloof because he keeps backing away. The North American may perceive the Latin American as pushy and aggressive because he keeps trying to come closer. Neither of the two intends this type of communication—it occurs by "accident." The impact such accidental communication creates can frequently be much greater than that of the communication that results from words actually spoken.

Throughout this book, unless specifically noted, when we use the term "communication," we shall be referring to the process of one individual *intentionally* trying to stimulate meaning in the mind of another individual. Thus we are approaching communication from the "stimulation" and "purposeful" vantage points. We should not, however, forget the other dimensions of communication. From time to time we will specifically refer to these dimensions.

Variables in Communication

The following sections of this chapter will be devoted to a variety of models of the communication process. Each of these models has been designed to provide insight into the workings of that process. Models are used extensively in a wide range of professions and vocations. Most people are familiar with the kind of models our children play with, such as model airplanes, which physically represent the larger, real-life version. This type of model has been referred to as an "iconic" model (Churchman, Ackoff, and Arnoff, 1957). Since communication is a process rather than a static thing, it is of course impossible for us to present an iconic model of communication. Therefore, the models that we will discuss are verbal, pictorial models. The purpose of the discussion of models is to help us understand the dynamics of the communication process. But first we need a rudimentary understanding of the terms included in the models. Almost all models of communication include certain variables. Therefore, before we look at specific models we will talk about these variables in order to gain a preliminary understanding of what they are.

Source

Almost all models of communication include the source variable. By "source" is meant the originator of the message in communication. The source may be a single person, a group of people, or even an institution. Thus, the source may be one of us, it may be the city council, or it may be the United States Department of Labor.

Message

By "message" is meant the stimulus that the source transmits to the receiver. This message may be either verbal or nonverbal. Verbal messages include words, phrases, and sentences. Nonverbal messages include a wide variety of stimuli. Such messages may include tone of voice, physical actions of the source, pictures, and the like. When one engages in oral communication, both verbal and nonverbal elements are necessarily present. And even if the message is transmitted on a telephone wire so that the receiver cannot see the source, the tone of voice would be a nonverbal stimulus. In written communication, such as a letter to a friend, our handwriting, while it presents words, also presents nonverbal stimuli in the way we shape the letters of the alphabet. Neat handwriting provides one kind of message, sloppy handwriting a different kind. The type of stationery we employ also provides a message.

Channel

The channel is the means of conveyance of the stimuli the source creates to the receiver. Channels include airwaves, light waves, and the like. The various channels through which information is received will be considered in Chapter 2.

Receiver

The receiver is the destination for the message. It is the individual who receives the simuli transmitted by the source and develops meaning in his mind as a result. All people are receivers of communication.

Models of Communication

The Shannon and Weaver Model

The Shannon and Weaver (1949) model of communication was one of the first models developed (see Fig. 1.1). It is often referred to as the telephone model because it explains telephone communication so easily. In this model communication begins with a source who creates a message and transmits it (by such means as a telephone speaker) through a channel (such as a telephone wire and sound waves) to a receiver (such as a telephone receiver) which recreates the message so that another person (the destination) can receive it. One of the very important elements included in the Shannon and Weaver model is the concept of "noise." "Noise" in this model refers to disturbances in the channel that may interfere with the signal transmitted and thus produce a different signal, which is the one then received. Later models have expanded on the concept of noise.

The Shannon and Weaver model can also be thought of as a model of human communication. We may think of the information source as the source who creates the message, his vocal apparatus as the transmitter, the sound waves being that which is transmitted, the air as the channel with the accompanying noise interference, the hearing mechanism of the person he is communicating with as the receiver, and the destination as what we have defined as receiver above. Viewed in this way this model is a fairly good representation of the communication process. However, it is over-

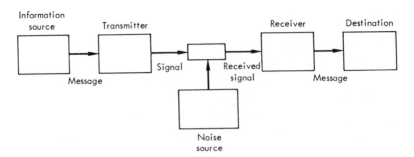

Figure 1.1 The Shannon and Weaver Model

Reprinted from *The Mathematical Theory of Communication* by C. E. Shannon and W. Weaver, (Urbana: University of Illinois Press, 1949), p. 98, by permission of the publisher.

simplified and omits some elements which we consider of great importance in interpersonal communication, and which we will discuss later.

The Lasswell Model

Lasswell (1948) presented a strictly verbal model and although it includes several important elements omitted by Shannon and Weaver, it still is a very limited model of the communication process. Lasswell's model may take the form of a question: "*Who* says *what* to *whom* through what *channels* with what *effect?*" To begin with, Lasswell calls attention to "who" introduces the message into communication. He also stresses "to whom" in his verbal model. In this way he points out that the nature of the source and the nature of the receiver are significant factors in the communication process. Finally, Lasswell introduces the element of "effect" into his model. Purposeful communication is designed to achieve effects in the minds of receivers. That is really what communication is all about. The Lasswell model, therefore, although very brief, introduces several highly significant variables in the communication process. Several later models were built upon Lasswell's contributions.

The SMCR Model

The SMCR model was first presented by Berlo (1960). It encompasses a representation of the four vital elements of communication discussed earlier: source, message, channel, and receiver (see Fig. 1.2). In his

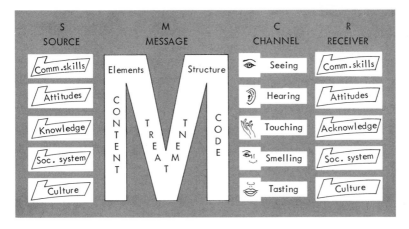

Figure 1.2 The SMCR Model

Reprinted from *The Process of Communication* by David K. Berlo. Copyright © 1960 by Holt, Rinehart and Winston, Inc. Reprinted by permission of Holt, Rinehart and Winston, Inc.

model Berlo notes several elements that will affect the communication of sources and receivers; notably their communication skills, their attitudes, their knowledge, the social system under which they live, and their cultural environment. The weaknesses of the SMCR model are that it fails to give the viewer the feeling of the communication process and that several important elements (noise, for example) are not apparent in the model.

The Carroll Model

Carroll (1955) has provided a model of purposeful communication. It is a very simple model (see Fig. 1.3) but indicates most of the important parts of the communication process. This model notes that at the outset of communication the source (speaker) has certain intention. As the target of communication Carroll notes the interpretive behavior of the receiver

Intentive behavior of speaker	Encoding behavior of speaker	Message	Decoding behavior of hearer	Interpretive behavior of hearer

Figure 1.3 The Carroll Model

(hearer). He also includes two terms that we have not discussed previously—encoding and decoding. By encoding is meant the process of translating an already conceived idea into a message appropriate for transmission. By decoding is meant the process of taking the stimuli that have been received and interpreting their meaning.

The McCroskey Model

The McCroskey (1968) model (see Fig. 1.4) is an expansion of the Carroll model. It includes the elements noted by Carroll, the concept of noise as introduced by Shannon and Weaver, and an element we have not observed in the preceding models—that of feedback. This model, like the

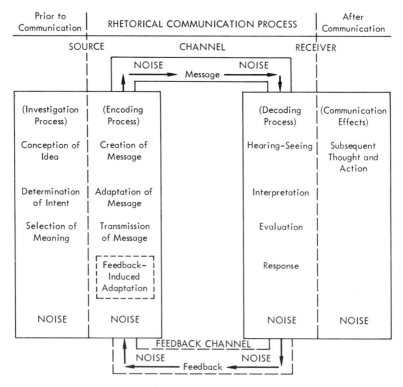

Figure 1.4 The McCroskey Model

Reprinted from *An Introduction to Rhetorical Communication* by James C. McCroskey, Englewood Cliffs, N.J.: Prentice-Hall, Inc., 1968, with permission from the publisher.

Carroll model, is one of intentional communication. It includes the source and the receiver but distinguishes that which occurs during communication from that which occurs in the source prior to communication and what occurs in the receiver after communication.

The inclusion of noise in this model is broader than that noted by Shannon and Weaver. This model indicates that noise can appear not only in the primary channel but also in the source, in the receiver, and in the feedback channel. The noise in the source, in what is referred to as the "investigation process," includes confused thinking in the source prior to communication. This type of noise prevents the communicator from clearly imparting his idea to his receiver because he doesn't understand it himself. The causes of this kind of noise are such things as education, background, past experiences, etc. Other factors contributing to this kind of noise are people's behavioral characteristics—their attitudes and prejudices. The noise noted in the *encoding process* in this model refers to things the communicator does in the process of developing a message for transmission that may interfere with the desired interpretation of that message. Included in this type of noise are such things as choosing inappropriate language or tone of expression of the message.

The noise noted in the *decoding process* includes such things as the attitudes of the receiver, his background, and his experiences. As we mentioned before, meanings are not in messages but are in people. Thus, the experiences of the receiver prior to a given communication event may have a major influence on how he will interpret it. He may, of course, interpret the message as intended, but it is equally possible that the receiver's experiences become noise elements. The noise noted in the "communication effects" area of the model refers to things that occur subsequent to an individual communication event, such as further communication with other sources. Finally, the noise in the feedback channel is very similar to the noise in the primary channel between the source and receiver, the type of noise to which Shannon and Weaver referred.

The concept of feedback in this model is an extremely important one for the understanding of the communication process. "Feedback" is a term that has been borrowed from the electronics field where it refers to a stimulus getting back into the system and recycling. We have all experienced this at one time or another when we have heard the squeal on a public address system. The sound goes through the microphone which is amplified by the speaker system and gets back into the microphone system. Feedback, as used in the area of human communication, refers to the response that a receiver may make to a source's communication, a response the source can perceive and which can subsequently cause him to modify his messages. This feedback, of course, is not present in all communication, but normally occurs in face-to-face interpersonal communication.

The Osgood Model

The model developed by Osgood (1954) does not follow the pattern of our previous models—from source through channel to receiver. This model notes that communication is a dynamic process and that a given communication event may begin with receiving stimuli (see Fig. 1.5). Osgood notes that messages are received by people and are interpreted through the decoding process and that these messages may cause the individual to become a source and encode messages for other receivers. The dynamics of the communication process are in evidence here. Because of this type of dynamic relationship between sources and receivers a person may be a source one moment, a receiver the next and, in turn, a source the following moment. This is particularly true in interpersonal communication.

Interpersonal Communication Models

Figure 1.6 presents the basic model of interpersonal communication occurring between two people. This model notes that each serves both as source and as receiver. It also shows the process of movement from source to receiver or from receiver to source. If we begin at an arbitrary point in person A with idea formation, we notice that the idea is encoded into a message that is transmitted through channel A → B to person B who functions as a receiver. Person B decodes the message and responds. This response contributes to idea formation in person B. The formation of ideas in person

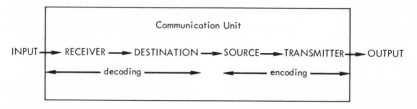

Figure 1.5 The Osgood Model

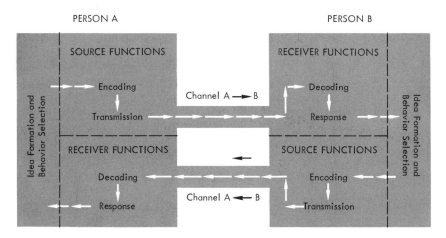

Figure 1.6 Two-Person Interpersonal Communication Model

B may cause him to function as a source and encode a message that he transmits through channel A ← B to person A who then functions as a receiver. He decodes the message from person B and responds to that message. This response in turn may affect his idea formation and cause him to function again as a source and to encode and transmit further messages. This is potentially a perpetual cycle, which may be begun at any point. If the two persons communicating are not in immediate proximity to each other, person A may encode a relatively extensive message and transmit it to person B before he receives any responding communication from person B. However, in a face-to-face interactive setting, the roles of source and receiver may shift much more rapidly, and the message that person A transmits to person B may be altered through person B's messages that A receives. We may think of the communication from person B to person A in the same context as feedback was considered in the earlier McCroskey model. However, we need not be concerned with feedback as such if we take cognizance of the fact that the person who starts out as receiver in interpersonal communication is unlikely to be only a receiver in the communication transaction. Feedback consists merely of messages transmitted by a source, whom we formerly called a receiver, to a receiver, whom we formerly called a source.

Figure 1.7 presents a model of interpersonal communication showing what occurs when more than two individuals are engaged in interpersonal communication simultaneously, as, for example, in any small group or

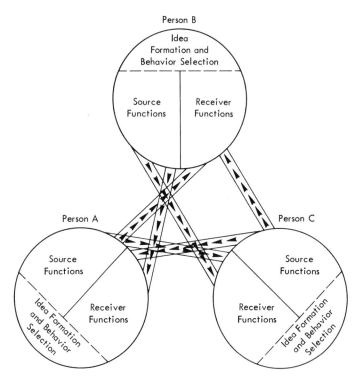

Figure 1.7 Multiple-Person Interpersonal Communication Model

conference setting. As the figures notes, a variety of channels are opened when more than two people are present. In fact, as the number of people increases arithmetically, the number of channels progresses geometrically. So that with three people we now have six channels of communication. The essential communication process, however, remains relatively unchanged, except that the communication between person B and person C may affect the communication between persons A and B or between persons A and C. The communication between two other persons also may be perceived as noise by a third person. This perception may be valid because the communication between these two persons may reduce the effectiveness of the communication of the third person.

Figure 1.8 presents a model of interpersonal communication appropriate for person-to-group communication. Very often one person will attempt to communicate with many people simultaneously. This occurs in what we normally call public speaking as well as in communication through the

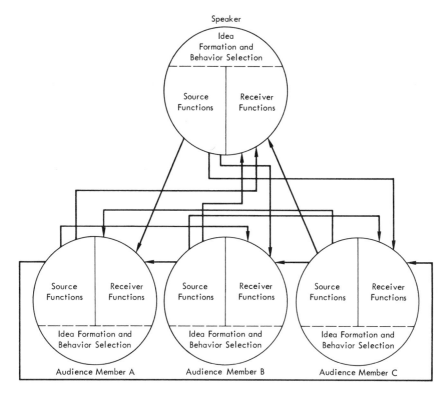

Figure 1.8 Person-to-Group Interpersonal Communication Model

mass media—radio, television, newspapers, etc. Because of the complexity of this process our model shows channels as lines with terminal arrows. The model represents a live person-to-group communication setting, not a situation involving the mass media. Under such conditions the primary source both transmits and receives messages from the primary receivers. Were we to substitute the mass media for the group of people, we would break the channel from primary receiver to primary source. We do not, however, necessarily break the channels that exist among primary receivers. Later we will consider the impact the media have on interpersonal communication, both as a deterrent and as a stimulus. At this point we merely wish to note that the process of communication does not change essentially from the simplest transaction, person-to-person, to the most complex transaction, mediated person-to-group communication.

Examination of the models has shown us several basic concepts that are important for us to remember: First, in interpersonal communication each individual involved will function as both a source and a receiver of communication. Second, the messages that we receive at one point in time will effect our idea formation and behavior and subsequently determine to some extent what, whether, and when we will attempt to communicate again. Third, the concept of noise. Noise is any element that interferes with the communication. If it is severe, the meaning that the source wants to convey to the receiver will not be stimulated by the source's message. To a large extent the success of communication is determined by the degree to which noise is overcome or controlled.

This chapter was intended to give you a general overview of the communication process. The following chapters will consider the variables in interpersonal communication in considerably more detail.

References

Berlo, D. K., *The Process of Communication*. New York: Holt, Rinehart & Winston, Inc., 1960.

Carroll, J. B., *The Study of Language*. Cambridge, Mass.: Harvard University Press, 1955.

Churchman, C. W., R. L. Ackoff, and E. L. Arnoff, *Introduction to Operations Research*. New York: John Wiley & Sons, Inc., 1957.

Hall, E. T., *The Silent Language*. Greenwich, Conn.: Fawcett Publications, Inc., 1959.

Lasswell, H. D., "The Structure and Function of Communications in Society," in *The Communication of Ideas*, ed. L. Bryson. New York: Harper & Row, Publishers, 1948.

McCroskey, J. C., *An Introduction to Rhetorical Communication*. Englewood Cliffs, N.J.: Prentice-Hall, Inc., 1968.

Osgood, C. E., ed., "Psycholinguistics: A Survey of Theory and Research Problems," *Journal of Abnormal and Social Psychology*, 49 (1954), Morton Prince Memorial Supplement.

Shannon, C. E., and W. Weaver, *The Mathematical Theory of Communication*. Urbana: University of Illinois Press, 1949.

Principal Outcomes of Interpersonal Communication

Much has been said and written about "how to communicate effectively." Too frequently "effective communication" is regarded as a single-faceted phenomenon. Effective communication, however, is one of those phrases that is misleading in its simplicity. There is a wide range of outcomes any one of which might warrant the judgment that communication between two people has been "effective." In some cases communication will have been effective if the individuals involved have arrived at a greater mutual understanding of attitudes, sentiments, opinions, etc. In other situations, communication will have been effective if the attitudes or beliefs of one or both parties change as a consequence of the interpersonal encounter. In still other situations, we are interested primarily in being liked or evaluated favorably by another. We could go on at great lengths identifying other outcomes, any one of which might be considered effective communication.

Section II is based upon the following assumptions: (1) The traditional and legitimate way of discussing interpersonal communication is in terms of those things that increase or decrease the probabilities of eliciting certain outcomes. (2) Some of the principal outcomes emphasized in interpersonal communication are accuracy (the extent to which two people understand each other), attraction (the extent to which two people like each other), and influence (the extent to which attitudes and beliefs are changed by the communicative encounter).

Chapter 2 discusses certain variables and the extent to which they contribute toward achieving accuracy in interpersonal communication. Chapter 3 discusses relationships between interpersonal communication and the development and maintenance of interpersonal attraction. Chapter 4 discusses to what degree variables are likely to influence attitudes, beliefs, and values in communicative encounters.

Accuracy and Understanding

"No matter what I say to that kid, I can't make him understand that. . . ."

"Nobody seems to understand me. . . ."

Greater understanding among men is one of the loud and persistent cries of this generation. Such a plea addresses itself to one of the most fundamental aspects in the study of communication—that of achieving a greater correspondence between messages sent and messages received. Simply, it is a matter of achieving greater accuracy—or greater understanding.

We say *greater* accuracy rather than *total* accuracy because achieving 100 percent accuracy between communicator and receiver is not possible—and never will be. Total accuracy in communication would require that both parties have a history of identical experiences in all things they discuss. Only then could they perceive exactly the same meaning for a given message, and only then would we have total accuracy, total understanding, or perfect communication. As long as people have different experiences we will never be able to evoke exactly the same idea in the listener's mind as the one we construct in our own mind. Fortunately, total accuracy is not necessary in order to function effectively. Effective communication can be accomplished by striving for the highest possible degree of accuracy (short of 100 percent) in each situation. To fully understand interpersonal encounters in which the expected outcome is accuracy and understanding, one must first examine the nature of the symbol system we use in such encounters.

We use words when we communicate with one another through verbal channels. Words are symbols. They are things that stand for or represent "something else." The "something else" is called a referent—the thing being referred to by the word. For instance, the word "rhino" stands for and refers to a particular type of heavy, horned animal found in Africa and parts of Asia—and many American zoos. If we were unable to discuss the concept "rhino" using symbols, it would be necessary to take a rhinoceros with us every time we wanted to talk about one. Korzybski (1933) suggested that this relationship between a symbol and its referent was much like the relationship between a map and the actual territory it represents.

The accuracy of communication is sometimes affected by the perception of this relationship of the referent's symbol to the actual referent itself. The label attached to the referent elicits a response that ignores close examination of the referent. Hundreds of students at the University of Wisconsin, Milwaukee, were the subjects of an experiment reportedly first tried by Irving Lee at Northwestern University. In this experiment the students received a cookie when they entered class, and before the lecture began most students had eaten the cookies. Ratings of cookie quality were taken that invariably indicated that about 95 percent of the students felt the cookie was either good or excellent. Then the students were told that the ingredients contained an oatmeal cookie base with the crushed biscuits from a medium-sized box of popular dog food replacing the oatmeal. As expected, the reaction was far from passive, but the experiment did serve to stimulate thinking about what the tasters were responding to—the label "dog biscuit cookies" or the cookies themselves.

Haney (1960) reports a similar experience with Jay's Potato Chip Company around the time of World War II. At that time the company was known as Mrs. Japp's Potato Chips. The label apparently kept many people from examining the quality of the potato chips themselves—the referent. Sales declined until the name change was made; then sales began to rise again.

Scientists are trained in maintaining a high level of objectivity—that is, their experiments should reflect a minimum amount of map-territory confusion. The following events reported by Klineberg (1954) make it clear that no one is exempt from such behavior.

> In connection with the qualitative characteristics of the brain, the early investigations of Bean (1906) have focused attention upon possible Negro-white differences. In a series of studies Bean arrived at the conclusion that the frontal area of the brain was less well-

developed in the Negro than in the white, and the posterior area better developed. He believed that this difference paralleled the "known fact" that the Negro is inferior in the higher intellectual functions and superior in those concerned with rhythm and sense perception. Another important difference was in the depth of the convolutions of the cortex, those of the Negro being much shallower and more "childlike" than those of the white. There were also differences in the shape of the *corpus callosum*, which connects the two hemispheres of the cerebrum, and in the temporal lobe, but these were not regarded as having any direct phychological significance. It happened that these studies were carried out at Johns Hopkins University under the direction of Professor Mall, head of the Department of Anatomy. Mall (1909) was for some reason uncertain of Bean's results, and he repeated the whole study on the same collection of brains on which Bean had worked; he took the precaution however, of comparing the brains without knowing in advance which were Negro and which were white. When he and his associates placed in one group those brains which had rich convolutions, and in another those with convolutions which were shallow, they found exactly the same proportions of Negro and white brains in the two groups. When further they measured the size of the frontal and posterior lobes in the two groups of brains, they found no difference in their relative extent. As a consequence, Mall came to the conclusion that Bean's findings had no basis in fact, and that it had not been demonstrated that Negro brains differed in any essential manner from those of whites.

Intellectually, we may agree that *words are not the things they represent.* As you read this book, detached from a given social situation, it is an easy concept to grasp. In actual practice it is not always so easy. The words used to label various objects and behaviors may have a profound influence on the responses—and ultimately the communication accuracy—between two people. The following news release (*Milwaukee Journal*, 1968) represents a concern for this kind of behavior on an international level:

United Nations, N.Y.—AP—In an effort to combat racial prejudice, a group of UN experts is urging a sweeping revision of the terminology used by teachers, mass media and others dealing with race.

Words such as Negro, primitive, savage, backward, colored, bushman and uncivilized would be banned as either "contemptuous, unjust or inadequate." They were described as aftereffects of colonialism.

The recommendations are contained in a study by a group assembled in Paris at the invitation of the UN educational, scientific and cultural organization (UNESCO) to work out plans to improve educational efforts against discrimination.

The experts did not say what words should be used to describe black people and others referred to by the words.

The report said, however, that these terms were "so charged with emotive potential that their use, with or without conscious pejorative intent, to describe or characterize certain ethnic, social or religious groups, generally provoked an adverse reaction.

The report said that even the term "race" should be used with care since its scientific validity was debatable and it "often served to perpetuate prejudice."

The experts suggested: The word "tribe" should be used sparingly, since most population groups referred to by this term have ceased to be tribes or are losing their tribal character.

A "native" should be called "inhabitant."

"Savanna" is preferable to "jungle."

The new countries should be described as "developing" rather than "underdeveloped."

The Chicago policemen at the 1968 Democratic Convention are a good case study in the myth that "sticks and stones may break my bones, but words will never hurt me." Words apparently had a tremendous impact on their ultimate behavior. They reacted violently to the obscenities from young girls and the persistent shouts of "Nazi Pigs" from the demonstrators. Clearly, *meanings do not lie in words at all—but in us.*

Some of the symbol-referent problems contributing to misunderstandings and inaccuracies are related to the nature of the referents involved. In some cases it is possible to achieve greater accuracy (greater agreement on meaning) because the referent, or territory, is structurally simple and concrete in nature. Thus, objects like chairs, tables, rhinos, and certain mathematical and technical terms seem to provide the greatest potential for common agreement on their meanings. Even with such relatively concrete and simple concepts—many with visible referents—total accuracy is not possible. We cannot cognitively process all the stimuli from any one of these objects so we select those stimuli that seem important to us and filter out all others. The image elicited in the mind of the South African game conservationist for the concept "rhino" would be different from the image evoked in the mind of a lifelong resident of Intercourse, Pennsylvania. Reportedly, in an executive training program, trainees were kept busy for three hours listing the characteristics of a piece of chalk. When they finished, the trainer pointed out the numerous things that they might have added to their list. Thus, in conversation, a simple object—such as a piece of chalk—may evoke any combination of two or more of the hundreds of characteristics it possesses.

Adding to the complexity of our symbol system are many words we use that have no concrete referent—nothing visible—nothing that can be easily felt, examined, measured, and tested. These words represent abstract concepts such as beauty, truth, love—and communication. In this case, the referent is entirely grounded in the personal experiences of each person, and in most cases is not completely stable. As new information is obtained about a concept, the referent becomes slightly different. The examples of misunderstandings engendered by symbols with abstract referents are found daily in our newspapers: "law and order" as seen by ghetto residents and law enforcement groups; "peace" as seen by the United States, Russia, North Viet Nam, South Viet Nam, antiwar protesters, and the war "hawks"; "religion," "love," "success," and "honesty," as seen by teenagers and their parents.

Sometimes the complexity of the referent makes the encoding process a difficult one. It is not easy to explain the color of the grass in my yard in August. It is a brownish-yellow-green. Encoding complex physical features and behavioral patterns is equally difficult and increases the chances for error in the communication process. This difficulty in encoding may cause some persons to filter through the complexities until they can deal with a simple concept. For example, "My wife's hair is, well, it's sorta brown . . . you know what I mean." Macy, Christie, and Luce (1953) conducted an experiment with marbles to illustrate this phenomenon. Subjects who tried to encode and communicate accurately the colors of marbles exhibited an averge rate of error of 10 percent for solid-color marbles; but for cloudy, indistinctly colored marbles the average rate of error was 50 percent.

With this brief introduction to the symbol system, let us examine the specific components of our interpersonal communication model to determine ways in which they may affect the accuracy of communication. The characteristics of the referent have already been discussed. Other components include: the communicator and the receiver, the communication channel(s), and the message. These factors will be discussed independently, but it should be clear that in most situations the degree of accuracy is determined by the combined effects of several of these factors.

Sender and Receiver

Physical and Psychological Equipment for Communicating

Perhaps the most obvious factor that might influence communication accuracy is the physical and psychological capability of the sender to send and the receiver to receive. Any neurological or sensory defect in the speaker or listener may increase the possibilities for inaccurate communication. A speaker may have difficulty with his articulatory mechanisms or a listener may have impaired hearing. In some instances this may only be a temporary condition brought about by such things as physical exhaustion or a high anxiety level. Under such conditions it is not unusual to manifest actual physical impairment of the equipment necessary for sending and receiving messages. In other situations, we are able to compensate for and adjust to factors that initially detract from accuracy. A case in point concerns what we refer to as "poor" vocal qualities (hoarseness, harshness, nasality, breathiness), poor pitch patterns, and other nonfluencies. With the exception of extreme cases, there will be an initial period of "getting used to" such sounds; then listening comprehension does not seem to be significantly affected. In one study, the stuttering of the sender was sufficiently adapted to by the listeners so that it did not significantly interfere with reception of the speaker's message (Petrie, 1963).

Mehrabian and Reed (1968) hypothesize that communication accuracy is also related to the lowest level of cognitive development (or cognitive complexity) represented by a member of the interacting pair—particularly with complex referents. One measure of cognitive complexity is represented by Vannoy's (1965) factor analytic study, which associated cognitive complexity with "a more varied and possibly more equivocal interpretation of experience" and with being able to differentiate one's own view of things from the view others might have. To illustrate this concept, Mehrabian and Reed assume that age is one index of cognitive development. Thus, they would predict that children are less accurate in their communication efforts than adults, and in situations involving child-adult pairs, the degree of accuracy will seek the lower level—represented by the child.

Cultural and Environmental Experience

Earlier we discussed our inability to achieve 100 percent accuracy due to each person's individual experiences with the objects and concepts about which we communicate. It is not surprising then to find that individuals who have had similar cultural and environmental experiences tend to have some advantage in obtaining greater accuracy. In some educational programs for black students there is a demand for black instructors. The usual defense of such a demand concerns this matter of similar backgrounds and is phrased, "blacks can understand blacks." In some cases, the similarity of experiences can be a great aid in achieving understanding. Harms (1961) recorded the responses of speakers from three different socioeconomic groups to questions about their favorite movies, television shows, and books. He then deleted every fifth word of these responses and presented them to people representing each of the three groups. The subjects were asked to fill in the words that had been deleted. Accuracy was greatest when speaker and receiver were from the same socioeconomic group.

Vick and Wood (1969) showed the importance of similar past experiences in an experiment using a form of the "password" game. Subjects were asked to complete a questionnaire about family background (father's occupation, family size, parents' education), formative experience (urban vs. rural environment, locale in the U.S., and neighborhood characteristics), and education (degrees obtained and the field of study). Communicating pairs were formed of highly similar and highly dissimilar backgrounds. Pairs played "password" for one hour. Results showed that those with highly similar backgrounds were able to communicate significantly more accurately than those from highly dissimilar backgrounds. Runkel (1956) found that students and teachers who were determined to have greater "cognitive similarity" were also those who communicated most effectively with one another. People may have cognitive similarity without having extremely similar backgrounds—but it is clear that cognitive similarity does increase the possibility for accurate communication.

One's environmental experiences and the influence of his culture also affect his coding rules. Differences in coding rules may also affect accuracy. If sender and receiver speak different languages they will use different coding rules; if a German is trying to speak English, he may use German syntactical codes while using English words; two speakers may speak the same language, but differ in coding on nonverbal channels, or two speakers may agree on coding rules in all channels individually, but may have different rules when using combined channels. Mehrabian and Ferris (1967) propose that receivers may differentially weight the effects of communications presented in three channels—the verbal message, the tone of voice, and the facial expression. In this instance, facial expression was weighted most heavily in interpreting the message. It is possible that people from different cultural and subcultural environments have different weighting systems for interpreting such multichannel messages which, in turn, accounts for varying degrees of accuracy in communication with someone who has learned a different system.

Communication Skills

For both the sender and the receiver, communication skills broadly include all those processes involved in analyzing and adapting to each communication situation. Such skills represent a wide range of behaviors. The extent to which these skills are present and implemented affects the accuracy of the communication taking place. In the field of speech, it is popular to talk about a skill called "listening ability." Some researchers, however, feel that listening test scores are more indicative of a general mental ability than of a special integrated capacity called listening ability. The procedures employed in testing listening ability and the potential influence of the test itself on the listener's score make generalizations about listening ability as a specific skill in interpersonal communication difficult. Kelly (1967) notes another problem:

> The most apparent deficiency in research to date is the neglect of a very basic relationship; the typical behavior of persons listening to consecutive discourse under conditions of ordinary life compared to the listening behavior of like persons when taking a test.

One thing we do know about learning any skill—whether it is speaking, arithmetic, or listening—is that a major ingredient for improvement is a strongly felt desire to improve. If a deficiency in "listening ability" is perceived, it seems a logical first step would be to develop one's motivation to listen.

Sometimes inaccurate communication occurs because we behave in certain ways: We divide our attention or let our mind wander while we are trying to communicate. For instance, a new teacher, while trying to lecture, may be seriously pondering whether his students like him; or the woman who overhears her name mentioned in a nearby conversation may try to determine what is being said about her while she carries on a conversation on another subject with another group. We all have different degrees of competence for handling such situations. When there is an overload, accuracy is impaired.

Attitudes

The role played by communicator and receiver attitudes will be discussed at length in Chapter 4 in the context of persuasion, but it should be mentioned that these attitudes can also affect accuracy. If we perceive the speaker as extremely favorable or extremely unfavorable, we may let our image of him "release" us from listening. This, then, may cause misperceptions or distortions of the content presented.

This same phenomenon may occur with attitudes toward the message. If we agree with the general content or subject matter of a message under discussion, we may perceive it as being almost exactly the same as our own position (even though it is not); if we disagree with the general content of the same message, we may perceive it as the exact opposite of our position (even though it is not). Figure 2.1 illustrates such a situation.

Hovland, Harvey, and Sherif (1957) report a study which can be viewed

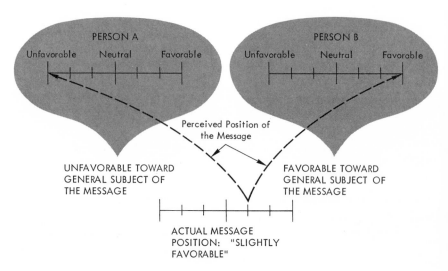

Figure 2.1

in the context of Fig. 2.1. The message concerned prohibition and was independently rated as a "moderately wet" position. Following the presentation of the message, subjects were asked to judge the speaker's opinion on the topic and to summarize the speaker's ideas. Subjects whose attitudes favored prohibition tended to look upon the message as being extremely wet rather than moderately wet.

These are only two examples of the many ways in which attitudes held by the sender and receiver can influence communication accuracy negatively. Both examples concerned distortions, inaccuracies, and misperceptions. Other attitudes such as "a deep concern to be understood by others" may act in a positive way.

Communication Channels

Availability of Channels

When messages are sent over more than one channel, you increase the redundancy—and at the same time, the accuracy. A boy is less likely to forget a girl if he can touch, smell, hear, and see her than if he were only able to hear her on the telephone. When you show a person a picture of an accident while telling him about it, you have increased the probabilities of being understood over a situation in which you could only present the description through the oral channel. The converse, then, is also true. You will decrease the probabilities for accuracy as you decrease the number of channels used for communicating a given message. For instance, if you were unable to see a person's smiling face when he greeted you with, "You ol' son of a bitch!" you might have a much different interpretation of his intended meaning. A brief but familiar dialogue reflects a concern for using more than one channel to increase accuracy.

"I've just got to let him know what I've done."

"Why don't you write him a letter?"

"Oh, I couldn't do that. I've got to explain it to him in person." Also implicit in this interaction is the desire by one person to be able to determine how the message will be received so that, if necessary, adjustments can be made. This is feedback.

Feedback

Feedback is the process by which the sender perceives how his message is being decoded and received. If he is not able to obtain information on how his message is being decoded, inaccuracies may occur and never be uncovered.

A classic study that resulted in the exposition of a number of feedback principles was that of Leavitt and Mueller (1951). A communicator was asked to describe a geometrical pattern (Fig. 2.2) to his audience. Audience members were then asked to draw what the speaker had described. The correspondence between the geometric pattern used by the sender and that drawn by the receiver was the measure of communication accuracy. There were four different feedback conditions. In the "zero feedback" condition speaker and audience were visibly separated, and the audience was asked not to provide any audible feedback for the speaker. In the "visible audience" condition, speaker and audience faced one another so that the speaker could react to nonverbal feedback cues. The third condition allowed the audience to ask questions that could be answered with yes or no. The final condition, "free feedback," permitted speaker and audience to talk freely to one another as needed. Results indicated the following: (1) Accuracy was highest under the free feedback condition; partial feedback was more accurate than no feedback; (2) as feedback increased, both sender

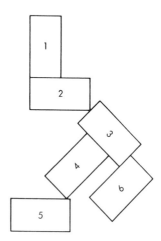

Figure 2.2

Reprinted from "Some Effects of Feedback on Communication" by H. J. Leavitt and Ronald A. H. Mueller in *Human Relations*, 4 (1951), 403, by permission of the publisher.

and receivers increased in confidence concerning their performance; (3) although zero feedback was the least accurate, it was the fastest method.

Just as we noted that the sender would do well to communicate through a variety of channels, it is also an aid to accuracy if feedback is available in a variety of channels. Faules (1967) found that accuracy increased as he added feedback channels—the optimum condition consisted of facial, vocal, and verbal cues; the least accurate condition consisted only of facial cues.

Although it is clear that accuracy in communication can be improved with optimum feedback conditions, there are times when we want to sacrifice accuracy in order to preserve our feelings. Few of us can tolerate continual evaluative feedback (accurate or not) concerning our statements, our manner of dress, or our ability to perform certain tasks.

Communication Noise in the Channel

"Noise" is a term frequently used in the study of communication to refer to any disturbance or interference impinging on the intended message, thereby significantly affecting comprehension on the part of the receiver. This perspective suggests that noise may occur in almost any phase of the communication process. In this section, we are primarily concerned about noise in the communication channels. The greater the source of noise, the less the accuracy in communication.

Noise may take the form of environmental sounds such as static on telephones or radios; it may be a speech problem such as stammering or stuttering; it may be an annoying or distracting mannerism such as a nervous twitch or a tendency to mumble; or it may be a distraction masking a message presented in visual channels outside the human organism.

One way of coping with noise is to eliminate its source. The noise created by some of the lines in Fig. 2.3 can be eliminated by placing a piece of

Figure 2.3

Reprinted from *This Week* Magazine by permission of the publisher.

paper across the top half of the figure. The visible bottom half should read, "nationality." Other sources of noise can only be reduced. Such reductions, though, can improve accuracy and understanding.

Multichannel messages tend to offset the effects of noise. Neely (1956) and others have reported that we get visual cues from the communicator's lips, which aid intelligibility.

In some cases, the effects of noise can be reduced considerably by changing the expectancies of the receiver. Fry (Cherry, 1957) made a Gramophone recording of two men holding a conversation, but their speech was distorted artificially so that it was almost unintelligible to listeners. After one playing of the record, listeners were informed that the speakers' discussion was on the subject of buying a new suit and referred to tailors, clothes, and styles. When the record was played a second time, most listeners were able to follow a high percentage of the conversation. Prior to the information about the recording's topic, the listener had to scan the whole range of human speech—all topics and words were a possibility—but having been given the hint, his range of possible messages was reduced and he developed his expectations around the key word "tailor." For example, Fig. 2.4 might just be a complex of lines . . .

Figure 2.4

Reprinted from *On
Human Communication*
by C. Cherry, New York:
Science Editions, by per-
mission of John Wiley &
Sons, Inc.

until you were told to look for something familiar . . . and finally, to look for a number.

Other methods for reducing the effects of noise will be discussed when we consider the nature of the message.

Rate of Information Processing

Information can be processed at a variety of speeds and this rate may vary for each individual and for each situation. Accuracy will certainly be increased if the receiver has some control over the speed at which he processes incoming information. If you've ever tried to read a book with another person you are familiar with that awkward moment when one of you is ready to turn the page and the other is savoring a particularly pleasurable passage halfway up the page. Programmed learning recognizes that not everyone learns at the same speed. Therefore, programmed materials are designed to give the learner control over his learning speed. In too many classrooms, students do not have such control and for some this detracts from the understanding that they should be gaining.

Another consideration, however, is that many of us can comprehend the spoken language at a much faster rate than that with which it is normally processed. In fact, Orr (1968) reports an experiment where subjects were allowed to vary their rates of presentation at will, and the average choice was one and one-half times normal speed. Recognizing that the ability to comprehend compressed or speeded speech varies substantially among people, Orr goes on to say:

> . . . clearly, humans find some degree of accelerated speech intelligible and comprehensible. There has been almost complete consistency in the research on this point. The exact degree of acceleration at which intelligibility and/or comprehension begin to decline significantly is a point of less agreement, though about 275–300 wpm seems to be about the right range. . . . (p. 288)

The Message

Redundancy

There are many reasons why people do not comprehend every word and idea the first time they hear it. The noise that exists in the message itself is one of them. One way of reducing noise in the message is to increase redundancy—or the repetition of a word, phrase, or idea. In the previous sentence, the clause following the dash was redundant. It repeated the same idea in slightly different words in order to make the concept clearer. When we repeat words, provide examples, use synonyms, analogies, or periodic summaries we are trying to increase redundancy—and accuracy. Accuracy will be increased if the redundancy does not go beyond what the receiver thinks he is capable of processing accurately. Too much redundancy may lead the receiver to think that the sender is "insulting his intelligence." Some of the humor in Arlo Guthrie's ballad "Alice's Restaurant" is found in its extreme redundancy—for example, "It all started four Thanksgivings ago—Four years ago on Thanksgiving Day." Ehrensberger's (1945) experimental results seem to add partial confirmation that there is a point of diminishing returns for redundancy in the message. He found that three spaced repetitions improved accuracy over the conditions containing only two repetitions, but that four repetitions did not seem to increase accuracy proportionally for the short speeches used in his study.

Fortunately, the structure of our language is highly redundant. This in itself assists our understanding in some instances. Shannon and Weaver (1949) calculated that the English language is 50 percent redundant if we consider its structure up to eight letters. If we adhere to the traditionally prescribed rules of sound and syntax for the English language you will note the tremendous prevalence of redundancy. If I tell you I am going to spell a word beginning with the letter *q* it is redundant to tell you that the next letter is *u*—you already guessed that when I told you what the first letter was. We also know that English belongs to a language family using a subject-predicate construction; we know that our sentence structure is based on an actor-action-actor sequence, just as the phonetic elements tend to be assembled on a "consonant-vowel-consonant" basis. If we follow syntactical rules, we will know the number, gender, and case of a noun even though it is garbled by noise if we hear the pronoun with which it is supposed to agree. Context also helps; if we hear only, "Fill up the . . . ," we begin to scan the range of things which can be filled up and which might be referred to in that given situation. Weaver and Strausbaugh (1964) even propose that a "reasonably intelligent person could guess up to 75 percent of a sentence you are thinking of from clues given only progressively." They explain it this way:

> Obviously, the sentence is quite unlikely to begin with the letter *x*. It is much more likely to begin with the letter *t*, since many of our sentences begin with the word *the*. If *t* is correct, the pattern of the languages makes *h* very highly probable for the second guess. Other letters are probable, too, but not so highly probable. If *h* turns out to be correct, the next guess might be *i*, *a*, *e*, *o*, or *u*. If *e* is the correct answer, the guesser will probably choose between *space* or *s*. *Space* is much more highly probable.

Thus far your guesser has been estimating phoneme frequencies. If the first word turns out to be *the*, his best guess is that you are now thinking of a noun, which will be the subject of the sentence. Now he is dealing with a different kind of context pattern, which we call verbal context. Words are arranged in regular ways—that is, in patterns. The article *the* precedes nouns, although not always directly. If the second word in our guesser's sentence does turn out to be a noun, let us say, *sun*, he will now expect a predicate, which is the other half of the most important feature of our lexical patterns. In most sentences the predicate follows the subject.

And so your guesser chooses a predicate. It might be *is*, but it might be *shines*, too. He weighs the probabilities (subjectively) and guesses. After a letter or two appears, he may know the whole word. And the farther he gets in the sentence, the more verbal context helps him. He knows what kinds of words to expect.

Organization

Many authors before us have noted man's apparent need to have things organized, and texts on public speaking are replete with suggestions on how to improve one's organization of a speech. It is argued that a well-organized speech will increase audience understanding. Thus far, however, research findings are far from consistent concerning organized speeches and almost nonexistent regarding organization of the less formal dialogue often found in interpersonal communication. Some experts feel the most that can be said is that if you want an idea to be remembered, present it either at the beginning or at the end. Thompson (1967) concluded from his review of research that: (*a*) climax and anticlimax methods of organization do not differ significantly in persuasiveness and probably do not differ in their effects on retention; (*b*) disorganization appears to affect comprehension in written communication, but effects on comprehension and effectiveness in oral communication are doubtful. Sharp and McClung (1966) found speakers with disorganized material to be less favorably perceived than those whose material was organized. In cases where organization seemed to help comprehension, the effects were short-lived and did not remain without being reinforced when measured a few weeks later.

Thompson suggests that in oral discourse the delivery of the message affords cues that permit listeners to comprehend disorganized material. He concludes by noting that in spoken dialogue it may not be so much a problem of ordering the units as it is one of clarity of thought and expression of the individual parts.

Probably the receiver's ability to structure the message for his own particular cognitive patterns is more important than the organization of the communication itself—particularly in interpersonal communication. Thus, while accuracy is certainly dependent on the receiver's level of intelligence, we are not sure that message organizational structure will significantly improve accuracy.

Forms of Emphasis

Accuracy can also be increased by using techniques that will emphasize and magnify the concept you want the receiver to understand. Under normal conditions, we may increase the loudness if we want to improve retention of a particular concept. In the late 1960s television advertising carried this concept to the ridiculous extreme. Recognizing the power of increasing the intensity of a stimulus, agencies would record the audio portion of the commercial at a high level. When the commercial was aired, the sheer volume attracted the viewer's attention. As time went on, though, almost every commercial was loud from beginning to end. In other words, all stimuli were again at the same intensity, and in order to regain the emphasis value, intensity either had to be increased or variety had to be injected into the sound level. Variety tends to maintain the attention of the receiver and having achieved this, the probabilities of accurate communication are increased.

An example of another method used to aid comprehension and retention of a particular idea is shown in this sentence: *This next point is an important one—you should read it carefully.* It is a form of reinforcement that accompanies the message. Sometimes a pause prior to the presentation of an idea can serve the same purpose.

A related form of reinforcement may derive from the behavior of the participants in the interaction. For example, if several members at a business conference make a written notation of an idea presented by the member who is speaking, it may give increased weight to the message, and others may also be induced to make a mental or written note of it.

Suggestions for Achieving Greater Accuracy

It is doubtful whether we could list all the factors that impinge on the interpersonal communication process and that affect accuracy and understanding—even if we wanted to. The factors we mentioned merely represent a beginning—an introduction. Other related factors will surely occur to you as you develop an analytical approach toward achieving greater accuracy and understanding. Some of these may include: the status of the speaker and receiver, the extent of their vocabulary, one's position in the sociocultural system, knowledge of the topic under discussion, and so on. One very obvious conclusion which we have reached after analyzing many communication situations is that inflexible, unvarying prescriptions for success in any situation are nearly impossible to establish. For this reason, any suggestions for success must be situational in nature, as the following list indicates:

A Communicator Wishing to Achieve Greater Accuracy Will:

A. have a desire to achieve greater accuracy and to understand the communication process more fully. He will analyze the listener, the situation, himself, and the special conditions of a particular communication event so he will be able to determine:

1. a realistic expectation for the degree of accuracy obtainable in a given situation.

2. the probable role of his own attitudes and those of the receiver toward the message, and toward each other.

3. the probable role of his own communication sending skills and the receiving skills of the listener.

4. an understanding of the sociocultural experiences of the receiver so adaptations can be made accordingly.

5. the probable response of the listener to certain ambiguous, complex, and emotion-laden symbols.

6. the channels available to him so that he can use as many channels as are needed for understanding.

7. ways of eliminating or reducing sources of noise if they are present.

8. ways of obtaining optimum feedback.

9. the optimum rate of transmission, given the information processing capacities of the channel and receiver.

10. the proper amount of redundancy for the message, given the knowledge and experiences of the listener.

11. the proper message structure and content, given the receiver's expectations.

12. the forms of emphasis that are needed for the message.

A Receiver Wishing to Achieve Greater Accuracy Will:

A. have a desire to achieve greater accuracy and to understand the communication process more fully. He will analyze the speaker, the situation, himself, and the special conditions of a particular communication event so he will be able to determine:

1. a realistic expectation for the degree of accuracy obtainable in this situation.

2. the probable role of his own attitudes and those of the sender toward the message, and toward each other.

3. the probable role of his own communication receiving skills and the sending skills of the communicator.

4. an understanding of the sociocultural experiences of the sender so that useful expectations can be established.

5. ways of eliminating or reducing sources of noise if they are present.

6. ways of providing useful feedback through as many channels as are necessary for understanding.

7. ways of avoiding excessive and immediate evaluative judgments—ways of suspending judgment until understanding is complete.

8. ways of directing his full attention to the speaker's message—ways of developing his motivation to listen.

References

Bean, R. B., "Some Racial Peculiarities of the Negro Brain," *American Journal of Anatomy*, 5 (1906), 353–432.

Cherry, C., *On Human Communication*. New York: Science Editions, 1957, p. 276.

Ehrensberger, R., "The Relative Effectiveness of Certain Forms of Emphasis in Public Speaking," *Speech Monographs*, 12 (1945), 94–111.

Faules, D., "The Relation of Communicator Skill to the Ability to Elicit and Interpret Feedback Under Four Conditions," *Journal of Communication*, 17 (1967), 362–71.

Haney, W. V., *Communication: Patterns and Incidents*. Homewood, Ill.: Richard D. Irwin, Inc., 1960, p. 196.

Harms, L. S., "Listener Comprehension of Speakers of Three Status Groups," *Language and Speech*, 4 (1961), 109–12.

Hovland, C. I., O. J. Harvey, and M. Sherif, "Assimilation and Contrast Efforts in Reactions to Communication and Attitude Change," *Journal of Abnormal and Social Psychology*, 55 (1957), 244–52.

Kelly, C. M., "Listening: Complex of Activities—*and* a Unitary Skill?" *Speech Monographs*, 34 (1967), 464. See also: Sam Duker and Charles Petrie, "What We Know About Listening: Continuation of a Controversy," *Journal of Communication*, 14 (1964), 245–52.

Klineberg, O., *Social Psychology*. New York: Henry Holt & Company, 1954. Cf. chapter entitled "Ethnic Differences."

Korzybski, A., *Science and Sanity*. Lancaster, Pa.: Science Press Printing Co., 1933.

Leavitt, H. J., and Ronald A. H. Mueller, "Some Effects of Feedback on Communication," *Human Relations*, 4 (1951), 401–10. See also: W. V. Haney, "A Comparative Study of Unilateral and Bilateral Communication," *Academy of Management Journal*, 7 (1964), 128–36.

Macy, J., L. S. Christie, and R. D. Luce, "Coding Noise in a Task-Oriented Group," *Journal of Abnormal and Social Psychology*, 28 (1953), 401–9.

Mall, F. P., "On Several Anatomical Characters of the Human Brain," *American Journal of Anatomy*, 9 (1909), 1–32.

Mehrabian, A., and S. R. Ferris, "Inference of Attitudes from Nonverbal Communication in Two Channels," *Journal of Consulting Psychology*, 31 (1967), 248–52.

Mehrabian, A., and H. Reed, "Some Determinants of Communication Accuracy," *Psychological Bulletin*, 70 (1968), 365–81.

Milwaukee Journal, "UN Experts Ask Care in Word Usage," September 30, 1968.

Neely, K. K., "Effect of Visual Factors on the Intelligibility of Speech," *Journal of the Acoustical Society of America*, 28 (1956) 1275–77. See also: W. H. Sumby and I. Pollack, "Visual Contribution to Speech

Intelligibility in Noise," *Journal of the Acoustical Society of America*, 26 (1954), 212–15.

Orr, D. B., "Time Compressed Speech—A Perspective," *Journal of Communication*, 18 (1968), 288–92.

Petrie, C., "Informative Speaking: A Summary and Bibliography of Related Research," *Speech Monographs*, 30 (1963), 79–91.

Runkel, P. J., "Cognitive Similarity in Facilitating Communication," *Sociometry*, 19 (1956), 178–91. See also: H. C. Triandis, "Cognitive Similarity and Communication in a Dyad," *Human Relations*, 13 (1960), 175–83.

Shannon, C., and W. Weaver, *The Mathematical Theory of Communication.* Urbana: University of Illinois Press, 1949, pp. 25–26.

Sharp, H., and T. McClung, "Effects of Organization on the Speaker's Ethos," *Speech Monographs*, 33 (1966), 182–83.

Thompson, W. H., *Quantitative Research in Public Address and Communication*, New York: Random House, Inc., 1967.

Vannoy, J. S., "Generality of Cognitive Complexity-Simplicity as a Personality Construct," *Journal of Personality and Social Psychology*, 2 (1965), 385–96.

Vick, C. F., and R. V. Wood, "Similarity of Past Experience and the Communication of Meaning," *Speech Monographs*, 36 (1969), 159–62.

Weaver, C. H., and W. L. Strausbaugh, *Fundamentals of Speech Communication*, New York: American Book Company, 1964, pp. 323–24. Copyright © 1964 by Litton Educational Publishing, Inc. by permission of Van Nostrand Reinhold Company.

Chapter 3

Attraction

Please bear with us while we try to make a point in a somewhat round-about way.

An interesting discovery has been made concerning the complex behavior of ants (Wilson, 1963). It relates to one small aspect of the very complicated organization that characterizes ant "societies." Consider the intricate pattern of tunnels through which thousands of ants travel as they go about their daily chores. You have probably never wondered what would happen if the bodies of some dead ants were to clog those underground tunnels.

It seems researchers have discovered that when an ant dies, its body emits substances that signal other ants that one of their brethren has passed away. Another ant encountering these signals "knows" that the dead ant must be removed from its present location and deposited on the pile of dead ants conveniently located so as not to interrupt the flow of traffic. The researchers were able to chemically duplicate these substances, which are called pheromones (a kind of chemical "odor"). They dabbed a little of these substances on a live ant and observed the reactions of the other ants. It seems that when the other ants encountered the live pheromone-"anointed" ant, they would immediately drag it to the pile of dead ants. No sooner had it landed there, than it would crawl back into the tunnels, where other ants would seize it and again dump it on the pile of dead ants. Again it would crawl back into the tunnel, and this cycle continued until the chemical substances wore off the body of the "living dead" ant.

The behavior of the ants can be described as an unmediated, necessary response to a property of an object. Given the occurrence of the signal, there seems to be nothing else the other ants can do except behave in narrowly prescribed patterns. These narrowly prescribed patterns characterize the behavior of a great many "lower" life forms. The human animal, on the other hand, is capable of controlling or regulating his responses to the properties of objects and to the properties of other human beings. The human animal is *capable* of regulating his response to the properties of other human beings, but there are times when we outdo the ants with respect to the narrowness of our response patterns and the persistence with which we reject those who possess certain properties.

Regardless of how haphazard and random much social communication appears to be, it is possible to identify systematic patterns that characterize relationships between interpersonal communication and the development and maintenance of interpersonal attraction. Indeed, it is sometimes surprising how systematic some of these patterns can be. For example, when we meet a newcomer to the faculty—be it at a meeting, a cocktail party, or a poker game—whenever the opportunity for informal social communication presents itself, he will invariably try to elicit answers to questions such as: What department do you teach in? Where have you taught before? What are your professional interests? Where did you get your degree? Where did you come from? Usually, this line of questioning will continue until the individual has elicited sufficient information to enable him to begin structuring his judgments of the other person.

The kinds of judgments with which we are presently concerned are judgments about whether we "like" another person, whether we desire to associate with or spend time with him, whether we "feel good" in his presence, etc. We call these sentiments "attraction," and we view attraction as one of the principal outcomes of interpersonal communication. There are, of course, other judgments that have important relationships to interpersonal communication. Chapter 5 discusses judgments concerning respect, trustworthiness, believability, and the like.

The bases underlying interpersonal attraction vary considerably from person to person. For example, I like people who are competitive, somewhat aggressive, inclined to be candid and even occasionally argumentative. However, such a person may not be attractive to you, but the odds are that you have some marked preferences of your own. Some of these may appear very reasonable to you, but somewhat bizarre to others. Consider the following exchange between two people: "I can't stand him." "How come?" "His butt's too big." Indeed, returning momentarily to the ants, we might profit from reflecting upon how similar we are to them in terms of our response to others on the basis of their "properties." Skin color, hair length, and dress style are but a few of the properties that have prompted rejection. Few of us are beyond worrying about our human "pheromones," body odors, and the commercial dramas constantly confronting us on television remind us that our success or failure may hinge on how we answer the crucial question, "Could it be . . . bad breath?"

We tend to view relationships between interpersonal communication and attraction as being more systematic than they might appear at first glance. Indeed, theory and research surrounding this topic will be deliberately simplified in the remainder of this chapter, and we will emphasize what we consider to be the important connections between communication and attraction. Berscheid and Walster's (1969) excellent summary of theoretical and empirical work on interpersonal attraction is worth investigating if you are especially interested in this particular aspect of interpersonal communication.

The systematic nature of our evaluative orientations toward others is illustrated in a different way through research conducted by Mehrabian (1968). Mehrabian has summarized and conducted investigations which suggest that we characteristically emit nonverbal cues indicating our evaluative orientations toward others. For example, we tend to have less eye contact with those we dislike; we tend to maintain greater physical distance when communicating with those we dislike; when seated, we tend to lean farther backward in the presence of those we dislike; and the orientation of our shoulders is one of turning slightly away from those we dislike. The systematic nature of interpersonal attraction is illustrated further by one of the findings of Priest and Sawyer (1967), who discovered among college students a kind of upper limit to the number of interpersonal attractions that may be formed. That is, even though the number of persons that the college students "knew" increased over time, the proportion of those people who were also "liked" decreased over time. At the very least this suggests a decreasing probability that new attractions will be formed at the same rate that new acquaintances are found. Horowitz (1966), in studying attraction among three thousand high school students, has gathered data illustrating the consistency with which people are either liked or disliked by other students of both sexes. Meyer and Barbour (1968), after investigating attraction patterns among children, concluded that the relative attractiveness of individuals varies little over situations, although the intensity of the attraction may vary considerably. That is, who is liked remains relatively consistent, even though how much he is liked may vary from situation to situation.

If we can agree at least temporarily that interpersonal attraction is not entirely haphazard and random, that there are systematic relationships between interpersonal communication and the development and maintenance of attraction, and that much informal and social communication is purposive, even if it is not recognized as such by the participants, then we can begin to explore the attraction system in a more orderly fashion.

Perspectives for Viewing Research

Interpersonal attraction, at least in its initial phases, is heavily dependent upon the kinds of judgments we make about others. Warr and Knapper (1968) distinguish between judgments we make about people as objects and judgments we make about people as people. If we attend to the fact that a person is tall, gray-haired, physically attractive, distinguished looking, etc., we are attending to that person in terms of *object properties.* If we attend to the fact that a person is friendly, happy, jovial, kind, and interested in us, then we are attending to that person in terms of *people properties.* The distinction is basically one between responding to people on the basis of their characteristics and responding to people on the basis of inferences we make about their personalities, interests, and habits. The distinction may be a hazy one, but it is important nevertheless, because the two types of judgments play differentially important roles in various phases through which attraction progresses.

In addition to the distinction between the two kinds of judgments discussed, there is another point of clarification and it concerns the accuracy of interpersonal judgments. An interpersonal judgment is accurate only if those things attributed to the object of judgment are valid. (The accuracy with which we judge others is considered in detail in the chapter on general response tendencies.) If you consider another person warm and sympathetic, then it is the attribution of these characteristics to the other person rather than the question whether, in fact, he possesses these characteristics that really matters in terms of your attraction toward him. We are not concerned here with the ligitimacy of the bases on which individuals form inter-personal attractions, but will focus on describing some of the more stable reasons why interpersonal attractions are formed and maintained.

The third point of clarification pertains to the theoretical framework through which we look at attraction. This framework is called "balance theory," and within this set of theories we are concerned primarily with the formulations of Newcomb (1953, 1961) and Heider (1946, 1958). Both formulations describe relationships among: (1) some focal person, "P"; (2) some other person, "O"; and (3) some object of orientation, "X."

The basic formulation gives attention to P's orientation toward O, P's orientation toward X, and O's orientation toward X. The system is con-sidered balanced, given the following two sets of conditions: (1) P likes O, and P's and O's orientations toward X are similar; (2) P dislikes O, and P's and O's orientations toward X are dissimilar. The system is con-sidered imbalanced, given the following two sets of conditions: (1) P likes O, and P's and O's orientations toward X are dissimiliar; (2) P dislikes O, and P's and O's orientations towards X are similar. To illustrate, if Bob (P) likes Carol (O) and if Bob likes skiing (X) and Carol likes skiing, the system is balanced.

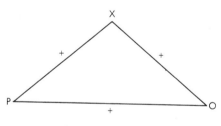

Figure 3.1

Or, if Bob dislikes Carol, and Bob dislikes skiing, and Carol likes skiing, the system is balanced.

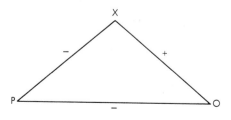

Figure 3.2

On the other hand, if Bob likes Carol, Carol likes skiing, and Bob dislikes skiing, the system is imbalanced.

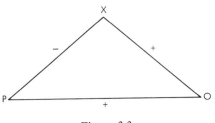

Figure 3.3

Or, if Bob dislikes Carol, Carol likes skiing, and Bob likes skiing, the system is imbalanced.

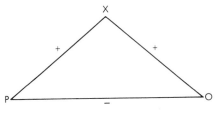

Figure 3.4

Obviously, the degree of balance or imbalance is a function of the importance of X and O to P and the importance of P's perception of O's orientation toward X. If Bob contemplates establishing a serious and prolonged relationship with Carol, and if Bob wishes to invest considerable time, energy, and devotion to skiing, then Carol's orientation toward skiing becomes an important determinant to the maintenance of Bob's attraction toward Carol.

The basic prediction of this formulation is that interpersonal communication will operate in ways that will bring systems into states of balance, preserve states of balance, or somehow resolve states of imbalance. The resolution of states of imbalance may take various forms. P may change his orientation toward O, his orientation toward X, or his perception of O's orientation toward X. P may reduce the importance with which he perceives X. Or he may sever the relationship.

An important variation on this basic formulation is provided by

Heider. He identifies orientations between P and O as "sentiment relations," or likes and dislikes. Relationships between P and X and O and X are called "unit relations." Thus, unit relations may be formed not only through agreements but through P's and O's perceptions of a common relationship toward X, such as belonging to the same organization, working for the same company, living in the same neighborhood. There is ample research evidence to support the basic formulations and predictions of balance theory. Let us consider only a few illustrative studies.

Aronson and Cope (1968) have demonstrated that we tend to like those who punish our enemies and reward our friends. Our liking for that other person appears to be independent of whether we have ever met or ever will meet him. The similarity of our orientations toward X is sufficient to result in interpersonal attraction regardless of the other person's motivation for rewarding or punishing X. It is our perception of the other's orientation toward X that determines our attraction toward him, rather than the real reason he may have for rewarding or punishing X.

Investigators concerned with the importance of the unit relationship have made some interesting discoveries (Darley and Berscheid, 1967). Female college students were led to believe that each would be paired with one of two other girls in a two-person discussion group for purposes of discussing sexual standards for college girls. Each subject was given two folders to review and was asked, presumably for another research study, to form a general impression of the girl described in each of the two folders. One of the folders described the girl with whom the subject subsequently would be paired. The subjects were aware of which folder described their future partner. After reviewing the folders, the subjects completed a questionnaire describing the impressions they had formed of the two girls. The results disclosed that subjects liked the girl with whom they were to be paired more than the other girl. They reported that a contributing factor to the attraction the subjects felt for their future partner was their perception of the girl they liked best as being the one most similar to themselves. Thus it seems that the formation of a unit relationship is sufficient in and of itself to increase the probability of interpersonal attraction. In a related study (Berscheid, Boye, and Darley, 1968), college girls believed they would be paired with either a "positive" or "negative" girl, and were then given the option of selecting either of the two girls as a partner. Subjects who believed they were to be paired with the negative girl evaluated her more favorably and showed a greater tendency to choose her voluntarily than did subjects who had not previously been paired with either girl.

Although much of the research we shall discuss later was never conducted as direct tests of balance theory, most of it supports this theoretical
framework. This brief introduction to balance theory should provide us
with a better vantage point from which to view the four bases of interpersonal attraction: proximity, physical attractiveness, personal rewards, and
interpersonal similarities. We will consider them one by one.

The Almost Sufficient Condition: Proximity

The number of city blocks separating people is related to the probability that they will marry (Katz and Hill, 1958). Persons occupying apart-
ments near stairways tend to be more popular than those living elsewhere
in the same building, and persons whose houses face directly into a court
of other houses tend to be more popular than persons in the same immediate area (Festinger, Schachter, and Back, 1950). Abrahamson (1966)
has summarized studies of housing projects, classrooms, and college dormi-
tories which have concluded that persons who are in a physically central
position are more likely to interact at higher rates and to form social bonds
more easily than individuals in less central positions.

One of the most recent investigations of proximity was undertaken on
the residents of a new dormitory housing 320 male students (Priest and
Sawyer, 1967). Over a period of four successive years, analysis of 25,000
distinct pairs from among the 320 students was completed. The study provided substantial support for a balance-theory orientation toward interpersonal attraction as well as support for the consistency of relationships
between proximity and interpersonal attraction. The results also established
that attractions were likely to form in order of increasing proximity, that is,
most frequently between roommates, then between students living in different rooms on the same floor, then between two persons on different floors
of the same house, then between two persons in different houses. Further
analysis disclosed that when attraction existed but distance was great, many
pairs changed proximity, so that the general result showed that whenever
either proximity or attraction increases, the other tends also to increase;
when either decreases, the other tends also to decrease.

To posit a relationship between proximity and attraction is probably
not very dramatic. Most of us are probably not overwhelmed by the statement that our attractions tend to form disproportionately toward those with
whom we come into frequent contact. But couple this statement with the

balance-theory prediction that unit relationships more likely than not result in interpersonal attraction, and you may arrive at a less obvious conclusion. Given proximity and the opportunity for communication, we will probably end up liking most of the people with whom we come into frequent contact. That we appear to limit the number of attractions we form from among those with whom we interact is even further support for the notion that our attractions are likely to be vested most heavily in proximal people. This is why we call proximity the almost sufficient condition, because in the absence of any other information we can still make some reasonable predictions about what kinds of attraction networks will form if we base our guesses on proximity alone. Even so, other bases for interpersonal attraction must be considered, because given reasonable degrees of proximity, other variables will emerge as the important ones.

The Initial Phases of Attraction:
The Person as Object

Weighing heavily as bases for the initial formation of attraction are judgments we make about the physical properties of others. The most consistent slant that related research has taken is its focus on physical attractiveness. This is not to imply that physical attractiveness is the only important determinant of interpersonal attraction in its initial phases. Nor is it to imply that physical attractiveness is relatively unimportant during subsequent phases. However, in view of our earlier distinction between judgments concerning people as objects and judgments concerning people as people a reasonable position would be that in the initial phases interpersonal attraction is more heavily dependent upon judgments concerning people as objects. Further, such judgments appear to be more important in determining attraction between people of opposite sexes than is the case between people of the same sex.

Warr and Knapper (1968) have summarized investigations that demonstrate considerable agreement concerning evaluations of the physical attractiveness of others. In a British study (Iliffe, 1960) 4,355 judges of different ages, sex, occupation, and geographical location exhibited high levels of agreement concerning the "prettinesss" of young women's faces. There is probably more agreement concerning properties of others that are physically attractive to us than we would suspect exists.

A team of researchers recently conducted a field study in which individuals were randomly paired with one another at a "computer dance" (Walster, Aronson, Abrahams, and Rottmann, 1966). These researchers gathered a battery of personality, intellectual, and scholastic aptitude measures in an attempt to predict which individuals would be liked best, how much a person would want to date his partner again, and whether or not he actually asked his partner out again. Even in the presence of all these measures, the only reliable predictor of one person's liking for the other was the other's physical attractiveness. A similar study by Brislin and Lewis (1968) randomly paired 58 unacquainted men and women at a dance. The variables that correlated with "desire to date again" were: (1) the other's physical attractiveness, (2) the other's sociability, (3) the other's perceived similar interests. Similarly, Byrne, London, and Reeves (1968) found among 89 subjects who evaluated strangers of the same or opposite sex who were either physically attractive or unattractive that interpersonal attraction was greater toward physically attractive strangers regardless of sex.

There are, of course, exceptions to these general conclusions. Occasionally individuals, or groups, or even generations claim to de-emphasize the importance of "object properties" in determining their evaluative orientations toward others. Most of these claims we tend to regard with some suspicion, perhaps as well-intentioned resolutions which one makes to oneself, but which one finds difficult to keep.

Personal Rewards

That we like people who like us and that we like people with whom interpersonal communication is a source of personal rewards for us are conclusions that appear on the surface to be rather obvious. Indeed, investigations have demonstrated positive attraction toward those who praise us (Landy and Aronson, 1968); that we are attracted to those from whom we have received reward during communication (Brewer and Brewer, 1968); that positive interpersonal evaluations result in higher levels of interpersonal attraction (Byrne and Griffitt, 1966); and even that we are more positively attracted to individuals from whom we *anticipate* positive reinforcement (Griffitt, 1968).

If we consider the relationship between personal rewards and interpersonal attraction more fully, we can identify some of the conditions that must be imposed upon this relationship. For example, Iverson (1968) has discovered that even though we like those who flatter us, we tend to dislike those who offer "phony" flattery. However, a further condition is imposed in that our dislike for those whose flattery is "phony" appears to be genuine when we are responding to lower-status others, but not genuine when we are responding to higher-status others. Similarly, Shrauger and Jones (1968) discovered that subjects who had reason to believe in the *validity* of the evaluations they received from others were more attracted toward the positive evaluator.

An interesting question raised by Jones and Schneider (1968) concerns individuals who have low opinions of themselves and who respond to positive evaluations. If we stick rigidly to our present conclusion concerning the relationship between interpersonal attraction and personal rewards, we would predict that individuals, regardless of positive or negative self-concepts, will respond positively to those who provide positive evaluation. But if we return momentarily to the balance-theory prediction we would arrive at a different conclusion. If P's orientation toward X (his own personal worth or value) is negative, that is, if P dislikes himself, and if O's orientation toward X is positive, then P liking O would imply an unbalanced state. If I dislike myself and you dislike me, then our two-person system is theoretically balanced. However, Jones and Schneider have argued that a mediating variable exists: Both predictions may be true if one takes into account the degree of certainty with which the person holds a derogating self-opinion. The results of the research confirmed their position. People who were relatively certain of their low self-opinions responded favorably to the negative evaluator, and people who were relatively uncertain of their low self-opinions responded favorably to the positive evaluator.

We may still hold to the general conclusion that we tend to like those who like us, or that we tend to like those who provide us with personal rewards during communicative encounters. However, in stating this conclusion we must impose certain restrictions concerning the relative sincerity or validity of the evaluations, the status of the evaluator, the kind of opinion we have of ourselves, and the certainty with which we hold that opinion.

Interpersonal Similarity

The most obvious prediction from balance theory is that we will tend to like those who like us or who exhibit similarities to us (not personality similarities, but attitudinal ones). A corollary prediction is that we will probably become more similar, at least in terms of our orientations toward a number of X's, to those that we like. In a sense, the pattern is circular and self-reinforcing. We will tend to become attracted toward another with whom we interact, especially if we share common attitudes toward a number of X's. Our communicative encounters with that other person are inclined to result in heightened attitudinal similarity, which in turn may increase the degree of interpersonal attraction between us and cause us to approach even higher levels of attitudinal similarity. Taylor (1967) has provided support for the prediction that unbalanced pairs will change toward balance after communicative encounters. Clore and Baldridge (1968) have documented the influence of attitudinal agreement on interpersonal attraction. Inglis (1965) has suggested that attraction leads to perceived similarity. Rogers (1968) has discovered that members of voluntary associations are more highly attracted to the group if they perceive that the group's leaders share opinions similar to their own. With respect to the corollary prediction, in addition to the evidence already cited in our discussion of balance theory, the results of an investigation by Brewer (1968) supports the conclusion that where interpersonal attraction exists attitudes are likely to become more similar as a result of communicative encounters.

Some Notions About Attraction Phases

We have focused on four variables that have emerged from research on interpersonal attraction: proximity, physical properties, personal rewards, and interpersonal similarities. Let us go beyond the results of the research and speculate about the way these variables operate in various phases of interpersonal attraction. Our model carries with it the following assumptions: (1) although each of the variables may operate during all phases of interpersonal attraction, it is possible to locate phases at which one variable may be more important than another; (2) although most of the research has been conducted on pairs with either no history or very little history of communicative encounters, it is possible to generalize to pairs with extended histories of communicative encounters; (3) employing the premise that individuals will respond on the basis of the information that is available to them in communicative encounters, it is possible to locate the aforementioned variables with respect to that point in an interpersonal communication history at which information related to the variables is most likely to emerge. With these assumptions in mind examine Fig. 3.5

	INITIAL PHASES	INTERMEDIATE PHASES	SUBSEQUENT PHASES
FOUNDATIONS FOR ATTRACTION	Properties of People Physical Attractiveness	Social Rewards Reinforcement	Interpersonal Similarity Evaluative Orientations
SOURCES OF THE FOUNDATIONS	Personal Tastes and Values	Orientations toward Self	Orientations toward Objects of Discussion
IMPORTANT COMMUNICATION VARIABLES	Perception of Object Characteristics Judger's Priorities	Nature of Feedback Self-Opinion and Perception of Evaluator	Perception of People Characteristics Degrees of Disclosure and Importance of Topics

Figure 3.5 Tentative Notions about Interpersonal Attraction Phases

With any simple description of communication and attraction one runs the risk of becoming too general and of obscuring the exceptions to the generalizations. Attraction is one of those things we frequently prefer to keep at least a little bit mystical. It is the stuff of which romantic fantasies are formed. And the fantasies become real just often enough to remind us that when we are dealing with the feelings individuals have for each other, all things are possible. History, literature, the entertainment and news media provide us with repeated examples, both factual and fictional, of the intriguing forms that intense likes and dislikes may take. And no matter what may be stated, either theoretically or empirically, about the ways in which interpersonal attraction works, these statements can never be completely descriptive of us individually. Others are not quite as capable of the intensities that characterize our relationships with other people. Others are not quite as discerning as we are in our judgment of other people. Some of our feelings for other people have never been and will never again be duplicated in the history of mankind. Our reasons for liking or disliking others are uniquely more legitimate and proper than are other people's reasons. These things we believe to be true, and no one is likely to convince us that we are wrong. We are willing to admit to similarities between our judgments and other people's judgments concerning the attractiveness of others. We will even grant that in most cases we form attractions on the basis of the variables discussed in this chapter, so long as we can note our own personal refinements of the theoretical and empirical conclusions. One of our friends owns a painting of a woman that is sufficiently unique so that many of his visitors examine it carefully. There is considerable consistency in their reactions to the color, the pose, the degree of clarity in the rendering, and the type of woman portrayed. But, as he pointed out, no one has yet noticed the small tear welling up in the corner of one of her eyes. Granting that each of us can provide our own refinements for whatever theoretical framework we wish to employ in looking at interpersonal attraction, let us examine the implications of Fig. 3.5.

Proximity may be regarded as an almost sufficient condition for the development of interpersonal attraction and as a variable that influences attraction at all phases. Proximity is probably more important in the initial phases of attraction formation, but can be expected to exert some influence even after stable and prolonged systems of attraction have formed. The theoretical prediction from balance theory is that when unit relationships are severed, even stable and well-developed systems of attraction may dissipate over time, at least in terms of the intensity that characterizes sentiment relationships.

With respect to the three foundations for attraction, any of these and others may be important in the initial phases if they are all we have during the initial communicative encounters. Much of the research reviewed earlier is based upon experimentally formed dyads consisting of strangers. Even in these conditions if information concerning the other's evaluative orientations toward P or the similarity in the attitudes of P and O is provided to P, then P's attraction toward O has been shown to be affected. Indeed, as some of the research has indicated P's attraction toward O may be affected by such information even before P and O directly encounter each other.

In the normal course of communicative encounters, we can reasonably expect certain kinds of information to emerge with greater frequency during different phases in the history of these encounters. In the initial phases information is immediately available concerning the characteristics or properties of the people involved. Recognizing the importance of object properties, we frequently adopt patterns of dress, deportment, personal mannerisms, and more visable signs of personal tastes so as to structure other people's perceptions of us. Indeed, even many people who profess considerable disdain for traditional criteria employed in evaluating each other will frequently take on properties of dress, taste, and mannerisms that are symbolic of their beliefs and attitudes. Properties thus assumed can carry considerable information in the initial phases of communicative encounters and are highly visible ways of "informing others" about ourselves. The criteria, that is, the properties we choose to emphasize, may change from time to time, but the attention given to the properties is still important in initial encounters. Even as some groups of college students reject traditional criteria for evaluating others, it is somehow important that they adopt new sets of properties, some of which may be of even greater informational value than the old ones.

As the history of the communicative encounters develops, greater emphasis may be placed on the social rewards derived from the encounters. If the other person appears to like us, if he appears to enjoy our company, if we derive pleasure from the interaction, then additional foundations for attraction emerge. This kind of information, however, is less visible than object properties. It takes more time for us to determine whether the image we are attempting to project, and which we consider a reasonable representation of ourselves, is being appropriately received and responded to by others.

As the history of communicative encounters progresses, we also receive information concerning the degree of interpersonal similarity between ourselves and others, that is, whether we share the same kinds of attitudes and values. We make the point in a later chapter that the degree of similarity we perceive between ourselves and another (not in terms of personality but in terms of attitudes and values) is related to our comfort level in the presence of that other person. As we get to "know" another person better, we have greater tolerance for silence and less need to force communication.

A point made earlier was that much informal social communication is more purposive than random or haphazard. It is appropriate to reemphasize that point. Individuals will seek ways of reducing uncertainty and ambiguity, providing greater structure for their perceptions of others, and arriving at information levels they consider reasonable bases for the formation of judgments. Relationships exist between communication and attraction. They are less clearly understood and less systematically investigated than are other basic communication processes. Nevertheless they are there, and they can be identified if we divest ourselves of the notion that there is not much going on in informal communication except random social behavior.

References

Abrahamson, Mark, *Interpersonal Accommodation*. Princeton, N.J.: D. Van Nostrand Co., Inc., 1966.

Aronson, E., and V. Cope, "My Enemy's Enemy Is My Friend," *Journal of Personality and Social Psychology*, 8 (1968), 8–12.

Berscheid, E., D. Boye, and J. Darley, "Effect of Forced Association upon Voluntary Choice to Associate," *Journal of Personality and Social Psychology*, 8 (1968), 13–19.

Berscheid, E., and E. Walster, *Interpersonal Attraction*. (Reading, Massachusetts: Addison-Wesley Publishing Co., Inc., 1969.

Brewer, R. E., "Attitude Change, Interpersonal Attraction, and Communication in a Dyadic Situation," *Journal of Social Psychology*, 75 (1968), 127–34.

Brewer, R. E., and M. B. Brewer, "Attraction and Accuracy of Perception in Dyads," *Journal of Personality and Social Psychology*, 8 (1968), 188–93.

Brislin, R. W., and S. A. Lewis ,"Dating and Physical Attractiveness," *Psychological Reports*, 22 (1968), 976, et passim.

Byrne, D., and W. Griffitt, "Similarity Versus Liking: A Clarification," *Psychonomic Science*, 6 (1966), 295–96.

Byrne, D., O. London, and K. Reeves, "The Effects of Physical Attractiveness, Sex, and Attitude Similarity on Interpersonal Attraction," *Journal of Personality*, 36 (1968), 259–71.

Clore, G. L., and B. Baldridge, "Interpersonal Attraction: The Role of Agreement and Topic Interest," *Journal of Personality and Social Psychology*, 9 (1968), 340–46.

Darley, J. M., and E. Berscheid, "Increased Liking as a Result of the Anticipation of Personal Contact," *Human Relations*, 20 (1967), 29–40.

Festinger, L., S. Schachter, and K. Back, *Social Pressures in Informal Groups*. New York: Harper and Brothers, 1950.

Griffitt, W. B., "Anticipated Reinforcement and Attraction," *Psychonomic Science*, 11 (1968), 355, et passim.

Heider, Fritz, "Attitudes and Cognitive Organization," *Journal of Psychology*, 21 (1946), 107–12.

———, *The Psychology of Interpersonal Relations*. New York: John Wiley & Sons, Inc., 1958.

Horowitz, H., "Interpersonal Choice in American Adolescents," *Psychological Reports*, 19 (1966), 371–74.

Iliffe, A. H., "A Study of Preferences in Feminine Beauty," *British Journal of Psychology*, 51 (1960), 267–73.

Inglis, R., "The Effects of Personality Similarity on Empathy and Interpersonal Attraction." Ph.D. dissertation, Duke University, 1965.

Iverson, M. A., "Attraction Toward Flatterers of Different Statuses," *Journal of Social Psychology*, 74 (1968), 181–87.

Jones, S. C., and D. J. Schneider, "Certainty of Self-Appraisal and Reactions to Evaluations from Others," *Sociometry*, 31 (1968), 395–403.

Katz, A. M., and R. Hill, "Residential Propinquity and Marital Selection: A Review of Theory, Method, and Fact," *Marriage and Family Living*, 20 (1958), 27–35.

Landy, D., and E. Aronson, "Liking for an Evaluator as a Function of His Discernment," *Journal of Personality and Social Psychology*, 9 (1968), 133–41.

Mehrabian, A., "Relationship of Attitude to Seated Posture, Orientation, and Distance," *Journal of Personality and Social Psychology*, 10 (1968), 26–30.

Meyer, W. J., and M. A. Barbour, "Generality of Individual and Group Social Attractiveness over Several Rating Situations," *Journal of Genetic Psychology*, 113 (1968), 101–8.

Newcomb, Theodore M., "An Approach to the Study of Communicative Acts," *Psychological Review*, 60 (1953), 393–404.

———, *The Acquaintance Process*. New York: Holt, Rinehart & Winston, Inc., 1961.

Priest, R .F., and J. Sawyer, "Proximity and Peership: Bases of Balance in Interpersonal Attraction," *The American Journal of Sociology*, 72 (1967), 633–49.

Rogers, D. L., "Correlates of Membership Attraction in Voluntary Associations." Ph.D. dissertation, University of Wisconsin, 1968.

Shrauger, J. S., and S. C. Jones, "Social Validation and Interpersonal Evaluations," *Journal of Experimental Social Psychology*, 4 (1968), 315–23.

Taylor, H. F., "Balance and Change in the Two-Person Group," *Sociometry*, 30 (1967), 262–79.

Walster, E., V. Aronson, D. Abrahams, and L. Rottmann, "Importance of Physical Attractiveness in Dating Behavior," *Journal of Personality and Social Psychology*, 4 (1966), 508–16.

Warr, Peter B., and Christopher Knapper, *The Perception of People and Events*. New York: John Wiley and Sons, Inc., 1968.

Wilson, E. O. "Pheromones," *Scientific American*, 208 (1963), 100, et passim.

Chapter 4

The Influence of Attitudes, Beliefs, and Values

In the preceding chapters we have examined the nature of the communication process and looked at the symbol system and the attraction system that operate within communication. Our purpose in these chapters has been to describe how the communication process functions. That will remain our purpose in this and other chapters, but before continuing, it is important to indicate *why* we communicate. One of the primary reasons man communicates with his fellowman is in order to influence him. If all men operated as completely independent agents, no civilized society would be possible. It is essential that men influence one another so that they may cooperate to achieve common ends.

When we attempt to influence other people, we are trying to modify their thoughts and actions. We seek to stimulate them to choose behaviors that are compatible with our interests. In order to accomplish this we seek to encourage other people to see the world as we see it, to evaluate the elements in the world as we evaluate them, and to agree with us as to what is "good" and "bad" in the world. The presumption on which we operate is that, if other people's thoughts and feelings are similar to our own with regard to given behavioral choices, they are likely to make choices similar to those we would make. The primary function of interpersonal communication is to establish this similarity of thought and feeling between people. In order to determine how this function can be facilitated and controlled, we need to consider several variables. Most important among these variables are *attitude, belief,* and *value.*

Attitude

No concept holds as central a position to the fields of social psychology and communication as does the concept of attitude. Although attitude is defined in various ways, social psychologists and communication theorists tend to employ the concept very similarly. Attitude may be defined, in the words of Fishbein (1965) as "learned predispositions to respond to an object or class of objects in a favorable or unfavorable way." Attitudes, then, are our evaluations of people, ideas, and things that we observe in the external world.

Attitude is what psychologists call an "hypothetical construct." The latter term is used to classify descriptions of things that we believe exist, but for which we have no sensory measure. We cannot prove that such constructs exist by pointing to them. Rather we must develop predictions for what would occur regarding such constructs and see whether such predictions can be confirmed. We may be able to understand the concept of attitude a bit better if we look for a moment at another hypothetical construct, "intelligence." We cannot see intelligence; we cannot touch intelligence; we cannot hear intelligence. But we can get people to complete what we call "IQ tests" that purport to measure what we call intelligence. Then we can predict that people with high scores will do better in school than those with low scores. If that prediction is borne out, we have some justification for believing in the reality of the concept of intelligence. Similarly, we can get people to fill out what we call "attitude tests," and those that have high scores may be predicted to engage in one kind of behavior, whereas those who have low scores may be predicted to behave differently. If those predictions are borne out in observation, we then have some reason to believe in the construct of attitude. There has been considerable research that indicates such predictions about the functioning of attitudes can be confirmed.

Attitudes as we will conceive of them in this chapter and throughout the remainder of this book must be thought of on a multidimensional plane. Although we live in a multidimensional world, the concept of multidimensionality is sometimes difficult for us to grasp. One of the simplest ways to understand it is to think of a multidimensional object—a box, for example. It has height, it has width, and it has depth—the normal dimensions of physical space. And not until we are given the height, width, and depth, can we gain a fairly good image of a particular box. If we translate this concept of multidimensionality from the physical to the psychological world, we will be able to understand more about the nature of attitudes.

What we call attitudes are human responses to things on three psychological dimensions: direction, intensity, and salience.

Direction

An attitude may be favorable, unfavorable, or neutral. These are the three possible directions an attitude may have. For example, on the question of nuclear disarmament, there are people who favor such a policy, people who oppose it, and people who are neutral. Other things being equal, we would predict that people who favor nuclear disarmament would be likely to engage in behaviors designed to make such disarmament come into effect, that people who oppose nuclear disarmament would be likely to engage in behaviors designed to prevent it, and that people who are neutral would be unlikely to engage in any behavior relevant to this issue.

Intensity

We qualified the above predictions with the phrase "other things being equal." Other things are very seldom equal. One of those "other things" is intensity, or strength, of attitude. As we noted above, we may classify people into those who favor, those who oppose, and those who are neutral on a given issue. This, while useful, is only a crude classification. Not all people who favor a policy, for example, favor it equally. Rather there are many variations of the strength of favorability and unfavorability. Some people who oppose the military draft would merely comment on it to a close friend. Others might make public statements in opposition to it. Others might burn their draft cards. Still others might leave the country and ask for political asylum in some other country. All of these people would be classified as opposed to the military draft. But their behaviors are quite different. And if we know the strength of their attitudes, we can predict these differences in behavior more accurately. Attitude strength, or intensity, should be viewed as a continuum ranging from zero to infinity. One person may have one unit of attitude strength, another person ten units, and still another may have five thousand units of attitude strength. Each person might be expected to behave differentially from the others. In general, the more intense the attitude, the more likely it is that the ensuing behavior will be extreme.

Salience

This third dimension of attitude refers to the perceived importance of the attitude to the individual holding it. To exemplify this dimension let us consider two women who have similar attitudes, in terms of direction and intensity, with regard to birth control. One is married to a very successful businessman with an income of over $50,000 a year and has only one child. The other woman has no husband, is living on welfare, and has eight children. The results of an unwanted pregnancy on the part of the second woman probably would be much more severe than for the first woman. Thus, the question of birth control would be much more important for this woman. In general, the more salient an attitude is to an individual, the more likely a person is to enage in behaviors predictable from the direction and intensity of that attitude.

To sum up, attitude is composed of our evaluative responses to our external world. Direction of attitude ranges over a continuum from "good" to "bad"; over a continuum of strength from very little to highly extreme; and over a continuum of the very important or salient to us to the very unimportant or nonsalient.

Belief

Another extremely important hypothetical construct is that of belief. "Belief" is the term we use to describe the way people view reality. Philosophers disagree on the meaning of the term "reality," so we will not attempt to define it here. However, to each of us, reality is as we see it. Before Columbus sailed to the New World, that the world was flat was a reality to most people. The belief that this was so was almost universal, and people thought that if you sailed out into the ocean you would eventually fall off the edge. Except for the few members of England's "Flat Earth Society," to most of us today it is a reality that the earth is round or almost so. This is an instance where the vast majority of the people have a shared belief or hypothesis, but on many other issues people's beliefs differ. Sometimes these beliefs differ from country to country. Most Americans, for example, believe that democracy is a better form of government than a dictatorship. However, in many other countries of the world this belief is not nearly so common. On an even simpler and more interpersonal level, Ted may believe the time is ripe to purchase a new carpet for the living room. But Ted's wife Alice may not share that belief. Beliefs, then, are the ways that we view reality. Beliefs, like boxes and attitudes, are multidimensional. The dimensions of belief are similar to those of attitude: direction, intensity, and salience.

Direction

Direction of belief differs somewhat from that of attitude in that it falls on a true-false continuum rather than on a good-bad continuum. People may fall into three categories according to the direction of their belief: There are those who believe that something is true; those who believe that something is false; and those who are undecided or do not "know." For example, in terms of religious beliefs, people who do not believe there is a God might be classified as atheists; those who believe the existence of a God is unknowable may be classified as agnostics; and those who do believe in a God may be classified as adherents to various religions such as Christianity, Judaism, Islam, Buddhism. Or on a simpler level of belief, John may believe that it is going to rain today, Bill may not believe it will, and the weatherman may be undecided.

Intensity

As is the case with attitude, so direction of belief tells us something about the way a person is responding to his external world. But knowledge of direction is not enough; we need to know considerably more if we are going to make a good prediction about a person's behavior. Although we may be able to predict certain religious behavior, such as church attendance, if we know a man is a Christian, not unless we know how strongly he feels about his religion can we predict his behavior more accurately. He may go to church very regularly, or may attend only rarely.

The strength or intensity of our beliefs runs on a probability continuum ranging from zero to 100 percent. While in most cases we view probability in an informal way, in some cases it can be precisely estimated. The concept of statistical inference used in the physical and social sciences represents the probability continuum of intensity or strength. The researcher reports a conclusion from his research at a probability level. He will say, for example, that at the .05 level of probability *X* statement is true. This means that he is at least 95 percent assured that his conclusion is correct, but recognizes a 5 percent chance of being incorrect. In our everyday lives we do not use such precise statistical estimates of the probability of truth of our beliefs; rather we use very informal probability statements such as "It will *probably* rain since the sun is behind the clouds." Or "It's so hot and humid this afternoon that we'll *probably* have a storm this evening." Or "It's so hot and humid this afternoon that we *might* have a storm this evening." Comparing the latter two statements of belief it would seem reasonable to suggest that the first speaker would feel that the probability of a storm is greater than would the second, because of the difference between "probably" and "might" in their two statements. If such a difference actually existed in their beliefs, we could probably predict some differences in their behaviors. For example, the first individual would probably be more likely to turn on the radio or the television to find out if a storm was predicted. Thus, while knowing the direction of belief is useful, knowing the strength of the belief gives us additional information about probable subsequent behaviors relevant to that belief.

Salience

Salience of belief is not unlike salience of attitude. It has to do with the relevance of the belief in a given case. Two people may share a belief, but in a given behavioral choice one may perceive that belief as relevant and another may not. For example, two gentlemen may believe that it is likely to rain during the afternoon, but one may decide to play golf anyway, whereas the other decides to stay home. The first gentleman may feel that the risk of getting wet on the golf course is worth the pleasure he will get from golf. But the second gentleman may feel that getting wet is a very important negative effect that might occur and thus he avoids going out on the golf course. This dimension, then, has to do with the importance or relevance of a given belief at a given point in time with a given behavioral choice.

Value

Our values are our enduring conceptions of the nature of good and bad. Whereas attitudes and beliefs are normally subject to modification and change, values tend to remain constant over much greater periods of time. Our values are central to our very lives. They form the basis for our beliefs and attitudes. They establish our criteria for evaluating people, actions, and things. Values, like attitudes and beliefs, are multidimensional. Their dimensions are also direction, intensity, and salience.

Direction

The dimension of direction for value is very similar to the dimension of direction for attitude, it is a matter of evaluation. The direction dimension of value ranges also over a continuum of from "good" to "bad." It is important, therefore, to distinguish attitude from value since these two constructs may on the surface appear very similar. An attitude is focused on a specific object or situation, but a value guides actions and judgments across specific objects and situations, beyond immediate goals to more ultimate states of existence (Rokeach, 1968). Let us take some examples to clarify this distinction. Our attitude toward stealing from the local discount store may be unfavorable. We may also have an unfavorable attitude toward cheating on examinations. These attitudes are related to a parent value —our value for honesty. Similarly, we may have an unfavorable attitude toward cancer and we may also have an unfavorable attitude toward automobile accidents because so many people die from these causes. These two attitudes are related to our parent value for human life. Thus, while we may have literally thousands of attitudes, we have a relatively small number of parent values. These values are the criteria by which we measure goodness. So, in terms of direction, our value may suggest that X is good, X is bad, or that we are undecided about the quality of X.

Intensity

The dimension of intensity of value is not as important as the dimension of intensity for belief and attitude because, of the three, values are the most central to our psychological comfort, to our way of life, to our standards. And just because our values are so important to us we tend to hold them very intensely—each of us in various degrees of intensity. For example, we all share the belief that killing other human beings is a bad thing —we place a high value on human life. However, some people hold this value in much higher regard than do others. They are the ones who take a pacifist position and refuse to cooperate in any endeavor that might lead to the destruction of human life, whereas some others are willing to serve in the armed forces knowing full well that they may have to kill another human being. The distinction between these people is based on the intensity with which they value human life.

Salience

As is the case with attitude and belief, salience has to do with the importance of a value in a given circumstance. Within a given society or culture, most people will hold similar values, although in varying degrees of intensity. When behavioral choices must be made, usually more than just one value will come into play. So the question of salience is which value or values are most relevant to this given behavioral choice. For example, we may have put our value of freedom above the value of taking a human life. When we are confronted with a choice of fighting in the armed services to protect our freedom, that is, perhaps to have to kill for it, these values come into conflict. We either serve and accept the possibility of having to kill another human being or we must allow the other human being (collectively) to take away our freedom. We may increase the accuracy of our predictions about a person's behavior if we know which value he feels is the more salient. Expressions such as "better dead than red" and "better red than dead" indicate the differences in the ordering of values on the basis of salience.

Formation of Attitudes, Beliefs, and Values

We have taken considerable space to clarify and explain the distinctions between attitudes, beliefs, and values; later we will stress the importance of these distinctions. But for the moment, let us consider the formation of attitudes, beliefs, and values together. Indeed, all are formed together. A baby is born without attitudes, beliefs, or values. These constructs are products of the totality of the human being's life experiences. People with essentially similar experiences will tend to develop similar attitudes, beliefs, and values.

Attitudes, beliefs, and values are learned. Many theories have been advanced as explanations of the learning process (Bugelski, 1964). Although scholars do not agree as to which theory is best, we have found the reinforcement theory to be particularly useful to describe the process of learning attitudes, beliefs, and values. The essence of the reinforcement theory is that we learn to respond to stimuli on the basis of whether or not those responses lead to rewarding or nonrewarding results for us. Responses we find rewarding (that are reinforced) tend to become part of our habitual response pattern. Those responses for which we do not receive reward, or for which we are punished (that are not reinforced), tend to decrease in frequency to a point where they eventually cease to be part of our response pattern. For example, if we were raised in a home where, when we attempted to communicate, we were rewarded, we tend to communicate more and to value communication quite highly. If, however, as children we were told to "sit down and shut up," or were told that "children are to be seen, and not heard," we tend to reduce the amount of communication in which we engage. Our value for communication may well decrease. Our attitude toward communication with our parents may become negative. We are likely to believe that attempts at communicating with our parents will result in punishment rather than reward. If we live in this type of environment for a considerable length of time, it is quite possible that we acquire very negative attitudes, beliefs, and values concerning communication. In the extreme, this type of negative reinforcement for communicative behavior may lead to psychological disturbances. Some children become stutterers, and others develop what we call communication apprehension or stage fright.

Not all of our attitudes, beliefs, and values are formed by such direct positive or negative reinforcement. Human beings have a capacity to generalize in their learning process. If we respond to a stimulus, we tend to generalize and respond to similar stimuli in much the same way. For example, if as children we have a very good relationship with a minister, we not only develop a favorable attitude toward him but also tend to develop a favorable attitude toward ministers in general. Unless other stimuli are presented to us later in life, we are likely to maintain a favorable attitude toward all ministers as a result of this early experience.

In addition to such direct experiences as described above that lead to the formation of attitudes, beliefs, and values, we gain many of our experiences at a vicarious level. Although most of us have never visited South Africa, nevertheless we have beliefs and attitudes about that country—beliefs and attitudes that we have formed from reading and from talking with people. Thus the beliefs and attitudes of other people tend to "rub off" on us. To a very large extent, then, we can predict a person's attitudes, beliefs, and values on the basis of the people with whom he associates. Many predictions can be made by knowing only the individual's cultural background, because each culture varies, particularly in its beliefs and values. These variations, of course, produce differences in attitude as well. But even within the same culture, the groups with which we associate or identify tend to produce varying attitudes, beliefs, and values in us. Sociologists call these groups "reference groups." Reference groups are more than just the groups of people with whom we associate; they may also be groups of which we are not members, but whose opinions we value. Our interaction with these groups can be satisfying or dissatisfying depending in large measure directly on the similarity of our attitudes, beliefs, and values to the attitudes, beliefs, and values of the other members of the group. If we express divergent opinions from those held by the rest of the group, we are likely to receive verbal punishment and will possibly be ostracized. If our views are similar to those of the group, however, we will most probably be accepted by the group and will be reinforced for our behaviors. Considerable research by psychologists and sociologists indicates that these propositions concerning reference groups are correct (cf. Newcomb, 1958). In fact, it seems that until now no better base for prediction of a person's attitudes, beliefs, or values has been developed than knowledge of that person's reference groups. The potency of the reference group variable is attested to by the high proportion of precise predictions made in public opinion polls. The pollster first identifies the major types of reference groups, and by sampling virtually only a few people in each of these groups, he is able to predict the attitudes of millions, usually with great accuracy.

To sum up, attitudes, beliefs, and values are learned responses. Responses are learned by our direct and vicarious everyday experiences. We often generalize these experiences so that an acquired attitude or belief with reference to one subset of a category (such as a minister or a policeman), is generalized to the category as a whole (all ministers or all policemen). In those areas in which we have no direct experience, we tend to lean upon the beliefs and attitudes of people around us—beliefs and attitudes that may or may not have been based on direct experiences of these individuals. Hence, since our life experiences never cease until life itself ceases, our attitudes, beliefs, and values are always potentially susceptible to change. Before we consider the topic of how such changes occur, let us consider the more typical situation—the persistence of attitudes, beliefs, and values.

Persistence of Attitudes, Beliefs, and Values

Some of our attitudes, beliefs, and values are formed in early childhood and remain with us throughout our lives. Others may persist a shorter period of time. But since attitudes, beliefs, and values are so deeply a part of us, it is essential for us to maintain some kind of stability in these areas of our personalities. Such stability is facilitated by our identification with our normal reference groups. In addition to the effects of our reference groups in maintaining such stability, several other factors often have an important influence. These are factors of selectivity: selective exposure, selective attention, selective perception, and selective recall.

Selective Exposure

Reinforcement theory suggests that people actually seek reinforcement. Consequently we can expect that they seek to get involved in situations where their attitudes, beliefs, and values will be reinforced by other people. By the same token, we expect people to avoid situations where they will not receive reinforcement. Considerable research suggests that this is precisely what we do (Mills, Aronson, and Robinson, 1959), although the research is not as yet extensive enough to specify the circumstances when this will occur. This process is referred to as selective exposure, by which is meant that we selectively expose ourselves to experiences on the basis of whether we consciously or unconsciously believe that these experiences will be reinforcing to our attitudes, beliefs, and values. This has a particularly important bearing on interpersonal communication. We tend to seek communication that we think will be consistent with our attitudes, beliefs, and values and to avoid communication when we think that we will not be reinforced. This is why we choose to talk with some people and why we avoid talking with others. We apply the same criterion to the mass media: We have a tendency to listen to those commentators and read those writers who express views similar to our own. We seem to avoid those who hold divergent opinions. In fact, our choice of reference groups and membership groups is often a matter of selective exposure. We are likely to join a particular church because we hold certain attitudes, beliefs, and values, and, having joined, we have become a member of a group that is very important to our lives. We will tend to be reinforced for our attitudes, beliefs, and values because our reference group shares them.

Selective Attention

We cannot always avoid being exposed to communicative stimuli that are inconsistent with our attitudes. When this happens the process of selective attention is often employed. Of course, all attention is, in a sense, selective: Since everything in our world makes some demand upon our attention, we cannot possibly pay attention to everything. Consequently, when we interact with people either on an interpersonal or mass communication basis, we necessarily will pay more attention to some parts of the communication than to others. In other words, we are selecting that which we attend most closely. Such selection is generally at the unconscious level. As a result we tend to pay closest attention to the communication that is consistent with our attitudes, beliefs, and values, and to pay the least attention to the inconsistent parts. Considerable research has borne out the hypothesis that this tendency exists in people. (e.g., Gilkinson, Paulson, and Sikkink, 1955).

Selective Perception

Because selective attention cannot screen out all inconsistent stimuli, some of them are attended to. This, of course, does not mean that we necessarily will perceive stimuli as inconsistent. Quite the contrary, there is a tendency in people to selectively perceive what the stimuli actually say. We may see what isn't there, or we may fail to see what is there. Extensive research has shown how this selectivity process works (e.g., Cooper and Johoda, 1947). For example, a study was conducted in which three messages with regard to bussing students to maintain racial balance in schools were variously attributed to Dr. Martin Luther King and Governor George C. Wallace of Alabama. One of the messages was a strongly worded message in favor of such bussing, one was clearly opposed to it, and one took a moderate position expressing both favorable and unfavorable views on the issue. When college students read the moderate statement, it made a considerable difference whether it was attributed to King or to Wallace. It is interesting to note that because the students believed King to be for such bussing and Wallace to be opposed to it, the same message was perceived as strongly supportive of bussing when attributed to King, but as strongly opposed to it when attributed to Wallace (Arnold and McCroskey, 1967). On the basis of this and similar studies, it appears that people often perceive what they want to perceive or what they expect to perceive whether or not such perceptions are in accord with what other people might consider reality. Thus, people frequently so distort communicative stimuli as to perceive them as reinforcing to their attitudes, beliefs, and values when the message could be perceived by others as being the exact opposite.

Selective Recall

When communicative stimuli or actual experiences manage to survive the screening processes of selective exposure, selective attention, and selective perception, there is still a selectivity process that may prevent change of the person's attitude, belief, or value: the process of selective recall. There is a tendency for people to forget unrewarding stimuli and to remember the rewarding ones. If we come in contact with another individual who holds a different belief than we do, or we have an experience that indicates that reality may be something other than what we believe it to be, we may simply forget that experience. In other words, if we are exposed to a message that presents both sides of a given question, we are inclined to remember the material that supports our own side, and to forget the material that supports the other side. Again, considerable research bears out the existence of this psychological process (Levine and Murphy, 1954).

Because of the existence of reference groups and the psychological processes of selectivity, our attitudes, beliefs, and values generally remain relatively constant as we advance in age. They are, however, subject to change in some circumstances and to elucidate how and why such changes take place has been one of the most central preoccupations of social psychologists and communication theorists. Most of this theorizing has gone under the label of "attitude-change theory." In the sense that we are using the terms attitude, belief, and value in this book, however, these "attitude" theories apply to all three. The following sections consider some of these theories.

The Principle of Consistency

A group of theories developed during and subsequent to World War II have come to be known as the "tension-reduction" or "homeostatic" theories. Heider's (1946) balance theory, Festinger's (1957) dissonance theory, and Osgood and Tannenbaum's (1955) congruity theory are representative of this group.

In Chapter 3 the balance theory provided a conceptual framework for discussing attraction as an outcome of interpersonal communication. The same theoretical formulations have been employed to account for outcomes associated with attitude and belief change. You will notice that the components of the conceptual model change slightly as we shift our focus to the relationship between sources and receivers (see Figs. 4.1 and 4.2).

All of these theories have in common the "principle of consistency" and also share the following basic assumptions: (1) The human mind has a need for consistency among its attitudes, beliefs, and values; (2) when man becomes aware of inconsistency among his attitudes, beliefs, and values this produces a state of tension; (3) man will seek to reduce this tension by altering one or more of his attitudes, beliefs, and values.

The principle of consistency may be applied to any pair or group of attitudes, beliefs, or values. However, most of the research has concerned

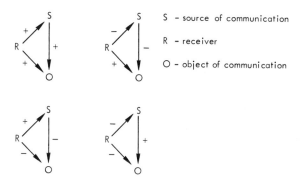

Figure 4.1 Consistent Relationships

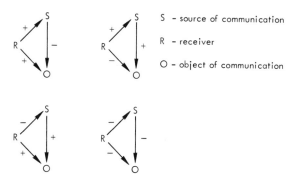

Figure 4.2 Inconsistent Relationships

a particular type—the receiver's attitude toward a source of communication, his attitude toward the object of communication, and his belief about the source of communication's attitude toward the object of communication. The principle of consistency assumes that as receivers we, at least potentially, are aware of our attitudes toward sources of communication and objects of communication. When entering into a communication transaction, therefore, it is assumed that we also have a belief about the source's attitude toward the object of communication. This may be based on prior knowledge of the source, or it may be generated from our own attitudes toward the source and the object of communication. With these particular types of attitudes and beliefs, the principle of consistency suggests that as receivers we expect sources of whom we approve to favor actions and objects of which we approve, and to oppose actions and objects of which we disapprove. Furthermore, it is presumed that as receivers we expect sources of whom we disapprove to disapprove of what we approve of and to approve of what we disapprove of. In each of these cases there is consistency between our attitudes toward the source and the object of communication and our belief about the source's attitude toward the object of communication. These relationships are indicated in Fig. 4.1. If the source indicates that his attitude is different from what would be consistent with our expectations, we have an unbalanced situation. Paradigms indicating such unbalanced situations are noted in Fig. 4.2.

The tension-reduction theories, operating on the principle of consistency, predict that no change of attitude or belief would be expected in the balanced situations indicated in Fig. 4.1. However, in the unbalanced situations indicated in Fig. 4.2, these theories would all predict that attitude change would occur.

Let us take a few examples to indicate in what ways we might change our attitudes. Presume that we approve of the source and that we approve of the object. Presume further that the object is capital punishment. Our expectation would be that the source would also favor capital punishment. If we hear the source discuss this topic and he states that capital punishment should be abolished, maintaining our previous attitudes and beliefs would be inconsistent. This body of the theory would then suggest that some alteration in our attitudes and/or beliefs is necessary. We might, for example, change our attitude toward capital punishment, or we might change our attitude toward the source.

An example from our everyday lives might be as follows. We have a close friend with whom we are sitting in a restaurant having coffee. We approve of him. We also approve of the football program at our university. Since those of whom we approve should approve of what we approve, we believe that our friend's attitude toward the football program is favorable. Thus there is no reason for us to change our attitudes. But let's presume that our friend indicates that he believes that football on the campus should be abolished. Now we are in a state of inconsistency. To regain consistency we might change our attitude toward the football program or we might change our attitude toward our friend. As you may perceive at this point, there are other alternatives for us to resolve our tension, but we will consider them later.

Another example that we may take from our everyday lives would be as follows. Presume that you are a student in a class in communication. You think highly of your instructor and consider him excellent. You have a favorable attitude toward the quality of work you are doing in the class. Since you approve of your instructor and approve of your work in the class, you believe that the instructor probably also approves of your work in the class. Thus you expect to receive a good mark in the course. Let's presume, however, that you receive a D at the end of the term. You are now in an inconsistent state. You must either change your attitude toward the quality of work you have done in class, or change your attitude toward the instructor of the class.

In each of the examples above you may note that in order for a state of inconsistency to be created, we must have obtained some type of message that was generated by the source and that concerned the object of communication. The message, then, is the element that produces the inconsistency and the tension in the receiver. Thus the type of message that is employed is extremely important in determining the type of change that will be produced. In the early formulations of the tension reduction theories it was postulated that the more extreme the message concerning the object, the more likely it would be that the attitude change toward the object would be greater. Recent writers have modified this postulation somewhat; however, before we go into this let us consider another area of the theory that has led to this modification.

Involvement Theory

Involvement theory, as set forth by Hovland and Sherif (1961) and by Sherif, Sherif, and Nebergall (1965), suggests that the more involved a person is with an attitude object, the more resistant he is to changing his attitude toward that object. Central to involvement theory are the concepts of "latitude of acceptance," "latitude of rejection," and "latitude of noncommitment." This theory speculates that there is a region of attitude positions relatively close to our own (latitude of acceptance) with which we could agree without suffering any considerable degree of inconsistency. Somewhat further removed from our own position is presumed to be a region of positions with which we neither agree nor disagree (latitude of noncommitment). Furthest from our attitude is presumed to be a region of attitude positions that are quite objectionable to us (latitude of rejection) and to which adherence would cause considerable inconsistency.

Involvement theory, contrary to consistency theory, would therefore predict that, if a source takes a position that is extreme, it would fall in the latitude of rejection and thus be much less likely to produce attitude change toward the object than would a more moderate position. Research by Whittaker (1967) clearly indicates that the involvement prediction is correct. Although on the surface this may appear to contradict consistency theory, we will note below that this is merely a further refinement of it.

Options for Reducing Inconsistency

When the receiver finds himself in a situation where he perceives that the source expresses a position contrary to what he believed the source would express, inconsistency is present. That inconsistency must somehow be resolved. The way that the source wishes the inconsistency to be resolved is to have the receiver alter his previous attitude toward the object of communication. This, then, is the first option for reducing inconsistency, but not the only one—or even in many cases the most likely one—that the receiver will exercise.

A second option that we mentioned earlier is to change attitude toward the source of communication. This option, of course, is not one the source wishes the receiver to employ in many cases. If the receiver thought highly of the source prior to the communication transaction, this option would probably mean that he would think less of the source as a result of the transaction. However, in some cases, this option is precisely what the source hopes the receiver will choose. This is true when the receiver has a low opinion of the source prior to the communication transaction. In such case the source may favor an attitude object that the receiver favors. This of course, will place the receiver in an inconsistent state. Resolution of this state may take the form of increasing the favorability of the source. This type of communication transaction is not uncommon in the field of business and politics as well as in our personal lives. We shall consider it further in the next chapter.

These options, change of attitude toward the source or toward the object of communication, are the two with which attitude theories are primarily concerned. The question, then, naturally arises as to which attitude is most likely to change when the receiver finds himself in a state of inconsistency. Research on this question indicates that the attitude most likely to change is the one that is held with the *least* intensity, or is least involving to the receiver. For example, if my wife disagrees with me on what should be done with penguins in Antarctica, I am much more likely to change my attitude toward penguins than I am toward my wife. But if a politician suggests that my salary should be reduced, I am a lot more likely to change my attitude toward the politician than toward my salary level. In many cases, however, I may avoid changing either attitude and exercise other options for reducing or avoiding inconsistency.

The third option for restoring consistency is sometimes referred to as "leaving the field." This withdrawal from the communication transaction may be either physical or psychological, but more commonly the latter. We have noted the phenomenon of selectivity earlier. Selectivity may be, and often is, employed either to avoid or reduce inconsistency in attitudes, beliefs, and values. If, for example, I know that my friend disagrees with me on a topic that is of considerable importance to me, I may avoid bringing up this subject when talking with him. This is, simply, a type of selective exposure. Or if I highly value my friend and the object of communication, I may unconsciously misinterpret what he is saying. I may perceive it to be the opposite of what he is saying, or, more likely, perceive a reason other than his true reason for why he is saying it. Further, in the face of inconsistent stimuli, I may just tune out and not pay attention to them. But probably the element of selectivity that is most often employed to resolve inconsistency is selective recall. I am aware that my beliefs and attitudes are inconsistent, but I find it extremely difficult to modify any of them; thus, I may just try to forget the entire transaction. This is particularly true when our own self-image is one of the attitude objects with which we are concerned.

Although the attitude change which we as sources seek may not be the option most often selected by the receiver, it is important for us to understand how this process does work when it is selected. In order to explain this occurrence we shall discuss in the next section a theory that stems from a combination of the tension reduction theories, involvement theory, and the work of Rokeach (1968).

Value Theory

Beliefs and values underlie all attitudes. Therefore—if values remain constant—as beliefs are altered, attitudes tend to be altered. Let us take a simple example. I believe that John is kind. I have a favorable attitude toward kindness, therefore, other things being equal, I have a favorable attitude toward John. But yesterday I saw him kick a dog. His act of cruelty is inconsistent with my prior belief that he is kind. And although this single incident may not lead me to conclude outright that John is cruel, my new belief reduces somewhat the expected probability of kindness on his part. The possibility of future unkind acts by John calls for some change in my attitude toward him. Although my attitude toward him may not become completely unfavorable, my overall evaluation of him should suffer somewhat.

In this example, we have no values explicitly concerned. Nevertheless, value is implicitly present, because our evaluations are hinged upon our values. The part values play may be more clearly perceived in the following example: I believe that the space program has enabled man to explore the moon. Further, I have a favorable attitude toward the discovery of new things. Therefore my attitude would tend to be favorable toward the space program. However, let us presume that I am a poor person. And I have been told that the dollars that have been spent on the space program have been taken indirectly from antipoverty programs. Since I have a favorable attitude toward governmental programs that help the poor, I would then tend to have a negative attitude toward the space program. In this case we have directly contradictory values. While I value discovery, I also value aiding poor people. If these two values become incompatible, as in the above example, then I must choose between these two values in terms of which I wish to satisfy most. So the question becomes which value is most important to me.

As has been suggested before, values are relatively enduring. For this reason a source will seldom change a receiver's values. However, he may cause the receiver to select a different value as central to the determination of his attitude than had been employed previously. In the preceding example, if the poor person was not aware of the relationship between the space program and the antipoverty program, his value concerning discoveries could be central to the development of his attitude toward the space program. If, however, a source were to point out the relationship between the space program and the antipoverty program, it may not only alter the receiver's beliefs, but it may also cause him to employ a different value in forming his attitude toward the space program. He may substitute the value for helping the poor, where previously his interest in new discoveries had determined his attitude. The paradigm of persuasion, therefore, may be diagrammed:

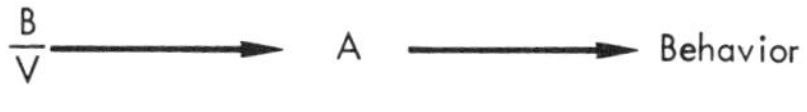

$$\frac{B}{V} \longrightarrow A \longrightarrow \text{Behavior}$$

Figure 4.3

The above paradigm indicates that behavior alteration is produced by attitude alteration, which, in turn, is produced by changing of belief and/or reordering of values. While this is the most common pattern in communication, change in human beings can work in a nearly opposite direction. This process is not considered persuasion by most people. Rather it is a form of coercion. The paradigm for change as a result of coercion is as follows:

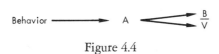

Figure 4.4

In the coercive situation, sometimes called "forced compliance," behavior is directly affected, which results in making behavior and attitude inconsistent. The individual must now choose either to alter his attitude or to "leave the field" by supplying a different attitude that is consistent with his behavior. If the latter choice is taken, no change in belief or value would be expected. But in the former case, if the attitude is changed, it then would become inconsistent with the beliefs and values upon which it is based. Thus, those beliefs and/or those values would need to be altered.

Retention of Change

Since the purpose of communication is to effect change in receivers, it is important to consider the question of what happens after such change occurs as a result of communication. For the most part the research tends to suggest that change as a result of a single communicative event tends to disappear over time. This tendency toward disappearance is referred to as "regression." By that we mean that the person's attitudes and beliefs tend to regress or return toward their original position. Several factors can account for this type of effect. The first is selective recall, which we have discussed at length before. A second is the matter of reference and membership groups with which an individual indentifies. Presumably he has been reinforced for his old attitudes by these groups prior to having his attitudes changed by communication, and when he goes back to these groups he will not be reinforced for his new attitude. Rather he will be encouraged to go back to his original attitude. A third element that contributes to this regression is the individual's habit patterns. If, for example, I have been smoking for many years and it has become a habit, a source may change my attitude toward smoking, but I continue to indulge in the habit, and the attitude change he produced tends to vanish. Some changes, however, are retained. Variables that seem to be related to the performance of change include awareness, retention of original stimuli that produce change, importance of the change, and the amount of original change.

Many attitude and belief changes occur at an unconscious level. As a result our habit patterns that were consistent with our old attitudes will tend to continue. However, if we are made aware of the change that has occurred, we are more likely to alter our habit patterns. Similarly, if the original stimuli that caused us to change are not particularly vivid or memorable, selective recall is facilitated. However, if the original stimuli were very vivid and memorable, this will tend to inhibit the process of selective recall.

While most research is done on relatively nonsalient topics, most of our important communication transactions are concerned with matters of considerable importance to us. For example, although we may change our attitude in an experiment toward apartheid policies in South Africa, this is not a particularly salient subject to most of us. As a result there will be a strong tendency for us to simply forget about the whole transaction. But, if the subject matter of the discussion has to do with our economic security, and we change our beliefs and/or attitudes, this type of change will tend to persist. Related to this is the amount of shift that occurs. If one crosses the barrier from favorable to unfavorable or the reverse, we may refer to this person as a "convert." This tends to be a very difficult change on any question important to us, and therefore our involvement and commitment to our choice are increased. Such choices tend to be retained over long periods of time, and, in fact, tend to become stronger as time goes on.

There are several things that a source may do in his message to increase the likelihood of retention of change. We will consider those in later chapters.

In the discussion above we have suggested that the receiver's attitude toward the source of the message may be the most important variable in producing change. The following chapter is devoted to this very important variable.

References

Arnold, W. E., and J. C. McCroskey, "Experimental Studies of Perception Distortion and the Extensional Device of Dating." Paper presented at the Speech Association of America Convention, Los Angeles, 1967.

Bugelski, B. R., *The Psychology of Learning Applied to Teaching.* Indianapolis: The Bobbs-Merrill Co., Inc., 1964.

Cooper, Eunice, and Marie Johoda, "The Evasion of Propaganda; How Prejudiced People Respond to Anti-Prejudice Propaganda," *Journal of Psychology*, 23 (1947), 15–25.

Festinger, L., *A Theory of Cognitive Dissonance.* New York: Row, Peterson, 1957.

Fishbein, M., "A Consideration of Beliefs, Attitudes, and Their Relationship," in *Current Studies in Social Psychology*, I. D. Steiner and M. Fishbein, eds. New York: Holt, Rinehart & Winston, Inc., 1965, 107–20.

Gilkinson, H., S. F. Paulson, and D. E. Sikkink, "Conditions Affecting the Communication of Controversial Statements in Connected Discourse; Forms of Presentation and the Political Frame of Reference of the Listener," *Speech Monographs*, 20 (1955), 253–60.

Heider, F., "Attitudes and Cognitive Organization," *Journal of Psychology*, 21 (1946), 107–12.

Hovland, C. I., and M. Sherif, *Social Judgment.* New Haven, Conn.: Yale University Press, 1961.

Levine, J. M., and G. Murphy, "The Learning and Forgetting of Controversial Material," *Journal of Abnormal and Social Psychology*, 49 (1954), 23–28.

Mills, J., E. Aronson, and H. Robinson, "Selectivity in Exposure to Information," *Journal of Abnormal and Social Psychology*, 59 (1959), 250–53.

Newcomb, T. M., "Attitude Development as a Function of Reference Groups; The Bennington Study," in *Readings in Social Psychology*, E. E. Maccoby, T. M. Newcomb, and E. L. Hartley, eds. New York: Holt, Rinehart & Winston, Inc., 1958, pp. 265–75.

Osgood, C. E., and P. H. Tannenbaum, "The Principle of Congruity in the Prediction of Attitude Change," *Psychological Review*, 62 (1955), 42–55.

Rokeach, M., *Beliefs, Attitudes, and Values*. San Francisco: Jossey-Bass, Inc., Publishers, 1968.

Sherif, M., Carolyn Sherif, and R. Nebergall, *Attitude and Attitude Change*. Philadelphia: W. B. Saunders Co., 1965.

Whittaker, J. O., "Resolution of the Communication Discrepancy Issue in Attitude Change," in *Attitude, Ego-Involvement and Change*, Carolyn W. Sherif and M. Sherif, eds. New York: John Wiley & Sons, Inc., 1967, pp. 159–77.

Limiting Variables

Now that we have discussed some of the basic interpersonal communication outcomes, we need to concern ourselves with a more general question. What are some of the variables that might limit the range of outcomes we might expect to observe from communication encounters? Specifically, in addition to the variables we have discussed in the preceding section, what are some of the general classes of variables ordinarily studied in terms of their relationship to interpersonal communication?

In Section III we discuss some general classes of variables, the presence of which might be expected to limit communication outcomes. We do not use the term "limit" in a value sense. Presence of high levels of empathic ability on the part of one or both participants may enhance mutual understanding as an outcome. On the other hand, the presence of certain nonverbal cues may decrease the likelihood of any of the principal outcomes. A limiting variable, then, is any variable that places considerable constraints upon the range of a particular outcome.

Each of the four chapters in Section III discusses a general class of variables that is important in understanding interpersonal communication. Chapters 5 and 8 discuss classes of variables usually associated with interpersonal influence. Chapter 6 (nonverbal variables) discusses a class of variables that may have marked consequences for any outcome. Chapter 7 (general response tendencies) discusses a class of variables usually associated with accuracy or influence.

Chapter 5

The Source-Sender

All messages in communication must originate somewhere. That point of origination is what we referred to in the preceding chapters as the "source." Who that source is perceived to be by the receiver will in many instances determine the success or failure of the message in communication. The importance of the source is suggested in a famous quotation by Emerson, "What you are stands over you the while and thunders so loudly I cannot hear what you say to the contrary." We might improve upon Emerson's thought by revising his statement to say "What I *think* you are. . . ." Nevertheless, his point is well taken. The most definitive result from communication research to date is that the impact of the source tends to dominate the effects in communication.

The term "source" is a singular noun. This rightfully suggests that most sources are individuals. However, it is important to realize that in communication the source can also be a collective entity. The source of a message could be a federal agency, a public relations firm, or the Student Affairs office, to name just a few. Many organizations exist in our society primarily to serve as sources of messages in communication. This is the function of many so-called nonprofit organizations.

In addition, the source of a message does not necessarily have to be human, either in a singular or collective context. When a dog barks, we have a message created by a nonhuman that may very well communicate meaning to the person who hears the barking. (This is why many of us own watchdogs.) Most of us have at one time or another seen movies set in the jungle. Do you recall the scene where the man in the jungle is warned of approaching danger by birds suddenly taking flight? By this act, these birds produce messages that stimulate meaning in the mind of the man. Obviously, there are differences between human communication and animal communication with human beings. But some of the distinctions commonly made are not really meaningful. For example, some people will suggest that people think about what they are communicating, whereas animals do not. In some cases, this is true. But we all communicate from time to time without thinking what we are doing, without considering our message before presenting it. Thus, the function of the animal as a source of communication is not necessarily unlike that of man. However, in these pages we shall not concern ourselves with communication between animals and human beings, rather we will restrict ourselves to human communication—not because people do not communicate with animals, but simply because the consideration of human communication is a task difficult enough in itself.

Source vs. Sender

In some cases we as receivers misperceive who the source of a message is. Simply because we read what someone says or what is attributed to someone or hear someone say something, we erroneously assume that that "someone" is the source. While this may be true in most instances, it is not necessarily true. A "sender" is a spokesman for a source. He is the person who transmits the message to the receiver.

Many sources employ senders to function as message transmitters. For instance, the press secretary to the President would be considered such a sender. Many of us remember Pierre Salinger, cigar in hand, conducting a news conference on behalf of President John F. Kennedy. Mr. Salinger as President Kennedy's personal press secretary was a sender close to the source, namely the President. However, some senders may be further removed from the actual source of the message, for example, television actors and actresses who do commercials that originated in advertising agencies. Similarly, a radio disk jockey who reads an advertisement on the air is a sender rather than a source.

The examples above should make it fairly easy for us to distinguish between the source and the sender. In some cases, however, it is much more difficult for us to make this distinction. Many prominent individuals employ ghost-writers to prepare speeches for them. Then this individual presents the speech to us, the receivers. As a rule we have no way of knowing whether this individual prepared his own message or whether he employed someone else to serve as a source. There is also the case of the "front man." Some people and some organizations employ other people to represent them in business and interpersonal relations. Of course, we frequently have no way of knowing whether the person with whom we are dealing is the real source of the message or only the source's employee. We become very concerned about this in instances where we have reason to suspect the motives of the real source, when, for example, a crime syndicate buys a legitimate business and retains the leaders in that business as front men for its criminal activities. The phenomenon of the illusive source is also present in many executive structures. In such cases the low-level executive is the one who has primary contact with the public. Often he is told precisely what to say and has little freedom to make up his own mind about much of anything. When we come into contact with him we may perceive him as the source of the message when, in fact, he is merely the sender for his superiors. This sort of thing occurs frequently on college and university campuses. Administration policies are determined by the elected or appointed officials, but they are normally communicated to the faculty and students of the institution by administrative assistants or secretaries.

Thus, in many circumstances, there is an important distinction to be made between the person who originates the message (the source) and the person who transmits the message to the receiver (the sender). This is not to suggest that such a difference is the rule. Actually it is the exception. In most of our interpersonal communicative activity we will serve as both source and sender of our messages, and the people with whom we interact will serve as both source and sender of their messages. However, situations in which we will interact and where we have to distinguish between source and sender occur often enough to warrant our concern with this matter.

Source Credibility

Probably the single most important element in interpersonal communication is source credibility. This element goes under a wide variety of names, such as prestige, ethos, interpersonal trust, charisma, and image. But whatever we label it, it represents the attitude of the receiver toward the source. It is what the receiver *thinks* of the source, not what the source *is*. A source may be a saint, but if the receiver thinks of him as being the opposite, he does not have high credibility with that receiver.

Dimensions of Credibility

The research on source credibility has indicated that this is a multidimensional attitude. Exactly what, or how many, dimensions of this attitude there are remains controversial (McCroskey, 1966a; Berlo, Lemert, and Mertz, 1966). However, for the purposes of explaining the nature of source credibility we will consider five dimensions: competence, character, intention, personality, and dynamism.

Competence

When we are trying to decide whether or not to accept the ideas a person presents to us, one of the first questions we ask is, "Does he know what he is talking about?" In essence, we are asking ourselves whether this man is competent in the subject matter he is discussing. Is he in a position to have relevant information on his topic? Is he qualified by background and experience? Is he an intelligent individual? Is he an expert in his subject matter? Other things being equal, we tend to accept the views of the competent source more readily than those of the source we believe to be less competent.

Character

Another important factor we normally take under consideration in determining whether or not to accept a man's views is what we perceive to be his basic nature, or his character. Can we trust him? Is he essentially decent? Is he noted for being honest and virtuous? Our concern with a man's character differs somewhat from our concern with his competence. As far as competence is concerned, we weigh the man's qualifications; when determining his character, we have to judge the man himself, his basic nature.

Intention

Closely related to the dimension of character is the dimension of intention. It is usually of importance to us to know the motives of the person who is communicating with us. Does he have our best interests at heart or are his intentions undesirable and manipulative? Essentially, does he or does he not bear us good will? He may be a very competent and basically honest man, yet he may, for personal gain, try to get us to accept something that is not althogether to our benefit.

Personality

Particularly in interpersonal communication we evaluate sources on the basis of personality. Is the source a friendly, pleasant individual, or is he an unfriendly, unpleasant person? Research suggests that we as receivers have some difficulty in separating our responses among the character, intention, and personality dimensions of credibility (McCroskey, 1966a). We tend to perceive an unfriendly individual as having a low character and evil intent. Conversely, there seems to be a tendency to perceive a source who is friendly to be of high character and to possess desirable intent. It may well be, therefore, that this dimension of credibility is the most important in interpersonal communication.

Dynamism

Research on source credibility indicates that in some cases receivers respond to sources on the basis of the dynamics of their communicative activity. The dynamic individual is perceived as aggressive, emphatic, and forceful. This research suggests that we tend to consider the dynamic individual more credible than his counterpart.

As may be surmised from the preceding discussion, it is possible for a source to be perceived as highly credible on one dimension, and low-credible on another or other dimensions. There is little evidence available from the studies on source credibility to suggest what dimension is the most important. But it would seem that a high-credible source is one who is perceived in a favorable light on *all* dimensions. On the other hand, a low-credible source is one who is perceived in a negative light on *any one* of the dimensions. For example, a high-credible source would be considered competent, of high character, having good intention, having a favorable personality, and being dynamic. A low-credible source could well be perceived as competent, of high character, having a favorable personality, being dynamic, but having undesirable intentions toward his receiver. It is vital, therefore, for us as sources to enhance our credibility on all dimensions. For if we do not do this—and research has made this clear—our receivers will tend to discount our message because of our inability to make ourselves appear credible in their eyes.

The Variability of Credibility

Source credibility is a variable in communication. It is not a constant. As we have suggested in the preceding section, source credibility is determined by the receiver's perception of the source, namely his attitude toward the source. Like all other attitudes, it is subject to change from time to time and from situation to situation. At least three things produce changes in a source's credibility: changes of receiver, changes of topic, and changes of time.

Changes of Receiver

Different people perceive sources in different ways. A person who is perceived by one receiver as a highly credible source, may be perceived by another receiver as a totally noncredible one. We may take the example of George Lincoln Rockwell, the late leader of the American Nazi party. Rockwell was perceived by his immediate followers and a tiny fraction of the rest of the American public as a highly credible individual. But for the vast bulk of society, Mr. Rockwell was perceived as an extremely low-credible source. Now let us look at the other side of the coin: President Kennedy was perceived by many millions of Americans as an almost godlike individual. His credibility could scarcely have been higher. For many other people within our society, however, President Kennedy's credibility was extremely low, so low as to make any message emanating from him unacceptable to these individuals.

Changes of Topic

We can perceive a person as high-credible on one topic, yet as very low-credible on another topic. A recent example is the case of Dr. Benjamin Spock, the famous baby doctor. Literally millions of women across the United States regard the writings of Dr. Spock as the best reference on child care and upbringing. But when Dr. Spock began speaking out against the draft and the Viet Nam war, many of these same women came to consider him to be low-credible. The distinction that was made in Dr. Spock's case was one on the competence dimension; he was perceived as competent on child care but not on international politics. Such a distinction could also be made on other dimensions of credibility for other sources.

Changes of Time

Times change and people change. As these changes occur, the individual's credibility may change with the same people. One of the most vivid examples of this was the change that occurred over time with President Lyndon B. Johnson. In 1964 he was the overwhelming favorite of the majority of the American public. His credibility was at an all time high; he reached peaks of credibility which exceeded that of all other presidents in the past. Within a span of three years, however, his credibility with the American public had dropped sharply, to the point where he considered it impossible to win reelection. Then shortly after his departure from office, his credibility again became quite high with the American public. Actually, it is not merely time that produced the change in Lyndon Johnson's credibility, but rather Lyndon Johnson's actions and other events that occurred throughout our country and the world were contributing factors. Nevertheless, it is useful to consider such changes on a temporal dimension.

The Effects of Source Credibility

Source credibility has been the most frequently researched variable in communication. And the results of this research are among the most consistent in the whole area of communication research. The outcome of a large and ever-increasing number of studies corroborates that source credibility has a major effect in the production of immediate attitude change in communication. For the most part, the higher the initial credibility of the source, the more immediate attitude change will be produced by that source (Andersen and Clevenger, 1963).

Before we consider some representative examples of the research on credibility, it would be helpful for us to distinguish credibility on a temporal dimension. *Initial credibility* is the credibility of the source prior to the beginning of a given communicative act. It is the credibility we have with our receiver just before we begin talking with him, or just before he begins to read what we have written. *Derived credibility* is the credibility of the source produced during the act of communicating. This is the credibility produced by the verbal and non-verbal messages transmitted by the source and by the circumstances surrounding the communication transaction. *Terminal credibility* is the credibility of a source at the completion of a communicative act. It is the product of an interaction between initial and derived credibility. It is what the receiver thinks of the source after a given communication transaction has been completed. With these distinctions in mind let us consider some of the research relating to source credibility.

Immediate Effects

Most of the research on source credibility that has been reported to date has been concerned primarily with the impact of initial credibility. The normal design of these studies has included sources of varying credibility levels, either selected or created, who are identified as the source of an identical message to different but comparable audiences. The effects of credibility have been most often measured by determining the amount of difference in attitude change between the various audiences exposed to the different sources.

The classic study of the effect of initial credibility was conducted by Haiman (1949). In his study three comparable audiences listened to the same tape-recorded speech. This speech was attributed to a different source for each group. One group was told that the source of the speech was Thomas Parrin, then surgeon general of the United States. A second audience was informed that the speaker was Eugene Dennis, then secretary of the Communist party in America. The final audience was informed that the source was a "Northwestern University sophomore." Analysis of the attitude-change data obtained in the experiment indicated that the "Parrin speech" was significantly more effective in changing the attitudes of the audience than either of the other two speeches. Strother (1951) obtained similar results in a comparable experiment.

Many other researchers have employed procedures similar to those of Haiman with comparable results for messages presented either orally or in written form. In most of these studies the dimensions of credibility were manipulated by introducing unknown speakers or writers or by identifying known individuals. The elements that presumably produced high or low credibility were those considered relevant by the researchers, and apparently by the experimental subjects as well. These characteristics included such things as affiliation with the Communist party, educational background, and criminal convictions. A smaller number of studies have considered elements that on the surface would appear to be objectively irrelevant to credibility in order to determine whether or not they would have an impact on the source's effect. Although, for the most part, these "objectively irrelevant" factors appear to have less impact in the communication process, some have been found to influence the source's effect. For example, Aronson and Golden (1962) found that the factor of the communicator's race had no effect when he was identified as an engineer discussing the value of arithmetic, but when the same communicator was identified as a dishwasher and discussed the same topic, race did have a major impact.

A study by Steffens (1967) tested the hypothesis that the sex of the communicator would influence his or her credibility and subsequently the attitude change that the source could produce. It was hypothesized that a male source would be perceived as more credible than a female source by female receivers, and that a female source would be perceived as more credible than a male source by male receivers. The results of the study provided no support for this hypothesis. Male and female sources were considered equally credible and were equally influential in producing attitude change. Mills and Aronson (1965), however, found that an attractive female could modify attitudes of male students more than could an unattractive girl. The two girls were actually the same girl with different makeup for the different experimental conditions. In both conditions the students were asked to complete some opinion scales. Before they began to complete the scales, the experimenters suggested that the students would find it easier to do so if there were a volunteer who would read the questions aloud and indicate what they meant. The volunteer, of course, was the girl who was planted in the audience. She read each question, interpreted it, and indicated what she thought was the correct answer. In the condition where she was made up to look very attractive, the male students tended to record the answers which she recommended. In the other condition, where the girl was made up to look quite unattractive, the students tended to record answers contrary to those she suggested.

On the basis of these two studies it would appear that the sex of the source is not relevant, but that the attractiveness of that source is. However, because the Mills and Aronson study included only male subjects, it may be argued that attractiveness and sex are interactive in producing credibility. Had Mills and Aronson examined the effects of attractiveness of their source on female subjects, they might have found different results. A study that throws some light on this question has been reported by Widgery and Webster (1969). In this study photographs from a college yearbook were shown to a group of students who were then asked to rate each picture for its attractiveness. After analyzing the ratings, the pictures of the most unattractive and the most attractive males and females were selected for further study. These pictures were presented to a separate group of experimental subjects who were asked to rate the individual's credibility on the competence, character, and dynamism dimensions. Great and significant differences between attractive and unattractive individuals were observed on the character dimension. No meaningful differences were observed on the other dimensions, and no differences were observed on the basis of the sex of the source. The results of these three studies taken together tend to suggest that the attractiveness of a communicator may have a major impact on that communicator's source credibility and subsequently on attitude change, but that the sex of the communicator is not a particularly relevant factor.

Initial credibility, then, has a major effect on immediate attitude change as a result of communication. There is reason to believe, as reported by Arnold (1966), that initial credibility has a similar effect on overt behavior change. In addition, initial credibility interacts with many message elements in the production of attitude change. For example, it has been observed that a high-credibility source profits little when he employs evidence in a message, whereas a low-credibility source may improve his impact sharply as a result of inclusion of evidence (McCroskey, 1966b). Such interactions with message elements will be considered in a later chapter.

The Effects over Time

Although the research findings we discussed above clearly indicate that initial credibility has an immediate effect on attitude change, and probably an effect on behavior, they have not completely established that credibility has any long-range impact. In fact, the studies suggest that the effects of credibility wear off in a very short time (Andersen and Clevenger, 1963). It has been established that in three or four weeks after a communication transaction the attitude change that is retained by the receiver will be no greater if he received his message from a high-credible source than if he received it from a low-credible source.

However, the studies that have examined the effects of credibility over time have done so in a person-to-group rather than an interpersonal communication setting. The studies reported by Hovland, Janis, and Kelley (1953) and by McCroskey (1966b) examined the effects of credibility in a condition where the experimental subjects received a one-way message and had no opportunity to interact with the source, nor did they have an opportunity to interact with the source at a later time. In a study by Hovland and Weiss (1951) the experimental subjects were reminded of the source they had previously heard, and the analysis of the data from the experiment indicated that this reinstatement of the source caused the degree of attitude change produced by the high-credibility source to be much higher over time than that of the low-credibility source. This suggests that in interpersonal communication where we continually interact with a high-credible source, his impact on us over time may be sustained. Similarly, a low-credible source would have little impact on us initially and little impact over time. However, this is still in the realm of speculation, because to date no systematic research on source credibility in an interpersonal communication situation has considered the effects of credibility over a given length of time.

The Importance of Source Credibility

Although most of the research in source credibility has been conducted in the environment of person-to-group communication rather than interpersonal communication, we should not let this mislead us to think that source credibility has less of an effect in interpersonal than in person-to-group communication. The reason for the emphasis on person-to-group communication in research programs is simply due to the fact that it is easier to do research in this area. It would seem reasonable to assume that source credibility might have an even larger impact in interpersonal communication than it has in person-to-group communication.

In person-to-group communication the transaction is normally much longer than in interpersonal communication. As a result it is possible in person-to-group communication to increase credibility by means of a skillfully developed message. In interpersonal communication, on the other hand, communication transactions are generally brief in nature. A person does not remain a source more than a few moments at a time. In a social setting, particularly, source credibility can have an important impact. The impact prabably is not primarily a result of the competence dimension as much as it is one of the character, intention, and personality dimensions. In our social environment we tend to react to people on the basis of whether or not we like them or whether they're pleasant and friendly, rather than whether or not we consider them to be experts. Our next-door neighbor may not be a political scientist, but if he is a friendly, pleasant, and helpful guy, his views on who should be elected to the presidency may strongly influence us. And if we are of a similar type, we may influence him. This principle also holds true within the business setting. Usually, in a business conference there is a specific person who is designated leader because of his administrative position. But in the absence of such a leader, the person who is most respected, who has the source credibility, will tend to become the leader, and as a result his views will have a major impact on the decisions of the group. If we are introspective for a few moments, each of us probably can perceive the effects of source credibility in our daily interpersonal communication. Who asks us for our opinion? Whom do we ask for their opinion? Those people who tend frequently to ask us, look to us as opinion leaders. Those to whom we turn for advice, are our opinion leaders. The term "opinion leader" is sociological in origin. It is just another way of saying high-credible source.

Interpersonal communication may be divided into two primary types: (1) those where we interact with others whom we consider equally credible, and who consider us equally credible; and (2) those interpersonal transactions in which one person considers the other person more credible than he is, and the feeling is shared. It is rare indeed for interpersonal communication to occur between two people who consider each other to be low-credible. These interpersonal communication situations are normally extremely strained, and we tend to avoid them because they make us uncomfortable.

Source credibility, then, may determine with whom we engage in interpersonal communication as well as how effective we as individuals are as sources in this communication environment.

Source Credibility as a Goal

Thus far in this chapter we have talked primarily about a certain aspect of source credibility, namely that it is something a source can use to be effective. This is true if we are considering source credibility in terms of initial credibility. But on the other side of the coin, there is terminal credibility. The concept of terminal credibility suggests something not to be used but to be obtained. Much, if not most, interpersonal communication has as its primary purpose the enhancing of credibility, or to put it another way, the achievement of high terminal credibility.

As we interact with acquaintances in our daily lives, we exchange pleasantries. Although an observer of this transaction may consider that what we are saying is meaningless jabber, still, this interaction on the pleasantries level has a significant purpose. The purpose on the other individual's part and on our part is mutually to increase our credibility with one another. We don't often think of it in these terms. Most of us are not that consciously manipulative. Nevertheless, this is the function of this type of communication.

In the world of business we also have to interact with our superiors. Frequently we will talk to them not to obtain information but only to make them more aware of our presence. Very often we will give verbal assent to things which we believe our boss approves of simply because we want to enhance our credibility with him. On a nonbusiness level similar activities occur in boy-girl relationships. While there may be certain ultimate intent involved, such as marriage, or conquest, most of the interaction that occurs between young men and young women is designed to enhance the credibility of one in the eyes of the other.

All of us at one time or another must undergo a job interview. Such an interview is a prime example of interpersonal communication that is designed to enhance credibility. As we walk into our potential employer's office, our specific goal is to make him think well of us so that he will hire us. Often, the same thing applies to him. He wants us to think well of him and his business so that we will accept the position he intends to offer us.

In short, most of our interpersonal communication activity is a form of public relations. We are trying to establish a favorable image in the minds of the other human beings with whom we must exist. To a major degree, our professional and social success depends upon our ability to enhance our credibility in the minds of our associates.

A similar type of activity is going on around us at all times with the other people with whom we come in contact. For example, most of us will listen to politicians' campaign speeches. Usually, these speeches are not designed to make us change our minds about a particular political issue, but rather to convince us that the speaker is on our side so that we will decide he is a good man for whom to vote. Similarly, the average newspaper editorial is intended to enhance the credibility of the newspaper, not to influence the opinion of the public. We find editorials extolling the virtues of charity and motherhood and patriotism and the flag and all sorts of things. That is not to say that the editor never takes an unpopular position, but in most cases he is trying to express the views of the public, not trying to mold them. Suffice it to say here, source credibility is at least as often a target as it is a tool of communication.

As mentioned above, source credibility is often the target of communication, but even when it is not, it is a potent variable nevertheless. For this reason it is important to consider what a communicator can do to enhance his credibility. Later chapters will discuss this in greater detail.

References

Andersen, K., and T. Clevenger, Jr., "A Summary of Experimental Research in Ethos," *Speech Monographs*, 30 (1963), 59–78.

Arnold, W. E., "An Experimental Study of the Effects of Communicator Credibility and Attitude Change on Subsequent Overt Behavior." Doctorial dissertation, Pennsylvania State University, 1966.

Aronson, E., and B. W. Golden, "The Effect of Relevant and Irrelevant Aspects of Communicator Credibility on Opinion Change," *Journal of Personality*, 30 (1962), 135–46.

Berlo, D. K., J. B. Lemert, and R. J. Mertz, "Dimensions for Evaluating the Acceptability of Message Sources." Research monograph, Department of Communication, Michigan State University, 1966.

Haiman, F., "An Experimental Study of the Effects of Ethos in Public Speaking," *Speech Monographs*, 16 (1949), 190–202.

Hovland, C. I., I. L. Janis, and H. H. Kelley, *Communication and Persuasion*. New Haven, Conn.: Yale University Press, 1953.

Hovland, C. I., and W. Weiss, "The Influence of Source Credibility on Communication Effectiveness," *Public Opinion Quarterly*, 15 (1951), 635–50.

McCroskey, J. C., "Scales for the Measurement of Ethos," *Speech Monographs*, 33 (1966), 65–72. (a)

————, "Experimental Studies of the Effects of Ethos and Evidence in Persuasive Communication." Doctoral dissertation, Pennsylvania State University, 1966. (b)

Mills, J., and E. Aronson, "Opinion Change as a Function of the Communicator's Attractiveness and Desire to Influence," *Journal of Personality and Social Psychology*, 1 (1965), 173–77.

Steffens, Gretchen E., "An Experimental Study of the Effect of the Sex of the Communicator on Perceived Ethos and Attitude Change." Master's thesis, Michigan State University, 1967.

Strother, E., "An Experimental Study of Ethos Related to the Introduction in the Persuasive Speaking Situation." Doctorial dissertation, Northwestern University, 1951.

Widgery, R. N., and B. Webster, "The Effects of Physical Attractiveness Upon Perceived Initial Credibility." *Michigan Speech Association Journal*, 4 (1969).

Chapter 6

Nonverbal Variables

Ray Birdwhistell, an authority on nonverbal communication, estimates that in a normal two-person conversation the verbal components carry less than 35 percent of the social meaning of the situation; more than 65 percent is carried on the nonverbal band. Initially, this may seem to be a surprising estimate, but if we begin to list the things that communicate information through nonverbal channels, the estimate becomes more realistic. For instance, we may communicate by our manner of dress, our body odor, our physique or posture, our body tension, our facial expressions and degree of eye contact, our hand and body movements, our punctuality or lack of it, the way we choose to position ourselves in relation to the other person, the vocal sounds accompanying our verbal messages, and many many more things. If we choose to think of nonverbal communication in its broadest sense, the potential sources for study would include such diverse areas as (1) Geldard's (1968) cutaneous communication laboratory where subjects are trained to receive a language through electrical stimulation of the skin; (2) Rhine's (1967) parapsychology laboratory where subjects have experimented with mentally transmitting a symbol from a card to a receiver at some distance; (3) Schutz's (1967) group encounter sessions conducted at the famed Esalen retreat. Some of these sessions rely heavily on nonverbal communication and are appropriately labeled body awareness workshops—

or by some, "group grope." At Esalen people purportedly increase their non-verbal sensitivity by engaging in such activities as "conversing" with their bodies, touching others' faces while blindfolded, and lying on the floor with other group members and rolling over and over.

Harrison (1965) attempted to demonstrate the frequency and importance of nonverbal variables in the communication process by the following picture:

Figure 6.1

Reprinted from *Dimensions in Communication: Readings*, edited by James H. Campbell and Hal W. Helper. © 1965 by Wadsworth Publishing Company, Inc., Belmont, California. Reprinted by permission of the publisher and the author.

We have used this picture with numerous student and adult groups and the reactions are generally the same. When asked to make judgments about power, trust, competence, sincerity, and honesty there is no hesitation. Some are even willing to risk judgments about intelligence, happiness, economic status, and age. When such groups are asked to list the cues in this simple drawing that caused them to make these important judgments, they are able to produce a rather lengthy list. When one considers the potential range of cues available from this drawing compared with the complexities of an actual human dialogue, one begins to carefully consider two things: (1) There is a great deal of nonverbal communication taking place—much of which we do not consciously take note, and (2) We make many important judgments and decisions based on these nonverbal cues.

In fact, when we receive conflicting information from verbal and non-verbal channels, we may make decisions by placing more credibility on the nonverbal message. Perhaps we feel it is harder to fake nonverbal responses. In situations where we receive conflicting messages through two different *nonverbal* channels, it is likely we will choose to believe the message which emanates from the channel we perceive harder to fake. When we want to communicate something unpleasant and do not want to be held accountable for such a statement, we magnify the nonverbal message. Thus, any argument as to our intent can be denied by asking for a review of what was *said*. If our nonverbal behavior is questioned we can dismiss such challenges and explain the behavior as random action. We have all been in situations in which we have observed or sent these conflicting messages on verbal and nonverbal channels—the mother who screams, "I WANT IT QUIET AROUND THIS HOUSE," or the professor who says, "Sure, I've always got plenty of time to talk to a student" while he glances at his watch and nervously begins packing his briefcase. In some instances printed verbal messages also carry nonverbal elements. In the example of the mother's scream, the capital letters support the verbal message. Sometimes the non-verbal dimension can add a great deal of information to the written message. For example:

detache d   maGNify   ↻ argle

Thus, it is difficult to study nonverbal communication in isolation because of its close interrelationship with verbal signals. Although this chapter may seem "isolated" from the context of the verbal systems previously discussed, nevertheless, it constantly interacts with each of them.

Effects of Environment

Many cues that affect our communicative behavior are found in the setting in which the interaction occurs. For example, architecture and room design are such factors.

Architecture and Room Design

Consider the architecture of your classroom. Does it promote a high frequency of interpersonal contacts? Does it influence your perceptual orientation? Does it influence your learning speed? Architects and interior decorators have long assumed relationships between structural-esthetic conditions and human behavior, but there has been little empirical verification of these intuitive judgments. The studies of Maslow and Mintz (1956) provide noteworthy exceptions. They placed their subjects in rooms that were designed to be "beautiful," "average," and "ugly" and asked them to rate a series of negative print photographs of faces. The description of the "ugly" room will be sufficient to illustrate the extreme conditions:

> It was 7' × 12' × 10' and had two half-windows, battleship-gray walls, an overhead bulb with a dirty, torn, ill-fitting lampshade, and "furnishings" to give the impression of a janitor's storeroom in disheveled condition. There were two straight-backed chairs, a small table, tin cans for ashtrays, and dirty, torn window shades. Near the bare walls on three sides were such things as pails, brooms, mops, cardboard boxes, dirty-looking trash cans, a bedspring mattress, and assorted refuse. The room was neither swept nor dusted and the ashtrays were not emptied.

Noise, odor, time of day, type of seating, and the experimenter were controlled. A follow-up study tested the effects of the rooms on the experimenters. The results showed that subjects in the "beautiful" room tended to give significantly higher ratings to the faces than did those participants in the "ugly" room. It was also found that the "ugly" room tended to promote a more rapid completion of the task. In some instances, the experimenter found excuses for avoiding the "ugly" room entirely. Observational notes showed that the "ugly" room produced responses such as monotony, fatigue, sleep, headache, discontent, irritability, and hostility. The "beautiful" room, on the other hand, produced responses such as feelings of comfort, pleasure, enjoyment, importance, energy, and a desire to continue the activity. Such visual-esthetic surroundings can indeed influence the nature of the human communication taking place.

The structural aspects of the architectural surroundings may also influence the nature of one's interpersonal communication. For instance, research seems to suggest that physical distance may have a great deal to do with friendship choices. In a number of studies conducted in housing developments, we consistently find more social contacts and more friendship choices among people from the same building—and particularly from the same floor (Festinger, Schachter, and Back, 1963). Some recent housing designs for the aged have tried to promote interaction by following a circular floor plan with all the doors on a given floor opening into a common entrance hall. This entrance hall provides a natural place to meet and talk, whereas a long narrow hallway would provide fewer opportunities for interaction. Whyte (1956), in his observations of suburban housing, noted that adjacent driveways would also serve to promote conversations among neighbors. Even the location of one's house may influence the number of interpersonal contacts—a centralized location, such as the middle of the block, would be more apt to result in a greater frequency of contacts than would be the case if the house were toward the end of the block. The interpretation that individuals give to architectural barriers and spaces brings us to some related environmental variables in the communication process: territoriality and personal space.

Territoriality and Personal Space

We carry our personal space with us. Sometimes we identify so strongly with a given location or space that we act as if we owned it. Hall (1959) suggests that this concept of territoriality can develop so fast that even during the second lecture of a series of lectures you will find many people sitting in the same seat they occupied during the first lecture. There may even be some irritation because someone took "your" seat. The tendency to identify one's territory during interpersonal encounters has sometimes led to heated debate. The concept of territoriality was the overriding environmental factor affecting the discussion on the size and shape of the negotiation table at the Paris peace talks in 1968. It took eight months to reach an agreement on the shape of the table. The diagrams in Fig. 6.2 mark the chronology of the seating proposals.

The United States (US) and South Viet Nam (SVN) wanted a seating arrangement in which only two sides were identified. They did not want to recognize the National Liberation Front (NLF) as an "equal" party in the negotiations. North Viet Nam (NVN) and the NLF wanted "equal" status given to all parties—represented by a four-sided table. The final arrangement was such that both parties could claim victory. The round table minus the dividing lines allowed North Viet Nam and the NLF to claim all four delegations were equal. The existence of the two secretarial tables (interpreted as dividers), the lack of identifying symbols on the table, and an AA, BB speaking rotation permitted the United States and South Viet Nam to claim victory for the two-sided approach. Considering the lives lost during the eight months needed to arrive at the seating arrangement, we can certainly conclude that territorial space has extremely high priority in some interpersonal settings.

The question of seating arrangements has been the subject of other

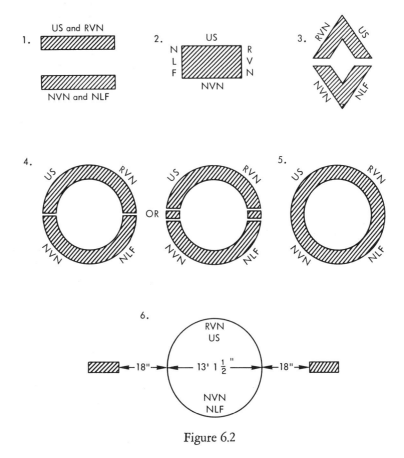

Figure 6.2

investigations concerning personal space. Generally, it seems fair to conclude that seating arrangements are not usually accidental. People sit opposite each other or facing each other across the corner of a table when they desire frequent conversation. The visibilty of the other person seems to be crucial here. Opposite positioning provides full visibility of the other person, and end-corner positioning preserves closeness, but does not require constant eye contact. Sommer (1961) found that elected group leaders were attracted to the end positions of rectangular tables, and Hare and Bales (1963) found that persons high in dominance seek focal locations in group meetings. A study, which included months of observation in a student union, a library, and responses to a student questionnaire, confirms the nonrandomness of seating behavior (Sommer, 1965). Students apparently select different seats depending on the type of interaction they are anticipating—for example, chatting before class, studying together for the same exam, studying together for different exams, or competing with another student on a given task. Chatting before class and studying for the same exam seem to require closer seating, whereas studying for separate exams and competitive tasks requires seating that creates distance between two parties at the same table.

The concept of personal space also includes the individual perception of what is "comfortable" conversational space. This varies from person to person, from situation to situation, and from culture to culture. Some conversations are difficult to complete if the conversational zone is not comfortable. Hall (1959) has even suggested a list of distances allied with certain kinds of information for the North American culture—for example, 3" to 6" is very close and top secret, 20" to 36" is neutral distance and personal subject matter, and 5½' to 8' is public distance and information for others to hear.

When we talk we make choices from the range of possibilities available to us on the verbal level; we also make choices on the nonverbal level regarding personal space. The study of such choices will bring us closer to understanding of the communicator's intent and the potential range of responses he will elicit.

We could not leave a discussion of environmental variables in nonverbal communication without mentioning the general influence of the total environment—the culture itself.

Cultural Factors

Much of what we know of the development and manifestation of nonverbal behaviors in various cultures comes from those who study intercultural communication—or communication between people from different cultural backgrounds. The analysis in such studies generally focuses on a violation by one party of some culturally-acquired custom, ritual, role, or expectation of the other and which has been learned from his culture. The following represents a few of the problem areas in intercultural communication and, at the same time, reminds us of some of our own nonverbal behavior specific to this culture.

Our culture generally discourages close physical contact except in intimate relations. We often tend to "hold ourselves in," avoiding bodily contact with strangers when in a crowded situation. Yet we know that in many countries it is perfectly natural for two adult males to embrace each other in greeting. In some countries it is common practice to place one's hand on the other person's arm while talking to him. The variance in the "proper" conversational space also seems related to the issue of physical contact. We mentioned in a previous chapter that Latin Americans desire a much shorter distance between the communicators—hence, we may find that a North American moves away from the Latin American in order to increase the conversational distance, while the Latin American advances in order to decrease the distance.

Another deeply embedded cultural orientation is our notion of time. Punctuality is generally highly regarded by our culture, but not in all quarters. The poor person in America often has to wait excessively long periods of time to see a professional caseworker. One of these poor people commented:

> It is one thing for the professional to objectively and analytically understand a client sitting and waiting seven hours in a clinic, but it is quite another thing for the professional to go to the clinic and sit for seven hours. (Daniel, 1968)

Latin Americans regard punctuality differently, too. Some have even suggested that if you can put up with a 5-minute wait in this country, you should be able to tolerate a 45-minute wait in some Latin American countries. The time it takes to "get to know someone" is also variously perceived. Our culture is highly dependent on schedules and deadlines, but in the Middle East the suggestion of a deadline may be interpreted as extremely threatening.

Culture also influences nonverbal emotional expression. From childhood we are taught that we should suppress our feelings. Emotional outbursts connote weakness. The "cool head" is revered. The Arab, on the other hand, is allowed and encouraged to express his feelings without inhibition. The Arab may think the "cool head" is hiding something and the American may think the Arab is being childish.

As previously noted, we do not have to leave our own country to experience differing cultural perceptions. The person who first referred to our nation's poor as "culturally *deprived*" was exhibiting the same blindness to cultural *differences* that characterizes so many of the "ugly Americans" overseas. Daniel's (1968) study of communication between professionals, nonprofessionals, and poor people found the following nonverbal factors to be critical in *effective* communication between these individuals.

1. When the professional goes to the poor person's home, the professional *sits* down, doesn't stand in the door as if afraid, is very informal, and relaxes—smokes a cigarette.

2. The professional allows the poor people to see him in the community, in block club meetings, on the street, in local restaurants, the church, or in the poolroom.

3. The professional does not use a rash, snappy, or demanding tone of voice—no harshness.

4. The professional always has a warm, friendly smile for the poor person.

5. The professional dresses in a clear, casual fashion, but not in a suit and tie when he visits a poor person in the poor person's home.

The following were critical nonverbal factors leading to *ineffective* communication:

1. The professional was white and working in a Negro neighborhood.

2. The professional wore a suit and tie and had a title such as Ph.D. or Supervisor.

3. The professional had a facial expression of fear and disgust when he entered a poor person's home.

4. The professional makes the poor person wait for a long period of time.

5. The professional used a snappy, harsh, and angry tone of voice.

6. The professional was very businesslike. Could only see poor people from nine to five. The professional does not greet the poor person with a smile, but asks a person to sit, and immediately begins asking the standard questions.

7. The professional wrote down what the poor person said as the poor person talked.

8. The professional mumbled to himself and fiddled with papers on his desk during the interview with the poor person.

9. White VISTA workers wore long hair, dirty, cutoff clothing and had body odor.

10. The nonprofessional was very impatient when talking with poor people.

11. The nonprofessional visited the poor person at the

wrong time—Sunday morning or when the poor person was trying to fix breakfast and clean house.

One of the obvious questions that may arise after a discussion of the
tremendous potential for intercultural misunderstanding is what can we do
—or what should we do. Hall and Whyte (1960) give a good answer:

> To work with people, must we be just like them? Obviously not.
> If we try to conform completely, the Arab, the Latin American, the
> Italian [the Negro], whoever he might be finds our behavior con-
> fusing and insincere. He suspects our motive. We are expected to
> be different. But we are also expected to respect and accept the
> other people as they are. And we may, without doing violence to
> our own personalities, learn to communicate with them by observ-
> ing the unwritten patterns they are accustomed to.
> To be aware that there are pitfalls in cross-cultural dealings is the
> first step forward. And to accept the fact that our convictions are
> in no respect more eternally "right" than someone else's is another
> constructive step.

Effects of Communicator's Appearance

Barnlund (1968) states, "Personal apparel is a major source of information about the identity and character of others." It seems plausible," he
continues, "that clothing may affect self-attitudes as much or more, than
observer attitudes." Although personal apparel covers a wide variety of
things from cosmetics to glasses, the little research available in this area
seems to have focused on clothing.

Clothing

Hoult's research (1954) suggests that the influence of clothing on ratings of attractiveness, personality, success, etc. is greater when the person
is unknown or socially distant to the rater. When raters and ratees were
well-acquainted, changes in clothing did not significantly influence ratings.
However, in another study subjects rated ten unknown male heads for attractiveness; then they rated a group of "outfits" for appropriateness in college. The high-rated heads were then put on the low-rated outfits. The low-
rated heads were placed on the high-rated outfits. This time clothing did

"No, this isn't my 'party get-up.' This isn't even my New Year."

Figure 6.3

Copyright 1967 by Saturday Review, Inc.
Reprinted by permission of the publisher and
the artist.

influence the perceptions. Previously high-rated heads (now with low-rated clothes) decreased in ratings; low-rated heads (now with high-rated clothes) increased in ratings.

Aiken (1963) was interested in the relationship of clothing attitudes of female students and their scores on other personality tests. He developed a clothing attitude scale that had five dimensions or factors—Decoration in Dress, Interest in Dress, Comfort in Dress, Economy in Dress, and Conformity in Dress. He obtained scores from his 160 women subjects on this scale and five other tests that surveyed a wide range of psychological and personality characteristics. As expected, he found those women who scored high on the Conformity in Dress category also revealed high scores on conformity variables in the other tests. Those who scored high in Interest in Dress and Decoration in Dress were characterized as "uncomplicated and socially conscientious." High scores on Interest in Dress also had indications of adjustment difficulties. Such difficulties were things like tenseness or insecurity. Those scoring high in Comfort in Dress were described as "controlled extroverts." And the high-scoring women on Economy in Dress revealed psychological characteristics of intelligence and efficiency.

Perhaps one of the most widely publicized incidents in which clothing contributed negatively to an already troubled situation was when Vice President Nixon visited Peru. After violating the custom which disapproved of political speaking on university property, he then found himself with an interpreter in full military uniform. Whether the clothing served to remind the audience of the military might of the United States or of the recently overthrown military dictators in Latin America, it did not contribute to affable intercultural relations.

Physical Attractiveness and Physique

"People believe that different temperaments go with different body builds." This is a conclusion from the research of Wells and Siegel (1961). In their experiments, subjects were shown silhouette drawings of various body types—ectomorph, endomorph, mesomorph, and average. The body types were then rated on twenty-four bipolar scales such as ambitious-lazy, fat-thin, intelligent-unintelligent. The ratings produced considerable agreement. For instance, the ectomorph was rated thinner, younger, more ambitious, taller, more suspicious of others, more tense and nervous, less masculine, more stubborn and inclined to be difficult, more pessimistic, and quieter. Barker (1942) had similar agreement on judgments of personal characteristics among strangers who had met each other for the first time. At one point in the study, these twelve strangers were asked to record any other member they considered good-looking or not good-looking. Forty responses were obtained and there was 100 percent agreement among the responses regarding those who were good-looking and those who were not. There was also a high degree of agreement among the strangers on which people were bossy or permissive, popular or unpopular, tidy or unkempt, talkative or skeptical. Wells and Siegel do not reject the notion that the stereotyped judgments in their study may be valid. Over half of the subjects in Barker's study (who selected seatmates solely on visual examination) chose to remain with their original selections when given a chance to change three months later. Regardless of whether we accept the validity of these judgments for the individuals concerned, such sterotyping does exist and must be considered as potential stimulus for communication responses.

In several instances, researchers have sought to determine the influence of physical attractiveness and physique in persuasive situations. Tentative conclusions imply that perceived physical attractiveness will enhance one's initial credibility and thus provide him with a persuasive advantage (Mills and Aronson, 1965; Haiman, 1949; Widgery and Webster, 1969). The only data available thus far on perceived tallness suggests that a persuasive speaker will not necessarily have a natural advantage by being tall (Baker and Redding, 1962). But as status is increased, perceived tallness also seems to increase (Wilson, 1968). Some studies show that there are situations in which a speaker elicits the greatest attitude change in the first few minutes of his persuasive speech. The data available on responses to the communicator's physical appearance and nonverbal vocal characteristics certainly cannot be dismissed in future research on attitude change.

Effects of Physical Behavior

There are many forms of physical behavior that provide stimuli for responses in interpersonal communication—body movements, facial expressions (especially of the mouth and eyes), hand and arm movements, walking style, posture, and many others. Another form of physical behavior that is extremely important to us at various stages in our development is tactile communication or, simply, touching.

Touching

Probably our first information about our world comes through tactile sensitivity during fetal life. In early infancy, the child develops his initial spatial orientation through tactile explorations. He also begins to learn about himself by feeling his own body. Perhaps more important to the child than his own efforts at tactile contact are the efforts by others toward him. A child deprived of being handled and touched may develop severe emotional and mental problems (Levine, 1960). It is through these tactile experiences that the child learns the nature and expectations of the world around him. Frank (1957) has stated that these early tactile experiences set the stage for later communicative experiences:

> It seems clear that the child's reception of verbal messages is predicated in large measure upon his prior tactile experience so that facial expressions and gestures become signs and symbols for certain kinds of tactile communications and interpersonal relations. . . .

Symbols, lacking primary tactile validation, may be less clearly and less effectively established as basic codes of communication later. (pp. 226–30)

After a latency period during middle childhood, tactile communication again becomes increasingly important during adolescence. At first we see members of the same sex freely touching one another; gradually such activity moves into heterosexual experiences such as petting, necking, and intercourse. The apparent success of the body awareness workshops at Esalen and Bethel testify that some of us have not been able to "free" ourselves on this level by the time we reach adulthood. Schindler-Rainman (1968) put it this way, "One thing is sure, that ours is a pretty hesitant culture when it comes to physical expression particularly for middle-class people."

In many cases tactile communication accompanies some other mode —for example, a smile, a gesture, a spoken sentence. It may support or contradict the message communicated in the other mode. For instance, the father who smiles and calmly explains to his three-year-old daughter, "Now you don't have to be afraid of the Ferris wheel. I'll show you how much fun it is by going with you." He then grasps the little girl's hand and she feels a nervous, shaking, clammy hand. An instance in which the linguistic and tactile codes seemed to work in harmony is found in an experiment conducted with nurses and patients. This study found touch gestures used by nurses would increase the verbal interaction between nurses and patients. It also improved patients' attitudes toward the nurses (Agulera, 1967).

Body Movements

Birdwhistell has given the label *kinesics* to the systematic study of body movements. The scope of such study is staggering. Mario Pei (1965) estimates that some 700,000 distinct and elementary physical signs can be produced by communicating man. La Barre's (1964) excellent work on kinesics and cultural anthropology takes the reader through such areas as Navajo motor habits; the silent language of European monks; hand language of deaf-mutes; sign languages of truck drivers and tobacco auctioneers; and gestures of greeting, kissing, contempt, beckoning, and politeness around the world. In this country, Birdwhistell (1965) claims to have isolated at least 23 different positions of the eyebrows that have separate meanings.

Body movements in the communicative behavior of man appear early in life and are closely related to one's culture. They are learned behavior and thus vary considerably from culture to culture. Spitz (1957) noted that children deprived of emotional support in hospitals tended to have unique physical reactions—unlike those of other children—to the approach of anyone except nurses with food at feeding time. This reaction was a rotation of the head from side to side resembling the gesture that signifies "no." Spitz explains that this motion occurs because contact with an emotionally deprived child builds tension in him and the head motion occurs as a regressive device to relieve that tension. Michael and Willis (1968) tested 80 children for their ability to send and interpret 12 common gestures and found middle-class children more skilled than those from lower socio-economic classes. Also, children with one year of school were more accurate in transmission and reception of these gestures than were children with no prior school experience. The gestures used indicated: yes, no, how many, how big, I don't know, come here, go away, shape, hi, good-bye, be quiet, and raised hand for attention. Although such results are tentative, they do tend to support the notion that these kinesic movements are learned and show that such learning begins at an early age. Brannigan and Humphries (1969) have proposed that some expressive gestures from early childhood appear in modified form in adult behavior. They use the example of the child, angered by a situation, who raises his hand with open palm as if to strike the other person.

Some researchers are concerned with studying extreme detail in body movements. Birdwhistell's notation system can record physical movements from moment to moment. His research is based on the theory that kinesics constitutes a language much like one that is written or spoken. A gesture can be performed in sequence to provide the equivalent of a sentence or paragraph. Like speech, gestures may have dialects or regionalisms. Further, just as we use only a small portion of the linguistic possibilities available to us in spoken English, we use only a small portion of the possible range of body movements available to us. Birdwhistell's work seems to support three important conclusions: (1) Body movement can be observed and recorded —even on what appears to be a microscopic level; (2) the compilation of a list of gestures and their meanings is useless without reference to specific contexts; and (3) movements in the area of the eye combined with hand motions are the prime situation definers for our culture. Ekman's research (1965) shows how the two areas may work in combination. He reports that the type of information communicated by the head area carries information about the affect being experienced while body cues communicate primarily information about the level of arousal or the degree of intensity of the affective experience.

Another detailed approach to kinesic study is the work done by Scheflen (1964, 1965). Scheflen made sound films of numerous therapeutic encounters. His content analysis of these films led him to conclude that there were consistent and patterned quasi-courtship behaviors being exhibited in this setting. He then developed a set of classifications for such behaviors. *Courtship Readiness* is characterized by constant manifestations of high muscle tone, reduced eye bagginess and jowl sag, lessening of slouch and shoulder hunching, and decreasing belly sag. *Preening Behavior* is exemplified by such things as stroking of the hair, touching up of makeup, glancing in the mirror, rearranging clothes in a sketchy fashion, leaving buttons open, adjusting suit coats, tugging at socks, and readjusting a tie knot. *Positional Cues* were reflected in seating arrangements that suggested "we're not open to interaction from others." Arms, legs, and torsos were so arranged as to inhibit others from entering the conversation. *Actions of Appeal or Invitation* include flirtatious glances, gaze-holding, rolling of the pelvis, crossing legs to expose a thigh, exhibiting wrist or palm, protruding the breasts, and other gestures. Some of these behaviors are shown in Fig. 6.4. As is often the case with nonverbal behavior, subjects reported little awareness of these behaviors.

Figure 6.5 is a sequence of events from Scheflen's films that further illustrates his observations. Two male therapists are treating a young schizophrenic girl. In Scheflen's words: "At the beginning of the sequence (6.5A) the therapist on the viewer's left turns to watch an attractive research technician walk across the room. The patient begins to preen (6.5B).

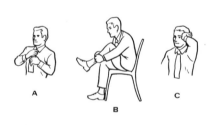

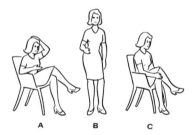

SOME PREENING BEHAVIOR
OF MALE PSYCHOTHERAPISTS
(A) Tie Preen
(B) Sock Preen
(C) Hair Preen

APPEALING OR INVITATIONAL
BEHAVIOR OF WOMEN PATIENTS
(A) Presenting the Palm with Hair Press
(B) Rolling the Hip
(C) Presenting and Caressing the Leg

Figure 6.4

Reprinted from "The Significance of Posture in Communicative Systems," by Albert E. Scheflen, in PSYCHIATRY 27 (1964) p. 323, by permission of The William Alanson White Psychiatric Foundation, Inc. Copyright 1964 by the Foundation.

QUASI-COURTING SEQUENCE THAT REESTABLISHED AN INTERRUPTED
DOCTOR-PATIENT RELATIONSHIP

Figure 6.5

Reprinted from "Quasi-Courtship Behavior in Psychotherapy," by Albert E. Scheflen,
in PSYCHIATRY 28 (1965) p. 252, by permission of The William Alanson White
Psychiatric Foundation, Inc. Copyright 1965 by the Foundation.

The therapist turns back to the patient and also preens (6.5C, 6.5D), but
he then disclaims courtship by an ostentatious look of boredom and a yawn
(6.5E). Immediately afterward, the patient tells him she is interested in an
attractive male aide." (Scheflen, 1965, p. 252)

The next section deals with facial expressions and eye contact. Even though we are discussing these two aspects of verbal communication separately, it is important to remember that in actual practice we generally respond to a stimulus that is a combination of several nonverbal cues. An experiment that includes a combination of body movement plus some facial cues demonstrates this. A shift of posture toward another person coupled with a smile and direct eye contact (Fig. 6.6B) seems to contribute to a perception of "warmth" and in turn contributes to the verbal output of the other person. (Reece and Whitman, 1962)

Facial Expressions and Eye Contact

The common phrase, "You should have seen his face," reminds us of our reliance on cues from facial expressions when making interpersonal judgments. We derive such cues primarily from the eye and mouth areas. When people are asked to make judgments about feelings displayed in facial expressions, there is a high degree of agreement among them. This is mainly due to a "learning" of facial stereotypes which, whether they are accurate or not, do influence the nature of interpersonal exchanges. On the question of accuracy of the judgments about feelings as seen in facial expressions, the literature reveals little consistency. There are many factors that may influence or determine accuracy in judging facial expressions, but the major ones can be classified as: (1) personality traits and other characteristics of those making the judgments, and (2) characteristics of the experimental method and the type of testing used.

Intelligence seems to be one factor that accounts for a small portion of our sensitivity to facial cues. Age may be another factor simply because

Figure 6.6

Reprinted from "Quasi-Courtship Behavior in Psychotherapy," by A. E. Scheflen, in PSYCHIATRY, 28 (August 1965) p. 245–57, by permission of the William Alanson White Psychiatric Foundation, Inc. Copyright 1965 by the Foundation.

we seem to have a decreasing ability in picking up visual cues in the facial area after age 39 (Farrimond, 1959). As yet, there is not enough evidence to support any perceptual superiority of one sex over the other. Perhaps the most provocative data related to accuracy differences in judging faces comes from research that investigated response sets—or typical response patterns. Shapiro (1968) has shown that some people may have a predilection for observing facial cues, whereas others may consistently choose to respond to linguistic ones. Other authors support the existence of a "general factor" or "general ability" which makes some people more accurate in judging than others. Thus, a person able to accurately identify emotional meaning in vocal expressions would also be able to accurately identify meanings in facial or musical expressions. Further, if a person can correctly identify emotional meanings, he will be fully capable of portraying or expressing these meanings to others.

Obviously, one of the most important aspects of testing facial expressions is the stimulus itself—the face and the emotion being expressed. Stritch and Secord (1956) found that very slight changes to facial details can make critical differences in personality and physiognomic judgments of faces. They had an artist retouch photographs so as to systematically change such things as grooming of the hair, mouth curvature, wrinkles about the eyes, heaviness of eyebrows, brightness of eyes. In some cases, such minute changes caused significantly different evaluations by the judges on dimensions of personality and physiognomic features. In the latter, for instance, when a mouth curvature was changed to look "straight" (rather than up or down) judges then perceived changes in lips (thicker) and complexion (lighter) although these had not been changed. Another common characteristic of many studies of facial expression is that the faces are frequently unknown to the judges. It seems possible that greater accuracy would be achieved with familiar faces. In addition to the faces themselves, variations in the length of observation, the kinds of discriminations asked, the method for making these discriminations, and the amount of contextual information provided, all tend to contribute to the consistently inconsistent results of studies in this area.

The discussion above illustrates the complexity involved in measuring one's reactions to facial expressions. Further complicating efforts to improve accuracy in judging facial expressions by teaching social conventions is the discovery that not all expressive facial patterns are learned (Davitz, 1964). Similarities in emotional expressions of the congenitally blind and of the sighted have been reported in several studies and tend to support this notion.

One area of the face that seems to convey a great deal of information is the mouth. For this reason, many scholars have chosen smiles as the subject worthy of further study. Generally, smiles communicate friendliness and cooperation in human relations. The smile is also used when seeking approval from others (Rosenfeld, 1966) or in communicating acceptance to others. We also know that the person who smiles *too* often is suspect and makes us uneasy. Because one's interpretation of a smile is nearly always bound up with movements and cues from other parts of the face, it is risky to isolate the smile as a unit of study. Figure 6.7 illustrates how additional cues can change the interpretation.

The other major source of information in facial expressions is in the eye region. Brannigan and Humphries (1969) have identified what they call *flash.* This is a sudden raising and then lowering of the eyebrows during conversation. This, they suggest, attracts the partner's attention and may indicate interest or emphasis on a certain phrase or word. Others have been concerned about eye contact. The following is a summary of the research findings on eye contact—largely based on a synthesis by Argyle and Dean (1965). Special patterns occur with mental patients, autistic children, and persons from other cultures, but they are not included.

When does eye contact occur?

1. When people are seeking feedback concerning the reactions of others. We tend to cast glances, ranging from three to ten seconds, at the other person more often when we are listening. When we are speaking, however, we tend to glance at our listener after we have finished our conversational "speech" or at some point where there is a natural break within the presentation of the "speech."

2. When we want to signal that the communication channel is open. In some instances eye contact can almost act as an obligation to interact.

3. When we want to convey our need for affiliation, involvement, or inclusion. Those who have high affiliative needs

Figure 6.7

tend to return glances more often. There appears to be more eye contact between people who like each other. When being introduced, eye contact is influential in determining partner selection for participation in experiments. This is true for male pairs and female pairs. Several investigators have noted that arousal leads to enlargement of the pupils of the eye and that men and women are more attracted to each other because of it—although they do not realize the cue they are responding to. (Stass and Willis, 1967)

4. Women seem to engage in more eye contact in a variety of situations than do men. This seems to be particularly true with other women.

5. Eye contact seems to increase as the communicating pair increases the distance between them. In this case eye contact psychologically reduces the distance between communicators.

6. Eye contact is also used to produce anxiety in others. You may remember the stare Mohammed Ali used against his boxing opponents while receiving instructions from the referee just prior to the fight. A gaze lasting longer than ten seconds is likely to produce an uncomfortable situation. Morris, in his book *The Naked Ape*, hypothesizes that this is due to man's biological antecedents—for example, the aggressiveness and hostility signified by the ape's stare.

When is eye contact absent?

1. When people want to hide something concerning their inner feelings they may try to avoid eye contact. In one experiment it was noticed that people who cheated tried to avoid eye contact. This may also be the case when discussing embarrassing topics, or in situations where feelings of humility or submissiveness occur.

2. In competitive situations, when there is dislike or tension, or when a recent deception has been practiced, the two participants will engage in less eye contact. This may be an attempt to insulate oneself against threats, arguments, information, or even affection from the other party.

3. Eye contact may also be lacking when the two parties are close to one another. Reducing eye contact will then psychologically increase the distance.

4. When a speaker begins a long utterance, the probability

that eye contact is avoided increases. Sometimes when listeners anticipate a long utterance they express their boredom by looking away.

5. When an individual wishes to disavow maintenance of any social contact his eye contact tends to diminish.

Effects of Communicator's Voice

The capacity to communicate information through vocal nuances is familiar to anyone who has ever tried to be sarcastic. Here the vocal message may contradict the verbal one. Thus, when you say to your friend, "That was really a great joke," but your tone of voice implies, "That was one of the dumbest stories I've heard," you are likely to be perceived as sarcastic. Studies of such conflicting messages on vocal and verbal levels suggest you will be more likely to respond to the vocal cues than to the verbal message. There are other situations in which we do not consciously try to communicate with our voice, but we do. We reveal emotional states and certain personal characteristics through vocal cues alone. Vocal cues include voice qualities as well as vocal continuity—for example, rate, duration, nonfluencies, and pauses.

Personality Judgments

Apparently we learn vocal stereotypes just as we learn facial and body stereotypes. This is demonstrated by the generally uniform personality judgments elicited from recorded voices that are not generally validated by other measures of personality characteristics. Again, however, it should be noted that the stereotypes do exist and will influence responses. The study of interpersonal communication should be equally concerned with "what *is* happening" as with "what *should be* happening."

One author who recognized that stereotyped judgments of vocal cues regularly occur decided to explore the nature of these stereotypes. He used male and female speakers to simulate nine vocal characteristics. Judges then responded to the voices by rating them on forty personality characteristics. He reaffirmed the vocal stereotype when he said: "It is nonetheless apparent that specific personality ascriptions are seldom unique to an individual listener; more often they are shared by many" (Addington, 1968). Addington's factor analysis of the personality data showed that "male personality was perceived in terms of physical and emotional power, whereas female personality was apparently perceived in terms of social faculties." Table 6.1 summarizes his results.

Simulated Vocal Cues*	Speakers	Stereotyped Perceptions
Breathiness	Males	Younger; more artistic
	Females	More feminine; prettier; more petite; more effervescent; more highly strung; and shallower
Thinness	Males	Did not alter listener's image of the speaker
	Females	Increased social, physical, emotional, and mental immaturity; increased sense of humor and sensitivity
Flatness	Males	More masculine; more sluggish; colder; more withdrawn
	Females	More masculine; more sluggish; colder; more withdrawn
Nasality	Males	A wide array of socially undesirable characteristics
	Females	A wide array of socially undesirable characteristics
Tenseness	Males	Older; more unyielding; cantankerous
	Females	Younger; more emotional, feminine, high strung; less intelligent
Throatiness	Males	Older; more realistic, mature; sophisticated; and well adjusted
	Females	Less intelligent; more masculine; lazier; more boorish, unemotional, ugly, sickly, careless, inartistic, naive, humble, neurotic, quiet, uninteresting, apathetic. In short, "cloddish or oafish" (Addington)
Orotundity	Males	More energetic, healthy, artistic, sophisticated, proud, interesting, enthusiastic. In short, "hardy and esthetically inclined" (Addington)

Simulated Vocal Cues*	Speakers	Stereotyped Perceptions
	Females	Increased liveliness, gregariousness, "increasingly proud and humorless" (Addington)
Increased Rate	Males	More animated and extroverted
	Females	More animated and extroverted
Increased Pitch Variety	Males	More dynamic, feminine, esthetically inclined
	Females	More dynamic and extroverted

*For description of these cues see: P. Heinberg, *Voice Training for Speaking and Reading Aloud*, New York: The Ronald Press, 1964, pp. 152–80.

Table 6.1

A related line of inquiry has concerned itself primarily with identifying general characteristics of speakers from vocal cues. Again we find judges extremely accurate in identifying some characteristics. Nerbonne's (1967) work is representative. He found listeners were able to differentiate accurately between male and female; Negro and Caucasian; big and small speakers; between speakers 20–30 years old, 40–50 years old, and 60–70 years old; between speakers with less than a high school education, high school graduates, and college graduates; and between speakers from the eastern, southern, and general American dialect regions. Interestingly, Nerbonne also found that some judgments were made more accurately when aural cues were provided by telephone speech—namely, those of age and dialect.

Status cues can also be accurately perceived from brief vocal samples (Harms, 1961). Nine speakers were tested and categorized as high, middle, or low status. Each speaker recorded a 40-to 60-second conversation in which he responded to such questions and statements as "how are you," "ask for the time." Adult listeners rated the speakers according to status and credibility. Results showed that these listeners were not only able to identify the speakers' status, but many of them said they had made their decision after only 10 or 15 seconds of the recording. Responses also showed those perceived as high in status were also perceived as the most credible.

Judgments of Emotions

There have been many methods used to measure the communication of emotion through vocal cues. Starkweather (1956) used actual speech from the Army-McCarthy hearings of 1954 and filtered it electronically to make the content unintelligible. It sounds rather like a mumble as one might hear through a wall. Starkweather admits that some aspects of vocal quality may be lost in the filtering process, but a listener can still adequately perceive pitch, rate, and loudness in order to make judgments of emotional content and intensity. Accurate judgments of "degree of liking" have also been obtained from electronically filtered voice samples. Davitz and Davitz (1959) had speakers express ten different feelings by reciting parts of the alphabet. Numbers and letters are used because they are thought to be neutral in emotional information. Judges are then asked to identify emotional meaning from a list of ten feelings as they hear the recordings. Russian scientists have used a spectroanalyzer to study intonational characteristics of the voice in order to estimate a person's emotional state. The application of such research centers on identifying emotional aspects of man's voice as he communicates from space vehicles. Using measures of pulse, respiration, etc., in addition to analysis of vocal characteristics, Popov (1966) reports being able to differentiate emotional tension and physical tension. Davitz (1964) summarized this area by saying, "Regardless of the techniques used, all studies of adults thus far reported in the literature agree that emotional meanings can be communicated accurately by vocal expression" (p. 23).

Most studies report the not too surprising fact that various feelings are communicated with differential accuracy. For instance, in one study joy and hate were the most accurately communicated, whereas shame and love were the most difficult to recognize; another study found anger identified 63 percent of the time, but pride was only identified correctly 20 percent of the time.

More information is needed concerning the vocal characteristics associated with various emotional states. Extremely tentative findings thus far show: (1) Anger is associated with a fast rate, shorter comments, and more frequent pauses; (2) fear is associated with high pitch, fast rate, shorter comments, and more frequent pauses; (3) happiness is characterized by a higher pitch than a sad or neutral state; and (4) grief and depression are characterized by a high ratio or pause to phonation time, slower rate, and longer comments.

While our main concern in this book has been with the interaction process, we cannot ignore the body of literature that describes the effects of various vocal behaviors on the speaker. Obviously, this will ultimately affect the interaction process and the responses of the other person, too. For instance, some investigators have been concerned with what might broadly be called "mistakes" in speaking—the use of unnecessary repetitions, stutterings, the omission of parts of words, and incomplete sentences. Some believe these "mistakes" become more frequent as one's anxiety or discomfort increases. Another fascinating finding concerns the role of filled and unfilled pauses in speaking. A filled pause is one that contains some form of vocalization like "ah," "er," or "um"; an unfilled pause lacks such a vocal insertion. Several experimenters using several different tasks find that when speakers use filled pauses they also impair their performance. Thus, in a heated discussion you may maintain control of the conversation by filling the pauses, but you may also decrease the quality of your contribution. Some feel pauses reduce anxiety, but jam cognitive processes (Livant, 1963).

Conclusion

The preceding chapter is only an appetizer for the total field of nonverbal communication. Cross-cultural studies and manifestations of disturbed nonverbal communication were largely neglected; hand and feet movements, body sounds, laughing, crying, coughing, and whistling were completely omitted. One source notes that the sweat of chronically schizophrenic patients emits a peculiar odor that rats and perfume experts are able to detect (Smith and Sines, 1960). The boundaries of the study of nonverbal communication are almost limitless.

In many of your interpersonal encounters nonverbal elements will only account for a portion of the total number of cues that structure responses. Nonverbal behavior acts and interacts with verbal behavior. However, our perception and the perception of others is frequently at a low level of awareness for nonverbal components. It has been the purpose of this chapter to raise the level of intellectual awareness. Whether this will carry over in actual practice is probably more a product of your attitudes and orientation toward communication and toward the other person. At present we do not know the correlates of sensitivity to nonverbal cues. What can you do to increase your sensitivity?

References

Addington, D. W., "The Relationship of Selected Vocal Characteristics to Personality Perception," *Speech Monographs*, 35 (1968), 498.

Agulera, D. C., "Relationships Between Physical Contact and Verbal Interaction Between Nurses and Patients," *Journal of Psychiatric Nursing*, 5 (1967), 5–21.

Aiken, L., "Relationships of Dress to Selected Measures of Personality in Undergraduate Women," *Journal of Social Psychology*, 59 (1963), 119–28.

Argyle, M., and J. Dean, "Eye Contact, Distance and Affiliation," *Sociometry*, 28 (1965), 289–304.

Baker, E. E., and C. Redding, "The Effects of Perceived Tallness in Persuasive Speaking: An Experiment," *Journal of Communication*, 12 (1962), 51–53.

Barker, R., "The Social Interrelatedness of Strangers and Acquaintances," *Sociometry*, 5 (1942), 169–79.

Barnlund, D. C., "Nonverbal Interaction: Introduction," in *Interpersonal Communication: Survey and Studies*, ed. D. C. Barnlund. Boston: Houghton Mifflin Company, 1968, pp. 518–19.

Birdwhistell, R., "Background to Kinesics," *ETC*, 13 (1955), 10–18.

Brannigan, C., and D. Humphries, "I See What You Mean . . . ," *New Scientist* (1969), 406–8.

Daniel, J. L., "Factors in Effective Communication Between Professionals, Non-professionals, and Poor People." Unpublished Ph.D. dissertation, University of Pittsburgh, 1968, p. 113.

Davitz, J. R., *The Communication of Emotional Meaning*. New York: McGraw-Hill Book Company, 1964, p. 19.

Davitz, J., and L. Davitz, "The Communication of Feelings by Content-Free Speech," *Journal of Communication*, 9 (1959), 6–13.

Ekman, P., "Differential Communication of Affect by Head and Body Cues," *Journal of Personality and Social Psychology*, 2 (1965), 726–35.

Farrimond, T., "Age Differences in the Ability to Use Visual Cues in Auditory Communication," *Language and Speech*, 2 (1959), 179–92.

Festinger, L., S. Schachter, and K. Back, *Social Pressures in Informal Groups*. New York: Harper and Brothers, 1950; Stanford, Calif.: Stanford University Press, 1963.

Frank, L. K., "Tactile Communication," *Genetic Psychology Monographs*, 56 (1957), 226 and 230.

Geldard, F. A., "Body English," *Psychology Today*, 2 (1968), 42–47.

Haiman, F. S., "An Experimental Study of the Effects of Ethos in Public Speaking," *Speech Monographs*, 19 (1949), 190–202.

Hall, E. T., *The Silent Language*. Garden City, N.Y.: Doubleday & Company, Inc., 1959.

Hall, E. T., and W. F. Whyte, "Intercultural Communication: A Guide to Men of Action," *Human Organization*, 19 (1960), 5–12.

Hare, A., and R. Bales, "Seating Position and Small Group Interaction," *Sociometry*, 26 (1963), 480–86.

Harms, L. S., "Listener Judgments of Status Cues in Speech," *Quarterly Journal of Speech*, 47 (1961), 164–68.

Harrison, R., "Nonverbal Communication: Explorations Into Time, Space, Action, and Object," in *Dimensions in Communication*, James H. Campbell and H. W. Hepler, eds. Belmont, Calif.: Wadsworth Publishing Co., 1965, p. 160.

Hoult, R., "Experimental Measurement of Clothing as a Factor in Some Social Ratings of Selected American Men," *American Sociological Review*, 19 (1954), 324–28.

La Barre, W., "Paralinguistics, Kinesics, and Cultural Anthropology," in *Approaches to Semiotics*, T. A. Sebeok, A. S. Hayes, and M. C. Bateson, eds. The Hague: Mouton & Co., 1964, pp. 191–220.

Levine, S., "Stimulation in Infancy," *Scientific American*, 202 (1960), 80–86.

Livant, W. P., "Antagonistic Functions of Verbal Pauses: Filled and Unfilled Pauses in the Solution of Additions," *Language and Speech*, 6 (1963), 1–4.

Maslow, A. H., and N. L. Mintz, "Effects of Esthetic Surroundings: I. Initial Effects of Three Esthetic Conditions Upon Perceiving 'Energy' and 'Well-Being' in Faces," *Journal of Psychology*, 41 (1956), 247–54.

Mintz, N. L., "Effects of Esthetic-Surroundings: II. Prolonged and Repeated Experience in a 'Beautiful' and 'Ugly' Room," *Journal of Psychology*, 41 (1956), 459–66.

Michael, G., and N. Willis, Jr., "The Development of Gestures as a Function of Social Class, Education, and Sex," *Psychological Record*, 18 (1968), 515–19.

Mills, J., and E. Aronson, "Opinion Change as a Function of the Communicator's Attractiveness and Desire to Influence," *Journal of Personality and Social Psychology*, 1 (1965), 173–77.

Nerbonne, G. P., *The Identification of Speaker Characteristics on the Basis of Aural Cues*. Unpublished Ph.D. dissertation, Michigan State University, 1967.

Pei, Mario, *The Story of Language*, rev. ed. Philadelphia: J. B. Lippincott Co., 1965.

Popov, V. A., "Analysis of Intonational Characteristics of Speech as an Index of the Emotional State of Man Under Conditions of Flight in Space," trans. from Russian, *Zhurnal Vysshei Nervnoi Deyatel'nosti*, 16 (1966), 974–83.

Reece, M., and R. Whitman, "Expressive Movements, Warmth, and Verbal Reinforcement," *Journal of Abnormal and Social Psychology*, 64 (1962), 234–36.

Rhine, L., *ESP in life and Lab*. New York: The Macmillan Company, 1967, pp. 26–27.

Rosenfeld, H., "Instrumental Affiliative Functions of Facial and Gestural Expressions," *Journal of Personality and Social Psychology*, 4 (1966), 65–72.

Scheflen, A. E., "Quasi-Courtship Behavior in Psychotherapy," *Psychiatry*, 28 (1965), 245–57. See also A. E. Scheflen, "The Significance of Posture in Communicative Systems," *Psychiatry*, 27 (1964), 316–31.

Schindler-Rainman, E., "The Importance of Non-Verbal Communication in Laboratory Training," *Adult Leadership*, 16 (1968), 383.

Schutz, W., *Joy*. New York: Grove Press, 1967.

Shapiro, J. G., "Responsibility to Facial and Linguistic Cues," *Journal of Communication*, 18 (1968), 11–17.

Smith, K., and J. O. Sines, "Demonstration of a Peculiar Odor in the Sweat of Schizophrenic Patients," *Archives of General Psychiatry*, 2 (1960), 184–88.

Sommer, R., "Leadership and Group Geography," *Sociometry*, 24 (1961), 99–110.

———, "Further Studies of Small Group Ecology," *Sociometry*, 28 (1965), 337–48.

Spitz, R. A., *No and Yes: On the Genesis of Human Communication*, New York: International Universities Press, 1957.

Starkweather, J., "The Communication Value of Content-Free Speech," *American Journal of Psychology*, 69 (1956), 121–23.

Stass, J. W., and F. N. Willis, Jr., "Eye Contact, Pupil Dilation, and Personal Preference," *Psychonomic Science*, 7 (1967), 375–76.

Stritch, T., and P. Secord, "Interaction Effects in the Perception of Faces," *Journal of Personality*, 24 (1956), 272–84.

Wells, W., and B. Siegel, "Stereotyped Somatypes," *Psychological Reports*, 8 (1961), 78.

Whyte, W., *The Organization Man*, New York: Simon and Schuster, Inc., 1956.

Widgery, R. N., and B. Webster, "The Effects of Physical Attractiveness Upon Perceived Initial Credibility," *Michigan Speech Association Journal*, 4 (1969).

Wilson, P. R., "Perceptual Distortion of Height as a Function of Ascribed Academic Status," *Journal of Psychology*, 74 (1968), 97–102.

Chapter 7

General Response Tendencies

A General Introduction

You must have encountered by now at least one instructor who believes that students are, by nature, lazy, indolent, and passive. This instructor may further believe that students will expend the least amount of energy necessary to receive the grade they desire, that students are devious in their designs and basically untrustworthy and unreliable. If you express interest in his class he regards this as an attempt to snow him. Conscientious and diligent work on your part may be interpreted by him as behavior motivated by a fear of not receiving a high enough grade. If you are alert, attentive, and frequently ask questions of him, he may regard this as a well-designed strategy for attaining greater visibility in his class. In specific instances his assumptions may be true, in others very much in error. He *behaves as if they were true*, and indeed his responses may tend to cause the very behavior in students that he disparages.

If this belief were based upon systematic empirical observations or research, you might influence this instructor by showing him empirical evidence that contradicts his belief. If the belief were based upon testimony by individuals considered to be authorities, you might influence him by exposing him to authoritative statements running counter to his belief. If the belief were based upon some kind of social consensus, you might influence him by demonstrating widespread social acceptance of the position contrary to his belief. But let us assume that, as is usually the case with such beliefs, this one is based upon the instructor's personal and peculiar interpretation of his own experiences. It is not based upon systematic empirical observation, research, expert testimony, social consensus, or anything else that might serve as a basis for influencing or changing his belief. Indeed, anything you might do which is designed to influence that belief may be interpreted by the instructor as proof of how clever and deceptive students really are.

If the instructor responds in essentially the same way to a variety of students, a variety of student behavior and messages, under a variety of conditions, he may be exhibiting a general response tendency. "General response tendency" is our way of defining any response or response pattern that remains relatively stable across a variety of sources, messages, and conditions. If we are attempting to explain or account for outcomes of interpersonal communication, general response tendencies may frequently be sufficient to account for most of what goes on, or most of what is produced by, interpersonal communication encounters. This is why we choose to call general response tendencies "limiting variables." We have already discussed some basic communication processes in interpersonal systems. A limiting variable is one whose existence or occurrence accounts for outcomes more efficiently than does an analysis of the communication process. A limiting variable might be environmental noise sufficient to render communication impossible. It might be the existence or occurrence of nonverbal cues that are so influential as to make communication outcomes predictable from the cues alone. It might be message content so loaded as to make communication outcomes predictable for a wide range of individuals and conditions. Or, it might be the operation of general response tendencies in the interacting individuals. To illustrate this point further, let us examine one of the most broadly outlined conceptual schemes for accounting for individual responses in communicative situations.

A Global Perspective

One of the most intriguing conceptual schemes for describing general response tendencies in their broadest sense was developed by Morris (1956, 1964). This conceptual scheme emerges from factor analyses of ways in which many people say they prefer to live.

These preferences were reduced by Morris (1964) to three dimensions of value: detachment, dependence, and dominance. He goes on to suggest some implications of acceptance of or adherence to these basic values. The implications are said to be particularly related to problem situations and take the following general forms:

1. Acceptance of or adherence to the detachment value implies a particular way of approaching problem situations and is labeled "designative" inquiry. Such a form of inquiry focuses upon what has happened, is happening, or will happen.

2. Dominance is associated with a form of inquiry labeled "prescriptive" and which focuses upon what to do.

3. Dependence is associated with a form of inquiry labeled "appraisive" and which focuses upon what is to be preferred or what is to be valued or evaluated favorably.

To illustrate differences among these forms of inquiry, let us assume that three students are meeting as a committee to discuss the case of another student who has committed some unacceptable act over which this student committee has jurisdiction. Student A says, "What we really need to find out first is why he did it, what prompted him to do it? What were the conditions? Let's get down to the facts of the matter." Student B says, "We all know what he did. Our job is to decide what to do about him. I think we should put him on social pro or maybe just issue a warning to him." Student C says, "Now wait a minute. The real issue here is whether the guy really did anything wrong in the first place. I mean, did he really hurt anybody or did he do anything that would have bad consequences for anybody?"

The point we believe Morris is attempting to make is that the individual's acceptance of or adherence to certain general values determines not only the form which his inquiry into the situation will take but his initial perception of the problem also. Indeed, it is not the same problem to each of the three students. To one, it is a problem of what happened. To one, it is a problem of what shall we do. To the other it is a problem of what is good or bad about it.

Our interest in this particular theoretical framework is that it provides an extremely general illustration of general response tendencies. If these three individuals characteristically approach problem situations with a specific and stable orientation, and if their communicative behavior is determined in part by their unique perception of the problem situation, then an analysis of the communication process and outcomes resulting from the interaction of these three individuals must take into account their general response tendencies. As the general response tendencies become more characteristic of the individual, more of the communication process and outcome can be accounted for primarily in terms of the general response tendencies. From this very general introduction we can now turn to some general response tendencies on which a great deal more information is available, and which have become important parts of the study of interpersonal communication.

Dogmatism

A concept that is particularly important to the study of human communication is open- or closed-mindedness, frequently called dogmatism. In one of his earlier publications Rokeach (1954, p. 195) defined dogmatism as "(*a*) a relatively closed cognitive organization of beliefs and disbeliefs about reality, (*b*) organized around a central set of beliefs about absolute authority which, in turn, (*c*) provides a framework for patterns of intolerance toward others." In his major work on the subject Rokeach (1960) has presented a complete description of open and closed belief-disbelief systems. We have abstracted from these descriptions characteristics that we believe are especially important in understanding the operation of dogmatism in interpersonal communication.

1. A closed person is more likely to respond to messages on the basis of irrelevant inner drives or internal pressures rather than considerations of logical consistency. For example, if I am a relatively dogmatic individual who believes blacks cause property values to decline, I can easily dismiss evidence to the contrary. I can dismiss as exceptions to the rule those cases in which the influx of blacks into middle and upper-middle class neighborhoods has not resulted in the decline of property values. The fact that in the past blacks have sometimes been absorbed by neighborhoods already on the decline, where physical, economic, and social conditions existing prior to their absorption may explain property value decline, these things I may dismiss as inconsequential or irrelevant to my basic position—that I have observed the physical deterioration of black neighborhoods. But note that it is not my conclusion which makes me relatively dogmatic, it is my intolerance for discrepant information or evidence and my unwillingness to accept

or to even consider alternative interpretations of an explanation for the conditions I have "observed." Some of the irrelevant internal pressures that may interfere with my realistic reception of information bearing on this belief are "unrelated habits, beliefs, and perceptual cues, irrational ego motives, power needs, the need for self-aggrandizement, the need to allay anxiety, etc." (Rokeach, 1960, p.57)

With respect to this first characteristic, one of the things we need to understand is the ease with which we can maintain beliefs in the face of evidence or information to the contrary. There are so many alternatives available to us when we are confronted with discrepant or contradictory information that most of us can defend our beliefs successfully with very little effort. The more closed a person, the more likely it is that he will turn to these alternative methods of defending his belief and dismiss the discrepant or contradictory information. The fact that there is an abundance of information and evidence documenting the negative effects of smoking troubles me very little if I wish to continue to smoke. Indeed, if I am threatened or anxious about this information, my reliance on irrelevant internal desires or pressures may be heightened. After all, I am not really a heavy smoker and I probably don't smoke enough to worry about the impact of smoking on my health; besides, there are a number of cigarettes on the market now that are relatively safe; and anyway, they are working on a cure for cancer and by the time I get it they'll have a cure for it; and the dangers of smoking are no greater than the dangers of driving or taking a bath; and what the hell, if I do die a lot of other people will go with me.

2. A closed person is more likely to see a wide discrepancy between his belief system and the belief systems of those who disagree with him. There are still politicians who perceive their opponents as Communist sympathizers. There are those who would perceive individuals suggesting examination and revision of welfare programs as greedy, rich conservatives. There are university officials who perceive as anarchists those who suggest examination or revision of policies these officials have established or are supporting. And there are those who perceive as apathetic incompetents those faculty members who oppose greater student involvement in the planning of academic programs. The magnification of differences between belief systems may lead a dogmatic Republican or Democrat to see no essential similarities between the goals and values of the Republican and Democratic parties. A central concept of dogmatism is that dogmatic individuals are characterized by greater degrees of anxiety and insecurity. Indeed, if I am prone to rigidly defend my beliefs, and if I am generally threatened or in-

secure, it seems reasonable for me to conclude that if you are not for me, you are against me.

3. The closed person is more likely to seek information about other beliefs from sources within his own belief system. The more dogmatic the Baptist, the greater are the chances that he knows what he knows about Catholics and Jews primarily from other Baptists, and the less likely it is that he has exposed himself to information from Catholic and Jewish sources. Those of us who are threatened by discrepant information and who actively defend our own beliefs know how easy it is to selectively expose ourselves to information or ideas from sources that will agree with our beliefs. This may not be a conscious or deliberate selective exposure. Indeed, even the "objective" scholar, when he develops a new theory, may unconsciously solicit reactions to this theory from those of his professional colleagues he knows will support him. The extent to which we are extremely selective in exposing ourselves to information and ideas bearing upon our beliefs and to the extent that we derive associated beliefs from sources within our own belief system, we are exhibiting one characteristic of dogmatism.

4. A closed person is more likely to respond to messages on the basis of his perception of the source rather than on the basis of message content. Underlying this characteristic is a central thesis in the study of dogmatism that authority, to a closed person, is absolute and that people may legitimately be evaluated on the basis of their acceptance or rejection of such authority. Of course we may all identify sources that we consider to be legitimate bases for influencing or forming our beliefs. However, for a closed person such identification of legitimate sources of influence tend to be absolute. We may better understand this reliance on absolute authority if we recall the basic hypothesis that dogmatic individuals tend to be more anxious and insecure. A greater reliance on absolute authority may be one way of combating anxiety and insecurity.

We may all exhibit these four characteristics to greater or lesser degrees. But when an individual characteristically responds to interpersonal communication situations by exhibiting these characteristics, then most assuredly we have identified a general response tendency that must be taken into account in our analysis of interpersonal communication processes and outcomes. A review of some of the research on dogmatism may provide us with greater understanding of its nature and operation, remembering as we review the research that almost all of it is based upon Rokeach's definition of dogmatism as operationalized in his Dogmatism Scale.

There is some evidence that dogmatism, as a concept, may be regarded as a general explanation of authoritarianism in that the dogmatism scale does not necessarily tap only that authoritarianism associated with political or religious conservatism. Plant (1960), Kerlinger and Rokeach (1966) and Hanson (1968) have obtained data supporting dogmatism as a concept that explains general authoritarianism. Barker (1963) obtained results that suggested that dogmatism was associated with commitment to a particular political position. That is, it is not whether one is a "liberal" or a "conservative" which determines his degree of dogmatism but rather it is whether he can tolerate alternative political ideologies. Of particular interest here is Simons and Berkowitz's (1969) review of validation studies on the dogmatism scale. One of their principal interests was in those studies in which liberals scored slightly lower than conservatives. Comparisons of the dogmatism scores of self-proclaimed liberals and conservatives showed that conservatives predicted about the same degree of dogmatism for the liberals as did the liberals predict for conservatives. The fact that the dogmatism scale was apparently perceived as a general measure of closed-mindedness by both groups and that the liberals scored significantly lower than the conservatives leads to the tentative conclusion that liberals may in fact be less dogmatic than conservatives.

There is at least some evidence that levels of dogmatism can be changed. Haiman (1963) and Larson and Gratz (1966) have demonstrated that dogmatism scores can change significantly as a result of certain kinds of communication-course work focusing on interpersonal and small group communication. Robinson and Spaights (1969) have also provided some support for the notion that levels of dogmatism can change. As part of Milwaukee's PROJECT UNDERSTANDING, which sought to change parental attitudes and value systems believed to generate prejudice in children, Robinson and Spaights assessed the impact of lecture and discussion workshops on the levels of dogmatism among participants. Significant changes on the dogmatism scale scores occurred among participants who were age 35 and under, participants who had some college education, participants who were in higher income groups, and Catholic participants. No significant changes were observed among those over age 35, who were among lower income groups, or who were Protestants. In this investigation significant decreases in dogmatism scores occurred primarily among those individuals whose initial dogmatism score was comparatively high. Although these investigations have demonstrated that dogmatism may change as a result of intensive communicative interaction with others, the stability of such changes over long time periods has not been assessed. Several investigations (Lehman, 1963; Plant and Telford, 1966) have discovered significant decreases in dogmatism among students attending college. These findings, coupled with the results of Rebhun (1967) which discovered close associations between the degree of dogmatism among children and the level of dogmatism among their parents, seem to indicate that the degree of dogmatism may change with the adoption of new norms or response patterns.

Considerable research supports Rokeach's original conceptualization of dogmatism. Studies of the personality characteristics of high dogmatic individuals have found that high dogmatics tend to be impulsive, defensive, and stereotyped in their thinking (Plant, Telford, and Thomas, 1965), less tolerant, flexible, and secure (Korn and Giddan, 1964), more conforming, restrained, and conservative (Vacchiano, Strauss, and Schiffman, 1968). Furthermore, in unstructured classroom interaction situations Zagona and Zurcher (1964) found high dogmatics to be much more structure- and leader-oriented and insecure when challenged by authority. Additionally, a review of the research on relationships between dogmatism and learning (Ehrlich and Lee, 1969) supports the frequently cited conclusion that dogmatic individuals tend to resist change and have greater difficulty learning new beliefs.

Two of the most important illustrative hypotheses, reliance on authority and basic insecurity, have been supported by a number of investigations. Powell (1962) found high dogmatics less capable of evaluating political statements independent of political candidates. McCarthy and Johnson (1962) found dogmatism to be associated with the extent to which people would or could accept official interpretations (versus peer explanations) of the causes of social demonstrations. Feather (1967) found dogmatism to be associated with membership in religious groups that are characterized by reliance on authority and little tolerance of variance in basic beliefs. With respect to basic insecurity and the need to defend existing beliefs there is considerable *empirical* support for the existence of these relationships. Vacchiano, Strauss, and Hochman (1969) have reviewed these investigations as well as many others not mentioned here.

Our discussion of dogmatism, its characteristics, and some of the research that establishes it as a valid concept is an attempt to underscore the fact that it may be regarded as one of the most crucial limiting variables in interpersonal communication. It is a limiting variable to the extent that high levels of dogmatism in interpersonal encounters may account for a great deal of what happens and what emerges from the encounters. A sec-

ondary hope is that we may, by considering the extent to which we ourselves exhibit dogmatic characteristics, take steps to correct these characteristics in our interpersonal communication with others. Or have you already
said to yourself "I'm not dogmatic, but I know a lot of other people who
are."

Agreeing Tendencies

It may have occurred to the reader that some of the characteristics of
dogmatic message processing should make dogmatic individuals more easy
to influence. Reliance on external authority and basic feelings of insecurity
might be the contributing factors in this, but not in the special case of dogmatic individuals. Messages that oppose existing beliefs, especially if those
beliefs are central to a person's belief system, are more likely to be rejected
by dogmatic individuals. Wright and Harvey (1965) have made the important theoretical distinction that an authoritarian individual may change
"central" beliefs less easily and "peripheral" beliefs more easily. In one of
Rokeach's later works (1968) centrality of beliefs is an important determinant of how resistant to change they are. Dogmatic individuals may be
easily influenced with respect to inconsequential or peripheral beliefs, but
this will be less so when responding to discrepant information not easily
incorporated into existing beliefs or information bearing upon central
beliefs.

Several interesting agreeing tendencies have been discovered. We do
not intend to go much beyond the original formulations of these tendencies
since we regard the original formulations as more productive of an understanding of general response tendencies than any subsequent minor revi-
sions. Two tendencies we will consider briefly are yea-saying and general
persuasibility.

Early articles by Cronbach (1946, 1950) have created increasing interest in the possible personality attributes of individuals who typically
agree or disagree with questionnaire items calling for yes-no, or agree-
disagree responses. Couch and Keniston (1960) constructed a test to derive
an Overall Agreement Score from a questionnaire they claim to be balanced
as to content. This OAS was then correlated with a number of personality
measures. Subjects were Harvard undergraduates. Approaching their results
from the point of view of communication reception and responses, let us
examine some of the results that may be of particular interest to students
of communication behavior.

1. The yea-sayer's general attitude is one of stimulus acceptance, by which Couch and Keniston mean "a pervasive readiness
to respond affirmatively or yield willingly to both inner and
outer forces demanding expression."

2. Yea-sayers seem to be impulsive and quick in their expression of themselves. They would be likely to accept or evaluate quickly the messages they receive, and their evaluations are
likely to be based upon their own wishes or desires rather than
upon "objective criteria."

3. Yea-sayers desire "novelty, movement, change, adven-
ture." Yea-sayers appear to be attracted by items that have an
enthusiastic, colloquial tone, whereas such items appear to repel
naysayers.

4. On the other hand, naysayers are likely to be extremely
careful and critical of messages they receive.

Couch and Keniston also report the results of a clinical study in
which two independent interviewers (clinicians) interviewed ten yea-sayers
and eleven naysayers. The clinicians were able to distinguish between yea-
sayers and naysayers accurately and reliably. Thus, the interactive behavior
of yea-sayers and naysayers would appear to be manifest (at least to clinicians). Consequently, although yea-saying may more appropriately be regarded as a specific response tendency relative to questionnaire completion,
yea-saying characteristics may manifest themselves in interpersonal communication situations and may therefore be regarded as a potential limiting
variable in communication.

General persuasibility is a somewhat broader concept growing out of
the Yale studies in communication and attitude change, part of which concerned investigations of individual differences in susceptibility to persuasion.
One of the Yale volumes (Hovland and Janis, 1959) and the later work
by Janis (1963) contain general summaries of their conclusions.

Most of the subjects were high school and college students, but samples of adults were also used. The most frequently used measure of persuasibility was a three-step design involving: (1) measurement of subject's attitudes on a number of issues; (2) measurement of these attitudes
after the subject had been exposed to a number of written persuasive messages on these issues; (3) measurement of attitudes on the same issues after
the presentation of messages directly opposing those used in step number
two.

Generally women were found to be significantly more persuasible than were men, a finding supported by many other investigators (Knower, 1936; Haiman, 1949; Paulson, 1954; Furbay, 1965; Scheidel, 1963). However, individual variations in persuasibility were found among men but not consistently among women. Even though women may generally be more persuasible, it is difficult to predict which women will be. On the other hand, there seem to be some relatively stable characteristics of persuasible men. Janis (1963, pp. 60–62) has hypothesized the following five characteristics associated with general persuasibility:

1. Men who openly display overt hostility toward the people they encounter in their daily life are predisposed to remain relatively uninfluenced by any form of persuasion.

2. Men who display social withdrawal tendencies are predisposed to remain relatively uninfluenced by any form of persuasion.

3. Men who respond with rich imagery and strong empathic responses to symbolic representation tend to be more persuasible than those whose fantasy responses are relatively constricted.

4. Men with low self esteem—as manifested by feelings of personal inadequacy, social inhibitions, and depressive affect—are predisposed to be more readily influenced than others when exposed to any type of persuasive communication.

5. Men with an "other-directed" orientation are predisposed to be more persuasible than those with an "inner-directed" orientation.

Neither yea-saying nor general persuasibility have been sufficiently researched in interpersonal communication contexts, but they appear on the surface to be potentially crucial concepts in understanding interpersonal communication. They are described here as potential means of accounting for communication outcomes wherein agreement or acceptance appear to be insufficiently accounted for by other communication variables.

Empathy—or Something

This "something" that we are about to discuss is one of the most difficult concepts to work with in the study of interpersonal communication. Many social and behavioral scientists are interested in it, but not many claim to know a great deal about it. It is regarded by many as an extremely important research focus, but there is considerable difference of opinion as to how to assess it. Most of us know that it exists but are not really certain what to call it. Information related to it is available under headings such as Empathy, Empathic Ability, Person Perception, Interpersonal Perception, Social Perception, Sensitivity, and other labels that probably have not yet found their way into articles summarizing or synthesizing theory and research related to it. Researchers have concluded that having it makes one a "better" teacher, counselor, parent, manager, or a "better" marital partner, but none of the researchers are likely to tell you how to get it or, indeed, whether it is possible to acquire it.

We intend to discuss it in terms of those definitions, concepts, and research conclusions in which we have considerable confidence. You will also find some material bearing on it in the chapters discussing communication and organizations, communication and marriage, and nonverbal communication. We will call it "empathic ability" because as an ability it appears to vary considerably from individual to individual, and because there is some evidence (Cline and Richards, 1960) that it is a general trait possessed by individuals in varying degrees. The longitudinal stability of this trait seems to be implied in the research conclusions of Irving (1965), who discovered that well-adjusted adolescents have parents who are more empathic than did the maladjusted adolescents.

Guiora (1967, p.376) has offered the following definition of empathy:

> Empathy is a process of comprehending in which a temporary fusion of self-object boundaries, as in the earliest pattern of object relation, permits an immediate emotional apprehension of the affective experience of another, this sensing being used by the cognitive functions to gain understanding of the other.

Or if you prefer brevity, empathic ability is the ability to understand another or to comprehend his feelings, attitudes, or sentiments. Most of the research studies conducted on empathic ability or accuracy of social perception have employed operational definitions. The usual operational definition of empathic ability has to do with one person's ability to predict how another person will describe himself or how another person will behave or what another person's attitude or values are. We stress this definition primarily because most of our focus here will be on research that has employed such an operational definition.

When we discuss your ability to enter into another's world, to get into his mind sufficiently so that you are able to judge his feelings, attitudes, or behavior, we are discussing a very complex ability. So complex is this ability that Marwell (1964) has identified twenty "operational components" of social perception measures. For approximately two decades social and behavioral scientists have argued the merits of various conceptualizations of and procedures for assessing empathic ability. Danielian (1967) has provided a recent summary of the methodological progress that has been made. Hobart and Fahlberg (1965) have developed a procedure for assessing empathy, a procedure that promises to resolve some of the methodological confusion that characterizes this field of study.

There are at least two types of judging accuracy (Cline and Richards, 1960). Stereotyped accuracy is a kind of global judgment that implies sensitivity to social norms and is usually interpreted as an individual's ability to predict the average responses of a wide range of people. Differential accuracy is a more analytical judgment implying sensitivity to and ability to predict differences between persons. Cline and Richards have concluded that a person who is accurate in judging others may be so because he has an accurate stereotype, or because he is sensitive to differences between people, or because of both. We are probably more accustomed to thinking of empathic ability in terms of differential accuracy. However, stereotyped accuracy is an extremely important component of empathic ability and warrants our further consideration.

Gage (1952) conducted some early experiments in which college and high school students predicted the responses of college students on self-description inventories. Some of the judges made their predictions only on the basis of stereotypes, that is, these judges might know only that they were judging "a typical male undergraduate in teacher training at the University of Illinois." Some of the judges made their prediction after having observed those they were judging. In two separate experiments Gage found that the stereotyped judgments were more accurate than the postobservation predictions. A somewhat related experiment is reported by Maier and Thurber (1968). In this experiment judges were trying to assess deception attempts by an interviewee during a role-played interview. Some of the judges watched and heard the interview, some only listened to a tape recording, and some only read a transcript of the interview. In this experiment the judges who only listened to a recording or only read a transcript were more accurate in assessing interviewee deception than were the judges who watched and heard the interview. The researchers suggested that the visual cues of the interview served primarily as distractors that lowered the accuracy of judgments. The frequent conclusion that global judgments tend to be more accurate than analytical judgments and that stereotyped accuracy accounts for much of the accuracy observed in interpersonal predictions makes sense in the light of Campbell's (1967) theoretical consideration of stereotypes. Campbell has referred to anthropological evidence and learning-theory formulations that suggest that if, indeed, there are group differences, these differences will tend to appear in the stereotypes groups have of each other. There is reason to believe that interpersonal communication will improve the accuracy of our perception of others if we have similar interests, attitudes, or characteristics, but that communication may not necessarily lead to a more accurate perception of others if we have dissimilar interests, attitudes, or characteristics (Wilkins, 1965; Brewer and Brewer, 1968; Hatch, 1961; Mellinger, 1956).

There is a tendency to regard stereotypes as "bad" and to regard the reckless and indiscriminate use, especially of religious and racial stereotypes, as "unjust." We may still adhere to these value judgments. Indeed, we would have preferred that the research on empathy and social perception had concluded that stereotyped judgments and global judgments were associated with extreme inaccuracy. Such appears not to be the case and we must consider stereotyped accuracy and global judgments to be an important part of empathic ability.

We know of course that empathic and sensitive people are not necessarily the kind who run amok with rash judgments of others. If we ask what characterizes accurate judges, we are much more likely to encounter answers that are more in line with our expectations. Cline (1955) discovered that among the characteristics of good judges were the absence of ethnocentric and authoritarian attitudes, superior intellectual ability, and a tendency for the good judges to describe themselves as "sympathetic" and "affectionate." Poor judges describe themselves as "dissatisfied," "irritable," "awkward," "praising," and "hurried." Fleishman and Salter (1963) found that industrial supervisors who scored high on empathy were more "considerate" toward their subordinates. Cooper (1967) found that individuals exhibiting greater empathy tended to ask more questions about the thoughts and feelings of others. Danielian (1967) has demonstrated that the relationship between authoritarianism and accuracy is a complex one. He discovered a positive relationship between authoritarianism and judging accuracy, a finding that runs counter to earlier studies. A partial explanation offered for these findings was that authoritarians might obtain a higher stereotype accuracy score by virtue of their greater sensitivity to social norms and greater commitment to a conventional picture of man, which on the average is correct. Although Danielian is unable to explain why the judges' differential accuracy scores are positively related to authoritarianism, we must remember that until recently crude measures of empathic ability have made it difficult to focus on characteristics of individuals who are accurate primarily in the differential accuracy component of judging effectiveness. Presently, the general portrait of an accurate judge would include global judgments apparently based upon personal feelings rather than upon analytic examinations of others, and would seem to describe persons who are sympathetic or considerate of others.

Other research provides support for some experiential conclusions that you may have arrived at from your own experience. (1) Morgenstern (1967) has found females to be more interpersonally aware than males. (2) Not everyone is equally "visible" to us, and the accuracy of our judgments depends to a certain extent on those we are judging (Shapiro, 1968; Brumbaugh, 1966; Morgenstern, 1967; Newman, 1967). (3) Within certain limits familiarity or similarity between the judge and the object of judgment improves judging accuracy (Wilkins, 1965; Hjelle, 1968; Taft, 1966). However, there is also evidence that similarity between the judge and the object of judging does not necessarily produce more accurate judgments (Inglis, 1965). (4) It would appear that individuals who have greater self-insight or who engage in more self-projection or who are more "transparent" are also more accurate in judging others (Dymond, 1948; Axelson, 1967; Morgenstern, 1967).

Now let us return to the question that might have occurred to you during our consideration of empathic ability. Why do we choose to call empathic ability a "limiting variable" in interpersonal communication? Part of our focus on interpersonal communication has to do with the accuracy with which individuals understand each other. High levels of empathic ability in one or both of the communicating individuals may account for more of the accuracy with which they understand each other than could be accounted for by a consideration of the other variables we have identified in our discussion of basic communication processes. If we are to be realistic in our study of communication, we must admit that sometimes interpersonal understanding or accurate interpersonal perception emerges relatively quickly and without prolonged communicative encounters.

We have considered only a few of the general response tendencies that are emerging from social science research. We have focused on those we consider especially promising. The concept "general response tendency" may be extremely helpful when we attempt an understanding of communication outcomes. There are instances in which certain outcomes are almost guaranteed, given the response tendencies of the interacting individuals. There are other instances in which certain communication outcomes are almost impossible, given the response tendencies of the interacting individuals. A rather simple illustration of this notion has occurred to the writer, one which many males are willing to discuss at great lengths. If a girl says "no," how do you account for this outcome? Some men will say that given the right conditions, the right time, the right place, the right words, and a complementary atmosphere, the girl will say "yes." But others argue that the outcomes of such encounters may be predicted much more accurately, not by carefully controlling the conditions, but by carefully selecting the girl.

References

Axelson, J. A., "The Relationship of Counselor Candidates' Empathic Perception and Rapport in Small Group Interaction," *Counselor Education and Supervision*, 6 (1967), 287–92.

Barker, E. N., "Authoritarianism of the Political Right, Center, and Left," *Journal of Social Issues*, 19 (1963), 63–74.

Brewer, R. E., and M. B. Brewer, "Attraction and Accuracy of Perception in Dyads," *Journal of Personality and Social Psychology*, 8 (1968), 188–93.

Brumbaugh, R. B., "Accuracy of Interpersonal Perception: A Function of Superordinate Role." The Center for the Advanced Study of Educational Administration, University of Oregon, 1966.

Campbell, D. T., "Stereotypes and the Perception of Group Differences," *American Psychologist*, 22 (1967), 817–29.

Cline, V. B., "Ability to Judge Personality Assessed with a Stress Interview and Sound-Film Technique," *Journal of Abnormal and Social Psychology*, 55 (1955), 183–87.

Cline, V. B., and J. M. Richards, "Accuracy of Interpersonal Perception—A General Trait?" *Journal of Abnormal and Social Psychology*, 60 (1960), 1–7.

————, "The Generality of Accuracy of Interpersonal Perception," *Journal of Abnormal and Social Psychology*, 61 (1961), 446–49.

Cooper, L. W., "The Relationship of Empathy to Aspects of Cognitive Control." Ph.D. dissertation, Yale University, 1967.

Couch, A., and K. Keniston, "Yeasayers and Naysayers: Agreeing Response Set as a Personality Variable," *Journal of Abnormal and Social Psychology*, 60 (1960), 151–74.

Cronbach, L. J., "Response Sets and Test Validity," *Educational and Psychological Measurement*, 6 (1946), 475–94.

————, "Further Evidence on Response Sets and Test Design," *Educational and Psychological Measurement*, 10 (1950), 3–31.

Danielian, J., "Psychological and Methodological Evaluation of the Components of Judging Accuracy," *Perceptual and Motor Skills*, 24 (1967), 1155–69.

Dymond, Rosalind, "A Preliminary Investigation of the Relation of Insight and Empathy," *Journal of Consulting Psychology*, 12 (1948), 228–33.

Ehrlich, H. J., and Dorothy Lee, "Dogmatism, Learning, and Resistance to Change: A Review and a New Paradigm," *Psychological Bulletin*, 71 (1969), 249–60.

Feather, N. T., "Evaluation of Religious and Neutral Arguments in Religious and Atheist Groups," *Australian Journal of Psychology*, 19 (1967), 3–12.

Fleishman, E. A., and J. A. Salter, "Relation Between the Leader's Behavior and His Empathy Toward Subordinates," *Journal of Industrial Psychology*, 1 (1963), 79–84.

Furbay, A., "The Influence of Scattered Versus Compact Seating on Audience Response," *Speech Monographs*, 32 (1965), 144–48.

Gage, N. L., "Judging Interests From Expressive Behavior," *Psychological Monographs*, 65 (1952), no. 18.

Guiora, A. Z., "Toward a Systematic Study of Empathy," *Comprehensive Psychiatry*, 8 (1967), 375–85.

Haiman, F. S., "An Experimental Study of the Effects of Ethos in Public Speaking," *Speech Monographs*, 16 (1949), 190–202.

————, "Effects of Training in Group Processes on Open-Mindedness," *Journal of Communication*, 13 (1963), 236–45.

Hanson, D. J., "Dogmatism and Authoritarianism," *Journal of Social Psychology*, 76 (1968), 89–95.

Hatch, R. S., An Evaluation of a Forced-Choice Differential Accuracy Approach to the Measurement of Supervisory Empathy, *Dissertation Abstracts*, 62 (1961), 3110.

Hjelle, L. A., "Accuracy of Personality and Social Judgments as Functions of Familiarity," *Psychological Reports*, 22 (1968), 311–19.

Hobart, C. W., and Nancy Fahlberg, "The Measurement of Empathy," *American Journal of Sociology*, 70 (1965), 595–603.

Hovland, C. L., and I. L. Janis, *Personality and Persuasibility*. New Haven, Conn.: Yale University Press, 1959.

Inglis, R., "The Effects of Personality Similarity on Empathy and Interpersonal Attraction." Ph.D. dissertation, Duke University, 1965.

Irving, G., "Parental Empathy and Adolescent Adjustment." Ph.D. dissertation, University of Florida, 1965.

Janis, I. L., "Personality as a Factor in Susceptibility to Persuasion," in *The Science of Human Communication*, Wilbur Schramm, ed. New York: Basic Books, Inc., Publishers, 1963.

Kerlinger, F., and M. Rokeach, "The Factorial Nature of the F and D Scales," *Journal of Personality and Social Psychology*, 4 (1966), 391–99.

Knower, F., "Experimental Studies of Changes in Attitude: II. A Study of the Effect of Printed Argument on Changes in Attitude," *Journal of Abnormal and Social Psychology*, 30 (1936), 522–32.

Korn, H. A., and N. S. Giddan, "Scoring Methods and Construct Validity of the Dogmatism Scale," *Educational and Psychological Measurement*, 24 (1964), 867–74.

Larson, C. E., and R. D. Gratz, "Problem-Solving Discussion Training and T-Group Training: An Experimental Comparison." Paper presented at the Speech Association of America Convention, 1966.

Lehmann, I. J., "Changes in Critical Thinking, Attitudes, and Values from Freshman to Senior Years," *Journal of Educational Psychology*, 54 (1963), 305–15.

McCarthy, J., and R. C. Johnson, "Interpretation of the 'City Hall Riots' as a Function of General Dogmatism," *Psychological Reports*, 11 (1962), 243–45.

McLaughlin, E. C., "An Investigation of the Effects of Stereotypy on Subjective Experience, Intellectual Performance, and Interpersonal Perception." Ph. D. dissertation, University of Georgia, 1966.

Maier, N. R., and J. A. Thurber, "Accuracy of Judgments of Deception When an Interview is Watched, Heard, and Read," *Personal Psychology*, 21 (1968), 23–30.

Marwell, Gerald, "Problems of Operational Definitions of 'Empathy,' 'Identification' and Related Concepts," *Journal of Social Psychology*, 63 (1964), 87–102.

Mellinger, G. D., "Interpersonal Trust as a Factor in Communication," *Journal of Abnormal and Social Psychology*, 52 (1956), 304–9.

Morgenstern, D. P., "An Investigation of Rogers' Theory of Congruence Through Measures of Self- and Other-Perception." Ph.D. dissertation, Temple University, 1967.

Morris, Charles, *Varieties of Human Value.* Chicago: University of Chicago Press, 1956.

——, *Signification and Significance.* Cambridge, Mass.: The M.I.T. Press, 1964. Used by permission of the publisher.

Newman, L., "A Study of the Effects of Generalized Expectancies upon Accuracy of Interpersonal Perception." Ph.D. dissertation, University of Southern California, 1967.

Paulson, S., "The Effects of the Prestige of the Speaker and Acknowledgment of Opposing Arguments on Audience Retention and Shift of Opinion," *Speech Monographs*, 21 (1954), 267–71.

Plant, W. T., "Rokeach's Dogmatism Scale as a Measure of General Authoritarianism," *Psychological Reports*, 6 (1960), 164.

Plant, W. T., and C. W. Telford, "Changes in Personality for Groups Completing Different Amounts of College over Two Years," *Genetic Psychology Monographs*, 74 (1966), 3–36.

Plant, W. T., C. W. Telford, and J. A. Thomas, "Some Personality Differences between Dogmatic and Non-Dogmatic Groups," *Journal of Social Psychology*, 67 (1965), 67–75.

Powell, F. A., "Open- and Closed-Mindedness and the Ability to Differentiate Source and Message," *Journal of Abnormal and Social Psychology*, 65 (1962), 61–64.

Rebhun, M. T., "Parental Attitudes and the Closed Belief-Disbelief System," *Psychological Reports*, 20 (1967), 260–62.

Robinson, R. D., and Ernest Spaights, "A Study of Attitudinal Change

Through Lecture-Discussion Workshops," *Adult Education Journal,* 19 (1969), 163–71.

Rokeach, Milton, *The Open and Closed Mind.* New York: Basic Books, Inc., Publishers, 1960.

————, *Beliefs, Attitudes and Values.* San Francisco: Jossey-Bass, Inc., Publishers, 1968.

————, "The Nature and Meaning of Dogmatism," *Psychological Review,* 61 (1954), 194–204.

Scheidel, T., "Sex and Persuasibility," *Speech Monographs,* 30 (1963), 353–58.

Shapiro, J. G., "Variability in the Communication of Affect," *Journal of Social Psychology,* 76 (1968), 181–88.

Simons, H. W., and N. N. Berkowitz, "Rokeach's Dogmatism Scale and Leftist Bias," *Speech Monographs,* 36 (1969), 459–63.

Taft, R., "Accuracy of Empathic Judgments of Acquaintances and Strangers," *Journal of Personality and Social Psychology,* 3 (1966), 600–604.

Vacchiano, R. B., P. S. Strauss, and L. Hochman, "The Open and Closed Mind: A Review of Dogmatism," *Psychological Bulletin,* 71 (1969), 261–73.

Vacchiano, R. B., P. S. Strauss, and D. C. Schiffman, "Personality Correlates of Dogmatism," *Journal of Consulting and Clinical Psychology,* 32 (1968), 83–85.

Wilkins, M. M., "A Study of the Conditions Which Influence the Accuracy of Interpersonal Perception." Ph.D. dissertation, University of Colorado, 1965.

Wright, J. M., and O. J. Harvey, "Attitude Change as a Function of Authoritarianism and Positiveness," *Journal of Personality and Social Psychology,* 1 (1965), 177–81.

Zagona, S. V., and L. A. Zurcher, "Participation, Interaction, and Role Behavior in Groups Selected from the Extremes of the Open-Closed Cognitive Continuum," *Journal of Psychology,* 58 (1964), 255–64.

Chapter 8

Verbal Message Variables in Interpersonal Influence

As we noted in an earlier chapter, communication can take place without words. However, communication seldom *does* take place in the complete absence of words. Man is a verbal animal. One of the things that distinguishes man from other forms of animal life is his ability to communicate with his fellow man by means of words. But our use of words is not always very efficient. We use them in an attempt to stimulate meaning in the minds of other people. But, often as not, the meaning stimulated is not that which was intended.

Let us take a very simple example, "cat." Just what does the word "cat" mean? To answer that question, first let's make it clear that that word, or any other word per se, doesn't "mean" anything. Words don't mean, people do. This is a simple, yet central, concept in communication. If we want to "look up" the meaning of "cat," we should not look in the dictionary. Instead we should look to see who is using the word "cat" and who is hearing or reading the word "cat." In addition we may need to consider the circumstance surrounding the person's use of that word "cat."

Mr. A. says to Mr. B, "I bought a cat last week." Just what did Mr. A buy? Presume that Mr. A is a construction man. The "cat" that he purchased may well have been a Caterpillar tractor. If he is a pet shop owner, he may have purchased a small, furry, four-legged animal. If he is a zoo-keeper he may have purchased a very large, ferocious, four-legged animal. Presuming that Mr. B doesn't know much about Mr. A, what kind of "cat" might he think was bought? That might depend on Mr. B's background. Is he a construction man, pet shop owner, or zookeeper? Possibly Mr. A, a pet shop owner, bought one kind of cat while Mr. B, a zookeeper, perceives that he bought another kind of cat. We need not belabor the point further. Suffice to say, your "cat" is not necessarily the same as my "cat." Nor is your "democracy" the same as my "democracy"; or your "comfortable income" the same as my "comfortable income."

Therefore, to determine the meaning we should attribute to a word, we must look at who is using the word and the circumstances in which he is using it. Similarly, if we wish to stimulate a particular meaning in the mind of another person, we need to determine as best we can what word he would use to give it that meaning and what kind of a context we might need for that word so that he will perceive the meaning we want him to derive. As we noted in an earlier chapter, messages (both verbal and non-verbal) give information about a source's attitudes and beliefs. The message connects the source with the object of communication. It is what is needed to produce inconsistency in the mind of a receiver and induce him to alter his beliefs or attitudes.

Common Message Elements

In interpersonal communication words are usually presented by sources to receivers in units or groups. These units or groups of words include phrases, sentences, and in some cases paragraphs. Three common message elements in interpersonal influence are a claim, a warrant, and data (Toulmin, 1958). These three elements provide information concerning the belief or attitude the source wants the receiver to accept and the reasons why the source thinks that this belief or attitude should be accepted. Let's take a closer look at each of these elements.

The Claim

A claim is any belief or attitude that a source wants his receiver to accept. Whenever a source makes an assertion, he is asking his receiver to accept a claim. Claims may indicate the way the source believes the world exists, what he believes should be done, or his attitude toward something in the world. Simple examples of each of these kinds of claims are as follows: "We won the football game last weekend." "We should schedule better opponents next year." "The team we played last weekend was a lousy football team."

Claims are not always expressed, sometimes they are implicit in the message. For example, if our friend tells us that he doesn't believe we can win a football game without a quarterback and that all of our quarterbacks have been injured, it is clear that he does not believe that we will win the game this weekend (his claim). He may choose to state that explicitly, or he may leave it implicit. In either case his claim is the same.

The Warrant

A warrant is a belief or attitude which justifies acceptance of the claim, if we accept the belief of the source concerning what exists in our world. If the source claims that prices of automobiles are going to go up and suggests that wage increases in the auto industry have always produced price increases (his warrant), and suggests that wages have recently increased in the auto industry, we have a complete message unit. If we concur with the source's view of reality concerning wages in the auto industry, we have reason to accept his claim. Warrants may express relationships among phenomena in our world, such as "wage increases normally produced price increases in the auto industry," or they may express attitudes. If someone tells us that Mr. X is an evil person and gives us the justification that Mr. X has embezzled money from his firm, the warrant that would link this data to the claim that Mr. X is evil is that "embezzlement is bad." That warrant is a statement of an attitude toward embezzlement. If we share that attitude toward embezzlement and concur with the source's view of reality (that Mr. X has embezzled from his firm), we then have reason to accept the source's claim.

The Data

Data are expressions of belief concerning the existence of phenomena in our world. There are three distinct types of data. First-order data consist of beliefs that are shared by the source and receiver. Second-order data are data that represent beliefs of the source, but are not necessarily shared by the receiver. Third-order data consist of beliefs of a source outside the communication transaction that are introduced by the source of communication.

The importance of distinguishing between these types of data will be noted in the following section. At this point, let us conclude our description of the verbal message unit by stressing what we have said about the parts of that unit. The claim is the expression of belief or attitude of the source that he wishes the receiver to accept. The basis for this acceptance comes from the warrant and the data. The warrant is an expression of belief or attitude on the part of the source that connects the data to the claim; the data being matters of belief concerning reality in our external world. Careful examination of Fig. 8.1 should help to clarify the distinctions between these parts and their relationships in the basic message unit.

Understanding message elements will help one to understand what is occurring in a given communication transaction, however, it certainly will not explain all of the outcomes of that transaction. At least as important as the message elements themselves, are what is included in a given message element. There are several variables that may or may not be present in any given message element. The remainder of this chapter is devoted to several of these variables. You are cautioned, however, that these are not all of the potential verbal message variables that are relevant in communication. Rather, these are some of the verbal message variables that have received

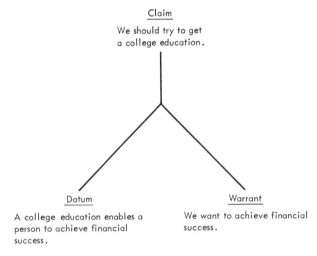

Figure 8.1   Common Message Elements

Reprinted from *An Introduction to Rhetorical Communication* by James C. McCroskey, Englewood Cliffs, N.J.: Prentice-Hall, Inc., 1968, by permission of the publisher.

attention from researchers so that we know something about how they function in communication. Most of this research was carried out within the framework of a person-to-group communication setting rather than a person-to-person or small group setting. This, of course, is because that format is more suitable to laboratory experimentation. The results of this research, however, should apply in most cases to small group and person-to-person communication as well.

Evidence

Evidence is what we referred to above as third-order data, or more formally, evidence consists of factual statements originating from a source other than the source of communication, objects not created by the source of communication, and opinions of persons other than the source of communication which are offered in support of the sources claims. Traditional theories of communication, particularly those stemming from classical rhetoric, suggest that evidence is one of the most important verbal message variables in producing effects on receivers. However, results of several studies of the effects of evidence in communication suggest that, while in some cases evidence may have an important impact, in others the impact of evidence is negligible.

Traditional theories that point to the importance of evidence in communication do not take into account the three orders of data and the fact that all three orders of data function in essentially the same way. As we have noted above, the presence of data in a message is necessary to effect attitude or belief. But from one communciation circumstance to another, the order of data most appropriate will vary. Early studies of the effects of evidence did not take this fact into account; consequently, some found evidence to have an impact (Bettinghaus, 1953; Cathcart, 1955) and some found evidence to have no impact (Gilkinson, Paulson, and Sikkink, 1954; Ostermeier, 1966; Anderson, 1958; Costley, 1958; Dresser, 1963; Gardiner, 1966; Wagner, 1958). More recent studies (McCroskey, 1966, 1967, 1969) have examined the functioning of evidence within the context of the three orders of data discussed above. The results of these studies suggest that including evidence has little, if any, impact on receivers' attitudes or beliefs if the source of the message is initially perceived to be high-credible, if the message is presented poorly, or if the receiver is familiar with the evidence prior to exposure to the source's message. However, including evidence may significantly increase immediate receiver attitude and belief change when the source is initially perceived to be moderate-to-low-credible, when the message is well presented, and when the receiver has little or no prior familiarity with the evidence included in the message.

The results of the McCroskey studies are consistent with what would be expected in light of the concept of three orders of data. If the receiver is already aware of the evidence that might be included, he either will have accepted it (believes it) or have rejected it, and to present the same evidence to that receiver again would be very unlikely to have any impact. If he were to be affected by that particular belief, it would be as a result of first-order data—beliefs jointly held by source and receiver. If those beliefs were not jointly held, that is, the receiver does not accept the belief, presenting the same old evidence to him would be most unlikely to have any impact on his belief. But presuming that the receiver is not familiar with this particular source, if he perceived the source as high-credible, there would be no need to bring in evidence from some person outside the communication transaction. Rather, the source's assertion would function as second-order data and provide the completion of the argument. For example, if I hold John to be high-credible and he tells me that wage increases have recently occurred in the auto industry, I am likely to believe that this is indeed what happened. I have no need for documentation from some other high-credible source to confirm John's statement.

That the evidence must be presented well to the receiver for it to have an impact should come as no surprise. Obviously, if the presentation of the evidence is poor, the intended meaning of that evidence is most unlikely to be stimulated in the mind of the receiver and for this reason it would have little or no impact.

One other finding from the McCroskey studies of evidence is worthy of note. This was the discovery that even when the source of communication was perceived by the receiver to be initially high-credible, and even when the receiver was familiar with the evidence employed by the communicator prior to his usage of it, including the evidence had an impact on the receiver's beliefs and attitudes over time. The reason for this is not completely clear. The only explanation that has been proposed at this time is that use of evidence may interfere with the process of selective recall. The evidence included in the McCroskey experiments was, for the most part, quite vivid and memorable, perhaps more so than the other elements in the messages, so that the elements that were more memorable would tend to have an impact over time, whereas less memorable elements would be forgotten. However, the finding that evidence has an impact on belief and attitude change over time suggests that evidence may be a potent variable for counteracting what future communicators may do. Thus if we are trying to influence a receiver and we know that he will be subjected to counterinfluence on the part of another individual at a later time, we may profit by including evidence in our initial message.

A study was designed by McCroskey to examine this possibility. Receivers were systematically exposed to either an "evidence" or a "no evidence" version of a message advocating federal control of education. They were then exposed to a message opposing federal control of education. The results of the study indicated that those receivers who had been exposed to the "evidence" version of the message advocating federal control of education were more favorable to such control after hearing the two messages (one pro and one con) than were the receivers who were initially exposed to the "no evidence" message favorable to federal control of education and then exposed to the one opposed to such control. The results of this study strongly suggest that evidence is indeed a potent verbal message variable in instances where we wish to produce long-range change in receivers' attitudes and beliefs.

A note of caution should be introduced at this point. Neither in our definition nor in our discussion of evidence above have we made a qualitative judgment. We have not suggested what is the difference, if any, between "good" and "poor" evidence. The research on evidence that is available at present does not definitively establish what is good and what is poor evidence. However, in our discussion of common message elements we noted that the data must be relevant to the claim (in the receiver's mind) and that a warrant must be present to link the two together. If the data are not relevant, then we would expect that the claim would not be accepted by the receiver. So it would seem that "good" evidence is evidence that bears upon the claim the source is asking the receiver to accept. Only one study has been conducted that attempted to determine if there is any difference in effect between relevant and irrelevant evidence (Dresser, 1963). However, the design of this study did not control for the variable of credibility of the source, making interpretation of the results difficult.

Message-Sidedness

We have indicated above that the use of evidence may have an effect on receivers' beliefs and attitudes over time, even in cases where it seems to have little immediate impact. Another variable, the so-called two-sided message, has been proposed to have a similar effect and has received considerable attention from researchers. But first let us explain what constitutes a one- and two-sided message. A one-sided message is one that merely sets forth the source's claim and the reasons why he thinks the claim should be accepted. A two-sided message not only sets forth the source's position but it also takes cognizance of opposing positions. In some cases that opposing position is merely acknowledged, and in other cases it is both acknowledged and directly attacked. Early research reported by Hovland, Lumsdaine, and Sheffield (1949) indicated that a one-sided message was more effective for changing immediate receiver attitudes when the receiver was initially in agreement with the communicator and when the receiver had less than a high school education. The research indicated, however, that a two-sided message was more effective when the receiver was initially opposed to the communicator's position and when the receiver had more than a high school education. Although the differences observed in these studies were statistically significant, they were not major differences. In several later studies, no such difference in effect on immediate attitude change has been observed.

Lumsdaine and Janis (1953) went further in their study. After the receivers had been exposed to an initial one-sided or two-sided message, they were systematically exposed to counterargument. It was found that the initial communicator was more effective in changing attitudes in the face of counterpersuasion when he presented a two-sided rather than a one-sided message. Based on the findings of Lumsdaine and Janis and some of his own research, McGuire (1961a) set forth a theory to explain this kind of effect. This theory is based on a medical analogy. In medicine we often immunize people against disease by innoculating them with a virus related to the disease but too weak to produce it in the individual. This process of immunization is what McGuire postulated as the rationale for the effect over time of the two-sided message. He suggested that giving the receiver a little bit of the disease (the opposing position) permitted him to build defenses against it, so as to avoid contracting that disease later. Several studies have been reported that support this immunization theory (McGuire, 1961b, 1962; McGuire and Papageorgis, 1961; Papageorgis and McGuire, 1961; Crane, 1962; Thistlethwaite and Kamenetsky, 1955; Manis and Blake, 1963; Anderson and McGuire, 1965). The results of these studies, as a group, clearly indicate that a source wishing to have a sustained effect on a receiver who is going to be subjected to counterpersuasion will be more successful employing the two-sided message.

The most extensive study of one-sided versus two-sided messages has been reported by Koehler (1968). Koehler's concern was not only with whether or not the initial source should use a one-sided or two-sided message, but also with what type of message the second source should employ. His results indicate that a source is at least as successful, and often more successful, employing the two-sided rather than the one-sided message except in the relatively unique case of a second source responding to an initial source who presented a one-sided message a week earlier. In that case the second source tends to be more effective if he uses a one-sided message.

An appropriate conclusion from all of this research seems to be that whenever we try to communicate with a receiver we are probably better off to employ the two-sided message than the one-sided one except in very rare instances. Such messages anticipate that the receiver will either think of objections by himself or be confronted with objections from a counter-persuader that might inhibit the long-range impact of the initial communicator. In order to counteract those objections or reservations with which the receiver might be confronted, either immediately or at a later time, the two-sided message indicates what is objectionable about those reservations. As we stated before, the research on message-sidedness has been primarily in person-to-group setting, but the results should be directly applicable to the person-to-person and small group settings. The fact that the latter settings are conditions of discontinuous discourse (meaning one person doesn't do all the talking), there is even greater opportunity to introduce the other side as a result of questions on the part of other people. But even if such questions are not forthcoming, the research would suggest that the wise source would anticipate what objections might be brought forth at a later time and answer them anyway.

Message Structure

Public-speaking theorists have long contended that message structure or organization is a vital component of effective communication. Classes in public speaking, therefore, normally devote considerable time and effort to teaching students how to organize their messages effectively. Research has provided little support for these theorists and this classroom procedure. Although several researchers have found that message structure in the person-to-group setting has an effect on immediate receiver recall of the content of the message (Thistlethwaite, deHaan, and Kamenetsky, 1955; Thompson, 1960; Darnell, 1963), this has not been a universal finding (Beighley,

1952). Further, the importance of message structure or organization in the production of belief and attitude change is even more suspect. It has been found that extreme disorganization has an effect on attitude change (Smith, 1951; McCroskey and Mehrley, 1969), but that less drastic disorganization does not have a similar effect (Thompson, 1960; Weaver, 1969).

It is important to stress that the conceptualization of message structure and organization in the above studies had a "logical" foundation. An organized message was one in which the parts followed in some kind of logical or rational pattern. The disorganized message was one in which this pattern was disturbed. Why this type of disorganization does not have much effect has been explained: Receivers have a capacity to organize that which comes to them in a relatively disorganized manner. Thus, until the message becomes chaotic, the receiver can still put it together in such a way that it makes sense. It would seem reasonable to speculate that in person-to-person and small group communication message disorganization would have an even smaller impact than it has in the person-to-group setting. This is because in these two settings receivers who do not understand what the source is trying to say have an opportunity to ask for clarification.

You may be asking yourself, why should we worry about message structure at all? The answer to this question is that there is more than one way to look at message structure. As we noted, the research cited above has looked at it from a logical foundation. It can also be looked at from a psychological foundation. It is from this vantage point that message structure becomes important in all forms of interpersonal communication. The kinds of questions asked by researchers approaching the effects of message structure from a psychological framework are questions such as the following: If I'm going to ask a receiver to adopt a new solution to a problem, should I talk about the problem first or the solution first. If I have several points that I plan to make with the receiver, and he has already agreed to one of them, should I present this point first? If I am presenting a two-sided message, should I present my side or the opposing side first? If I am citing evidence in my message, should I cite the source of that evidence before I present the evidence or afterward? Should I make the point that I want the receiver to accept very clear, or should I leave it implied? Should I inform the receiver that I intend to influence him, or should I mask my intent? Let's consider some of the tentative answers that research has provided for these questions.

Problem or Solution First

I am a vacuum cleaner salesman sitting in a living room with a man and his wife in order to sell them one of my machines. Should I first explain how my cleaner works and then talk about their need for a new one, or should I discuss with them their need for a new vacuum cleaner first and then talk with them about how my vacuum cleaner works? The most extensive study related to this question was reported by Cohen (1957). Cohen presented two different messages to comparable groups of receivers. In one message he presented an argument concerning problems of grading and necessary reforms, and followed it with a proposal with grading on a curve, suggesting that this would solve the problems. In the other message, he presented his grading-on-the-curve solution first, and then explained the problems. The problem-solution pattern was found to be significantly more successful in producing attitude change in the receivers. Cohen explained these results in terms of clarity in the message. He suggested that when the need was developed first and followed by the solution, the message was more interesting and the solution was better understood. On the other hand, when the solution was presented first, Cohen hypothesized that the audience could not see its relevance until after the need had been developed. By that time they probably already had forgotten much of the solution because they failed to pay close attention to it when it was originally developed. Thus, it would appear that if we are trying to sell a receiver a vacuum cleaner or an idea for a grading system, we should first of all develop a need in the receiver for that vacuum cleaner or grading system and then provide him with the solution.

Point of Most Agreement

If I am talking with a friend and trying to get him to accept a new idea, and I know that we have some beliefs in common and some that we disagree upon, when should I talk about those points on which we are in agreement? McGuire (1964) hypothesized that if a source presented ideas that a receiver liked at the beginning, and then discussed less desirable ideas, he would be more successful than if he followed the opposite procedure. McGuire explained his hypothesis in terms of attention. If we hear something we like, presumably we pay attention to it, and our attention is likely to carry over to the next idea even though we are not particularly in favor of it. This permits greater opportunity for the undesirable idea to penetrate the selectivity processes of the listener and have an effect on his attitudes and beliefs. The results of McGuire's research support this theory. Many salesmen employ a technique that is based on this theory. This technique is called "yes response." The salesman attempts to design his interaction with his potential customer in such a way that he can get his customer into the habit of agreement. This whole pattern leads to the final point of agreement, that the customer should buy the salesman's product. The fact that this technique does work suggests that the findings of McGuire's laboratory studies do generalize to the everyday world. We should begin an interaction with another person with ideas we have in common rather than with our points of disagreement.

Pro or Con First

My wife is trying to get me to hire a housekeeper so that she will have more free time to engage in her hobbies. She is well aware of the fact that I know there are some reservations to her arguments. Being a sensible communicator she will use a two-sided message. But should she present the arguments for hiring a housekeeper first, followed by the arguments against hiring a housekeeper and refutation of those arguments? Or should she talk about the reasons why we should not hire a housekeeper and refute those arguments first and then discuss why we should hire a housekeeper? Results of studies reported by Miller and Campbell (1959) and Anderson and Barrios (1961) suggest that she would be well advised to give me her arguments why we should hire a housekeeper first. In these studies, the con arguments were not even refuted, but still the pro arguments gained greater acceptance. The basic theory is that if the receiver receives the pro arguments first, he is already convinced to some extent and thus on the source's side when he attacks the opposition. If, however, he attacks the opposition first before presenting his own side, he may very well be attacking his receiver. In the case of my wife, if she were to raise the issues of why we should not hire a housekeeper first, she would be talking about the things with which I agree. And when she attacked those arguments, she would be attacking beliefs that I hold. I doubt that she would be effective in either case, but the research says that she has a better chance if she gives her reasons why we should hire a housekeeper first.

When to Cite the Source

Presume that I want to convince my wife that we should buy a new car now instead of waiting until the new models come out. To get her to agree I need to convince her that the price of the new model will be substantially higher than the price of this year's model. To gain her acceptance on this point I call forth the warrant that wage increases in the auto industry normally produce major price increases. So I need to get her to believe that substantial wage increases have occurred in the auto industry. Now, she knows I am not an expert on labor-management relations or wages in the auto industry, so I choose to use some evidence to support my position. When should I tell her who the source of that evidence is? Should I cite the source before I present what the source says, or should I present what the source says and then indicate who said it? The answer to the question is "it depends." A study by Greenberg and Miller (1966) indicates that the answer depends on how the receiver perceives the source of the evidence. Let's go back to the above example: If my wife considers the source of the evidence to be high-credible, then it really doesn't make any difference whether I cite the source before or after I give her the evidence. However, if she perceives the source of the evidence as low-credible, it is clear from the Greenberg and Miller results that I had better not let her know who that source is until after she's heard the evidence. Surprising as it may seem, the results of the Greenberg and Miller study suggest that evidence from a low-credible source is as effective as evidence from a high-credible source so long as we hear the evidence *before* we hear who the source is. Since the source of communication may not know what the receiver's opinion is of a source of evidence he wishes to use, (as in the case above I was not sure what my wife thought of my source on the auto industry), it would appear that the wise source would always cite his references after presenting the evidence rather than before. He may not gain anything if the evidence source is high-credible, but he has much to gain if it is low-credible.

Implicit and Explicit Conclusions

Earlier in this chapter we noted that some of the elements in messages may be implied rather than explicitly stated. Research has not given us much information bearing directly upon the question of the effects of implied data or warrants. However, data are available concerning the effects of leaving claims implied as opposed to explicitly stating them. For example, I want my receiver to believe that the Ed Sullivan Show will soon go off the air. I tell him that the Ed Sullivan Show has low ratings and that low ratings usually cause a show to be canceled. The question is, do I need also to draw the conclusion that therefore the Ed Sullivan Show will be canceled. Most of the laboratory research suggests that directly stating the conclusion will have a greater impact than leaving the conclusion implied (Hovland and Mandel, 1952; Thistlethwaite, deHaan, and Kamenetsky, 1955; Leventhal, Singer, and Jones, 1965; Biddle, 1966).

Clinical observations, however, indicate that in some cases the reverse may be true. For example Rogers (1947), an exponent of the nondirective school of psychotherapy, claims that decisions made by clients are more lasting when they are reached independently by the client than when they are explicitly recommended by the therapist. Although research data are not available to either support or deny our position, we may hypothesize that there are at least two circumstances under which implicit conclusions might be more effective than explicit conclusions. The first circumstance is when the source is perceived by the receiver to be moderate-to-low-credible. On the basis of the consistency theories discussed in an earlier chapter, we would predict that under this circumstance attitude change would be more likely to move against the conclusion explicitly drawn by such an individual rather than toward it. Thus the moderate-to-low credible source might be more effective by attaining as little identification with his conclusions as is possible. It seems reasonable to assume that implicit conclusions provide less identification with the source than do explicit conclusions. The second circumstance under which implicit conclusions might be more effective than explicit conclusions is the circumstance of the type to which Rogers refers. When the conclusion to be drawn has a highly involving relationship for the individual drawing it, the receiver may be more resistant to the conclusion when it seems to be someone else's rather than his own. This is the case in psychotherapy, and it may well apply much more generally.

Statements of Intent

Since we have noted above that in most cases it is probably better to make our conclusion explicit than to leave it implied, the question arises as to *when* should we make it explicit. On the surface it might seem that the time to make it explicit would be at the earliest possible moment. Research findings, however, suggest quite the opposite. People are more resistant to influence when they know that someone is trying to influence them. Several studies have pointed to this effect (Allyn and Festinger, 1961; Kiesler and Kiesler, 1964; Brock and Becker, 1965). Some studies, however, indicate that this effect of "forewarning" the receiver of the source's intent does not have a serious negative impact if the source is perceived as high-credible by the receiver (Mills and Aronson, 1965; Mills, 1966).

To summarize this section, we should stress that although the logical structure of a message may not have too much impact on the way a receiver responds to it, the psychological structure of the message is extremely important. The source would do well to consider the questions that have been raised above whenever he engages in interpersonal communication in an attempt to influence other people.

Fear Appeals

No verbal message variable has received as much attention from researchers as has the variable of fear appeals. The impetus for this massive body of research was the assumption that people must be emotionally aroused before their attitudes or beliefs are likely to be affected. As we noted in an earlier chapter, for attitude or belief to change, inconsistency must be produced. What better way is there to arouse a receiver and create inconsistency than to "scare the hell out of him"? If one is to judge by the number of studies conducted, one could certainly conclude that researchers are in full agreement: There is no better way.

A fear appeal message is one that notes the harmful consequences that will befall the receiver if he fails to comply with the source's recommendations. A strong fear appeal is one that explicitly and vividly expresses those harmful consequences. This type of message has on occasion been referred to as a "hellfire and brimstone" or a "blood and gore" message. A mild fear appeal, on the other hand, while also alluding to the potentially harmful consequences that might befall the receiver if he does not comply with the source, does so in a less vivid and dramatic way.

A question, of course, arises as to which type of fear appeal is most effective in producing change in the receiver. On the surface, it might appear that the strong fear appeal would be best because it would create the most tension in the receiver and the most inconsistency. On the other hand, as we noted in an earlier chapter, if a message is perceived as too discrepant from the receiver's own attitude, it will have much less effect and in some cases even have a negative effect (Whittaker, 1967). As might be expected, therefore, the results of the studies on fear appeals have been very inconsistent. Some have found that a mild fear appeal produces the most change (Janis and Feshbach, 1953; Janis and Terwilliger, 1962), and some have found that a strong fear appeal is the best (DeWolfe and Governdale, 1964; Insko, Arkoff, and Insko, 1965; Leventhal, Singer, and Jones, 1965; Rosenblatt, 1965). From these confused and conflicting findings it is obvious that some other variables must interact with fear appeals. A few studies have been reported that indicate reasonably clear results concerning how fear appeals interact with other communication variables. Let us consider some of these studies.

Hewgill and Miller (1965) hypothesized that the effectiveness of fear appeals would vary with the credibility of the source of those appeals. They presented the same message in two forms to four different audiences. One form was a strong fear appeal and the other a mild fear appeal. Two of the audiences heard the strong fear message, one hearing it attributed it to a high-credible source and the other hearing it attributed it to a low-credible source. The other two audiences heard the mild fear message, one hearing it attributed it to a high-credible source and one hearing it attributed it to a low-credible source. The results indicated the high-credible source was significantly more effective in persuading his receivers when he employed a strong fear message than when he employed a mild fear message. For the low-credible source, no differences in attitude change between the strong and mild fear conditions were observed. However, the low-credible source received significantly lower credibility ratings when he employed the strong fear message than when he employed the mild fear message. The results of this study strongly suggest that a high-credible source will be more effective with a strong fear message, but that a low-credible source has nothing to gain from a strong fear message and will probably find his credibility reduced even further.

Research reported by Powell (1965) suggests that it makes a difference to whom the fear appeal is directed in determining whether strong or mild fear appeal will be most effective. Powell manipulated both the level of fear appeal (strong and mild) and the target of that appeal (the receiver himself or the receiver's "valued other," for example, family member). His results produced a significant interaction between level of fear appeal and referent of the appeal. When the appeal was directed toward the receiver himself, the mild fear appeal produced more change, whereas when the appeal was directed at a valued other, the strong fear appeal produced more change. These results suggest that while it may be possible for us to discount strong fear appeals directed to ourselves, we find it difficult to discount them if they are addressed to our loved ones. We may rationalize that all we're doing is hurting ourselves if the fear appeal is addressed to us and consider that to be no one else's business. However, if the fear appeal is directed to our children it is not possible for us to take the same rationalization. We may feel increased societal pressure to conform to the source's request.

In a recent study Gardiner (1969) attempted to examine the possible interaction between the level of fear appeal and the exclusion or inclusion of evidence in a message. Gardiner constructed a strong fear and a mild fear message opposing the use of seat belts in automobiles. He then constructed a version of each message that was carefully documented with evidence and another version of each message that included only generalized assertion and no evidence. When these four messages were presented to comparable audiences, it was found that all of the messages produced significant attitude change but the strong fear message with evidence produced significantly more change than any of the others. An interesting observation from the Gardiner data that may help to explain this finding is that the subjects reported significantly more anxiety as a result of listening to the strong fear plus evidence message than they did for any of the other messages. Since the source's credibility in the Gardiner study was moderate, this is a case where increased inconsistency produced by evidence and a strong fear appeal resulted in greater change than other conditions that produced less anxiety.

Other interesting results drawn from the Gardiner study are that the source of the strong fear message was perceived to be more dynamic and authoritative than the source of the mild fear message regardless of whether or not evidence was included. However, over time, a two-week delay period, the interaction on attitude change between fear appeals and evidence disappeared. The attitudes of the subjects who heard the two messages that included evidence continued to differ significantly from their initial attitudes. But the two messages without evidence failed to maintain significant attitude change over time. The effects of fear appeals were completely erased.

To summarize all of the research on fear appeals in order to draw some conclusions for practical usage is both a risky and speculative process. However, it would appear that in most circumstances a strong fear appeal will have a more positive effect than a mild fear appeal. As was noted above, this would be true when the source of the message is high-credible, when the referent of the appeal is a loved one of the receiver, or when the message is well supported. In interpersonal communication it is not unreasonable to expect that in most cases at least one of these circumstances will be present. In fact, in most instances of interpersonal communication the source of the message is of at least moderately high credibility or the communication transaction does not take place. Obviously, we should not carry this conclusion to extremes. If a message is so frightening to a person, so vivid and gory, that it loses touch with reality, we certainly should not expect it to be more effective than a more moderate message. But strong fear appeal, judiciously employed, seems to be an effective verbal message element in producing change in receivers.

Language Intensity

Language intensity may be defined as the verbal indication of the degree of deviation from neutral of a source's attitude or belief. Probably no word is absolutely neutral, but some words indicate a much stronger attitude than do others. Although the perception of intensity will vary somewhat depending upon the receiver, it is useful to examine some of the characteristics of words that increase the perceived intensity of language.

The work of Bowers (1964) suggests that two types of words or phrases can produce considerable increases in intensity. The first type can be referred to as "qualifying words." These are words that indicate probability or extremity. For example, "probably" is likely to be perceived as less intense than "absolutely." "Totally unworthy" is likely to be perceived as more intense than "undeserving." "Completely ridiculous" is likely to be perceived as more intense than "erroneous." The second type of term that can indicate intensity is use of metaphor. Metaphorical words tend to increase intensity. We may say that a word is being employed metaphorically when it is being used in a somewhat unconventional way. For example, to say that the dog "follows the herd" of sheep is not metaphorical. But to say that a man "follows the herd" when he conforms to some social practice is metaphorical. Sex and death metaphors are particularly common. The use of these may be exemplified in such expressions as the "prostitution" of education, the "perversion" of our national goals, the "seduction" of the United Nations, the "death" of the Republican party, the "ghastly" conditions in the ghetto, and the "decay" of American morality.

There has not been much research that has systematically, and under controlled conditions, investigated the effects of language intensity on receivers. If, however, we accept the work of Whittaker (1967) on message discrepancy as related to language intensity, we have a base for predicting the effects of language intensity. Figure 8.2 presents the kind of results that Whittaker observed. It shows that as message discrepancy increases, up to a point, attitude change in the desired direction also increases. However, as message discrepancy continues on beyond that point, desired attitude change tends to decrease and at a certain point attitude change tends to become negative. As attitude change tends to decrease, the probability of source derogation tends to increase. Thus, as message discrepancy gets very great, no positive attitude change occurs, or negative change occurs, and the source is the recipient of extensive derogation. If we may think of the attitude change curve represented in Fig. 8.2 as representing change as a result of language intensity causing the message discrepancy, it will predict that increased language intensity will increase attitude change, to a point, but increased intensity beyond that point would tend to reduce attitude change. The shape of the curve in Fig. 8.2, of course, is arbitrary. We would pre-

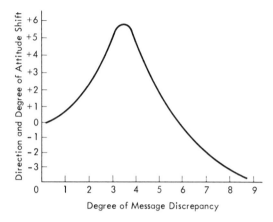

Figure 8.2 The effects of message discrepancy on attitude change. Numbers were arbitrarily selected to illustrate the relationship between attitude change and message discrepancy and are not meaningful in themselves.
Reprinted from *An Introduction to Rhetorical Communication* by James C. McCroskey, Englewood Cliffs, N.J.: Prentice-Hall, Inc., 1968, with permission from the publisher.

sume that the point of inflection of the curve would be further out toward the extremity of language intensity if the source of communication were high-credible. Similarly, we would assume that it would be nearer to the minimum level of language intensity if the receiver held an extremely intense and involving attitude on the subject.

Some research, which concerns opinionated language, tends to support the above speculations. Non-opinionated statements convey information relating simply to the source's attitude or belief on a particular topic ("I believe that the United States should withdraw its troops from Viet Nam.") By contrast, opinionated statements convey two kinds of information; they indicate the source's attitude toward the idea and his attitude toward those who agree or disagree with him. ("Only a warmonger would oppose the withdrawal of United States troops from Viet Nam.") This latter type of statement has been referred to as opinionated rejection statements. There are also opinionated acceptance statements. ("Any intelligent person knows that the United States should withdraw its troops from Viet Nam.")

Studies by Miller and Lobe (1967) and Miller and Baseheart (1969) conform to our above prediction for the effects of intense language. Specifically, the prediction was confirmed that opinionated rejection language would be more intense than non-opinionated language, and therefore would be more effective for a high-credible source but less effective for a low-credible source. In a study by Mehrley and McCroskey (1970) it was hypothesized that opinionated rejection language would be more effective than non-opinionated language when the receiver was relatively neutral on the topic, but when the receiver held an intense attitude on the topic it was hypothesized that non-opinionated language would be most effective. The results of the study supported both hypotheses.

In the presence of so little controlled research concerning language intensity, we may draw only tentative conclusions from the above discussion. It would seem that a communicator should be careful not to make his language too intense unless he is perceived by his receiver as very high-credible. Similarly, if the receiver is known to hold a very strong attitude on the subject, it would seem wise to keep the language intensity at a relatively low level.

In this and the preceding chapters we have examined several models of communication, the basic systems and outcomes of communication, and the primary source, receiver, and messsage variables that affect communication. In the next section two chapters are devoted to practical application of the theory set forth in the preceding chapters in circumstances common to almost all people—interpersonal communication in marriage and interpersonal communication on the job. The final chapter of this work will consider interpersonal communication within the context of the totality of communication that surrounds mankind.

References

Allyn, Jane, and L. Festinger, "The Effectiveness of Unanticipated Persuasive Communications," *Journal of Abnormal and Social Psychology*, 62 (1961), 35–40.

Anderson, D. C., "The Effect of Various Uses of Authoritative Testimony in Persuasive Speaking." Master's thesis, Ohio State University, 1958.

Anderson, L., and W. J. McGuire, "Prior Reassurance of Group Consensus as a Factor in Producing Resistance to Persuasion," *Sociometry*, 28 (1965), 44–56.

Anderson, N. H., and A. A. Barrios, "Primary Effects in Personality Impression Formation," *Journal of Abnormal and Social Psychology*, 63 (1961), 346–50.

Beighley, K. C., "An Experimental Study of the Effect of Four Speech Variables on Listener Comprehension," *Speech Monographs*, 19 (1952), 249–58.

Bettinghaus, E. P., Jr., "The Relative Effect of the Use of Testimony in a Persuasive Speech upon the Attitudes of Listeners." Master's thesis, Bradley University, 1953.

Biddle, P. R., "An Experimental Study of Ethos and Appeal for Overt Behavior in Persuasion." Doctoral dissertation, University of Illinois, 1966.

Bowers, J., "Some Correlates of Language Intensity," *Quarterly Journal of Speech*, 50 (1964), 415–20.

Brock, T. C., and L. Becker, "Ineffectiveness of 'Overheard' Counterpropaganda," *Journal of Personality and Social Psychology*, 2 (1965), 654-60.

Cathcart, R. S., "An Experimental Study of the Relative Effectiveness of Four Methods of Presenting Evidence," *Speech Monographs*, 22 (1955), 227–33.

Cohen, A. R., "Need for Cognition and Order of Communications as Determinants of Opinion Change," *The Order of Presentation in Persuasion*, ed., C. I. Hovland. New Haven, Conn.: Yale University Press, 1957, pp. 102–20.

Costley, D. L., "An Experimental Study of the Effectiveness of Quantitative Evidence in Speeches of Advocacy." Master's thesis, University of Oklahoma, 1958.

Crane, E., "Immunization; With and Without the Use of Counter-arguments," *Journalism Quarterly*, 39 (1962), 445–50.

Darnell, D. K., "The Relation Between Sentence-Order and Comprehension," *Speech Monographs*, 30 (1963), 97–100.

DeWolfe, D. S., and C. N. Governdale, "Fear and Attitude Change," *Journal of Abnormal and Social Psychology*, 69 (1964), 119–23.

Dresser, W. R., "Effects of 'Satisfactory' and 'Unsatisfactory' Evidence in a Speech of Advocacy," *Speech Monographs*, 20 (1963), 302–6.

Gardiner, J. C., "An Experimental Study of the Use of Selected Forms of Evidence in Effecting Attitude Change." Master's thesis, University of Nebraska, 1966.

———, "An Experimental Study of the Effects of Evidence and Fear Appeals on Attitude Change and Source Credibility." Research monograph, Department of Communication, Michigan State University, 1969.

Gilkinson, H., S. F. Paulson, and D. E. Sikkink, "Effects of Order and Authority in an Argumentative Speech," *Quarterly Journal of Speech*, 40 (1954), 183–92.

Greenberg, B. S., and G. R. Miller, "The Effects of Low-Credible Sources on Message Acceptance," *Speech Monographs*, 33 (1966), 127–36.

Hewgill, M. A., and G. R. Miller, "Source Credibility and Response to Fear-Arousing Communications," *Speech Monographs*, 32 (1965), 95–101.

Hovland, C. I., A. A. Lumsdaine, and F. D. Sheffield, *Experiments on Mass Communication* (*Studies in Social Psychology in World War II*, Vol. 3). Princeton, N.J.: Princeton University Press, 1949.

Hovland C. I., and W. Mandell, "An Experimental Comparison of Conclusion-Drawing by the Communicator and by the Audience," *Journal of Abnormal and Social Psychology*, 47 (1952), 581–88.

Insko, C., A. Arkoff, and V. Insko, "Effects of High and Low Fear-Arousing Communications upon Opinions Toward Smoking," *Journal of Experimental Social Psychology*, 1 (1965), 256–66.

Janis, I. L., and S. Feshbach, "Effects of Fear-Arousing Communications," *Journal of Abnormal and Social Psychology*, 48 (1953), 78–92.

Janis, I. L., and R. F. Terwilliger, "An Experimental Study of Psychological Responses to Fear-Arousing Communications," *Journal of Abnormal and Social Psychology*, 65 (1962), 403–10.

Kiesler, C. A., and Sara B. Kiesler, "Role of Forewarning in Persuasive Communications," *Journal of Abnormal and Social Psychology*, 68 (1964), 547–49.

Koehler, J. W., "Effects on Audience Opinion of One-Sided and Two-Sided Speeches Supporting and Opposing a Proposition, Examining Opinions on Speaker's Ethos, the Topic, and the 'Open-Mindedness' of Listeners." Doctoral dissertation, Pennsylvania State University, 1968.

Leventhal, H., R. P. Singer, and S. Jones, "Effects of Fear and Specificity of Recommendation upon Attitudes and Behavior," *Journal of Personality and Social Psychology*, 2 ,(1965), 20–29.

Lumsdaine, A. A., and I. L. Janis, "Resistance to 'Counter-Propaganda' Produced by One-Sided and Two-Sided 'Propaganda' Presentation." *Public Opinion Quarterly*, 17 (1953), 311–18.

McCroskey, J. C. "Experimental Studies of the Effects of Ethos and Evidence in Persuasive Communication," Doctoral dissertation, Pennsylvania State University, 1966.

————, *Studies of the Effects of Evidence in Persuasive Communication,* Report SCRL 4–67, Speech Communication Research Laboratory, Michigan State University, 1967.

————, "A Summary of Experimental Research on the Effects of Evidence in Persuasive Communication," *Quarterly Journal of Speech,* 55 (1969), 169–176.

McCroskey, J. C. and R. S. Mehrley. "The Effects of Disorganization and Nonfluency on Attitude Change and Source Credibility," *Speech Monographs,* 36 (1969), 13–21.

McGuire, W. J., "The Effectiveness of Supportive and Refutational Defenses in Immunizing and Restoring Beliefs Against Persuasion," *Sociometry,* 24 (1961), 184–97. (a)

————, "Resistance to Persuasion Conferred by Active and Passive Prior Refutation of the Same and Alternative Counterarguments," *Journal of Abnormal and Social Psychology,* 63 (1961), 326–32. (b)

————, "Persistence of the Resistance to Persuasion Induced by Various Types of Prior Belief Defenses," *Journal of Abnormal and Social Psychology,* 64, (1962), 241–48.

McGuire, W. J., and D. Papageorgis. "The Relative Efficacy of Various Types of Prior Belief-Defense in Producing Immunity Against Persuasion," *Journal of Abnormal and Social Psychology,* 62 (1961), 327–37.

McGuire, W. J., cited in A. R. Cohen, *Attitude Change and Social Influence.* New York: Basic Books, Inc., Publishers, 1964, p. 12.

Manis, M., and J. B. Blake, "Interpretation of Persuasive Messages as a Function of Prior Immunization," *Journal of Abnormal and Social Psychology,* 66 (1963), 225–30.

Mehrley, R. S., and J. C. McCroskey, "Opinionated Statements and Attitude Intensity as Predictors of Attitude Change and Source Credibility," *Speech Monographs,* 37 (1970), 47–52.

Miller, G. R., and J. Baseheart, "Source Trustworthiness, Opinionated Statements and Response to Persuasive Communication," *Speech Monographs,* 36 (1969), 1–7.

Miller, G. R., and J. Lobe, "Opinionated Language, Open- and Closed-

Mindedness and Responses to Persuasive Communications," *Journal of Communication*, 17 (1967), 333–41.

Miller, N., and D. T. Campbell, "Recency and Primacy in Persuasion as a Function of the Timing of Speeches and Measurements," *Journal of Abnormal and Social Psychology*, 59 (1959), 1–9.

Mills, J., "Opinion Change as a Function of the Communicator's Desire to Influence and Liking for the Audience," *Journal of Experimental Social Psychology*, 2 (1966), 152–59.

Mills, J., and E. Aronson, "Opinion Change as a Function of the Communicator's Attractiveness and Desire to Influence," *Journal of Personality and Social Psychology*, 1 (1965), 173–77.

Ostermeier, T. H., "An Experimental Study on the Type and Frequency of Reference as Used by an Unfamiliar Source in a Message and Its Effect upon Perceived Credibility and Attitude Change." Doctoral dissertation, Michigan State University, 1966.

Papageorgis, D., and W. J. McGuire, "The Generality of Immunity to Persuasion Produced by Pre-Exposure to Weakened Counter-arguments," *Journal of Abnormal and Social Psychology*, 62 (1961), 475–81.

Powell, F. A., "The Effects of Anxiety Arousing Messages When Related to Personal, Familial, and Impersonal Referents," *Speech Monographs*, 32 (1965), 102–6.

Rogers, C. R., "Some Observations on the Organization of Personality," *American Psychologist*, 2 (1947), 358–68.

Rosenblatt, P., "Enhancement of Persuasion by Threat." Paper read at Midwest Psychological Association Convention, Chicago, 1965.

Smith, R. G., "Effects of Speech Organization Upon Attitudes of College Students," *Speech Monographs*, 18 (1951), 292–301.

Thistlethwaite, D. L., H. deHaan, and J. Kamenetsky, "The Effect of 'Directive' and 'Non-Directive' Communication Procedures on Attitudes," *Journal of Abnormal and Social Psychology*, 51 (1955), 107–18.

Thistlethwaite, D. L., and J. Kamenetsky, "Attitude Change Through Refutation and Elaboration of Audience Counter-arguments," *Journal of Abnormal and Social Psychology*, 51 (1955), 3–12.

Thompson, E., "An Experimental Investigation of the Relative Effectiveness of Organizational Structure in Oral Communication." Doctoral dissertation, University of Minnesota, 1960.

————, "Some Effects of Message Structure on Listeners' Comprehension," *Speech Monographs*, 34 (1967), 51–57.

Toulmin, S. E., *The Uses of Argument*. New York: Cambridge University Press, 1958.

Wagner, G. A., "An Experimental Study of the Relative Effectiveness of Varying Amounts of Evidence in a Persuasive Communication." Master's thesis, Mississippi Southern University, 1958.

Weaver, J. F., "The Effects of Verbal Cueing and Initial Ethos upon Perceived Organization, Retention, Attitude Change, and Terminal Ethos." Doctoral dissertation, Michigan State University, 1969.

Whittaker, J. O., "Resolution of the Communication Discrepancy Issue in Attitude Change," in Carolyn W. Sherif and M. Sherif, eds., *Attitude, Ego-Involvement and Change*. New York: John Wiley & Sons, Inc., 1967.

Social Contexts of Interpersonal Communication

Section IV discusses the unique situational constraints associated with interpersonal communication in various social contexts. The preceding sections of this book have attempted to assist you in developing greater perceptiveness and diagnostic ability in understanding and coping with interpersonal communication in general. However, the three chapters in Section IV illustrate that interpersonal communication always occurs in a social context and, frequently, this social context will force us to refine some of our generalizations, conclusions, and predictions about interpersonal communication. Section IV builds upon everything we have discussed so far, but additionally attempts to elicit from you a sensitivity toward social contexts. We have selected social contexts to illustrate situational constraints on interpersonal communication. The three social contexts—marriage, work, and mass communication—are situations that you already have or *probably* will in the future, experience directly.

Chapter 9

Interpersonal Communication
in Marriage

A Basic Point of View

Our own perspective on marital communication is a relatively simple one for such a complex and foreboding topic. We intend to let this perspective emerge in the next several pages, rather than state it at the outset. Perhaps the following example will help us get started.

A husband and wife, driven to the point of spontaneous combustion by their three small children and a few dozen other eroding pressures, escape for the evening to a party in their neighborhood. They have been looking forward to this evening out for a week. The party is great. In about an hour, however, the wife develops a headache. After waiting a short while to make sure that the headache is not going to leave her, she dismays her husband with her entreaty, "You'd better take me home." He resists momentarily. "Every time we start having fun, you seem to get a headache." She doesn't feel like arguing. "You take me home and then you come back to the party." He pauses, rehearses in his mind all the reasons why he should return to the party and says, "Okay, let's go." They are both quiet during the drive home. Arriving home, he escorts her into the living room, asks if there is anything to do to help her get comfortable, and announces his departure. "Where are you going?" she asks. "I'm going back to the party." He notices the pained expression and a small tear welling up in the corner of her eye. "What's the matter now?" "You're leaving me alone." "But you told me I should go back to the party." "I know, but if you really loved me, you wouldn't want to."

Let's stop the example at this point, allowing you to end the story in your own words. If you reflect upon this and other examples you may have experienced in marital or other similarly intense communication contexts, perhaps you can agree with the following observations.

1. If you try to analyze such examples by commenting on the logic or rationality of the behavior involved, you are engaging in a foolhardy activity. Everything that the husband or wife does seems logical and reasonable to them while they are doing it. The rules of formal logic and principles of reasoning do not provide you with a productive approach to marital communication. Indeed, in one investigation to be described in greater detail later, we found that husbands who tended to evaluate their wives in terms of criteria associated with "logic" or "rationality" are markedly deficient in their abilities to understand their wives' attitudes on a range of topics. When we are considering a two-person communication system in a marital context, we must remember that the system was established, is based, and is maintained primarily on affective or nonrational sentiments. Why, then, should we attempt to impose principles of logic or rationality upon that system?

One important implication of this observation must be pointed out, however obvious it may already be to you. We tend to develop habitual ways of responding to others. And these habitual response patterns may be more characteristic of marital communication than of other interpersonal contexts. When we fall into the pattern of evaluating the logic or rationality of another's behavior, we encounter problems whenever the other's "logic" is different from our "logic." It is easy for us at this point to do one of two things. First, we may simply dismiss the other as unreasonable, messed up, unintelligent, or even in need of professional help of some kind. And since we all know how useless it is to talk to someone who is incapable of thinking straight, or following our own clear and concise patterns of reasoning, why bother. Second, if we decide to try to resolve the differences, it is easy for us to invest all our energies and resources into "correcting" the faulty thinking of the other; hence, we enthusiastically embark on a small but holy crusade to convert the other, to save him from the pitfalls of his own thinking; to prove that he is wrong and we are right. Either of those two courses of action is likely to be unproductive.

2. The second observation that discloses our basic perspective also emerges from the example. It concerns the question of who determines the outcomes of interpersonal communication. We would suggest that in the example given, regardless of whether you assume the role of the husband or the wife, it should be evident that the other person determines the outcomes of the interpersonal encounter. If the husband wishes to adopt a particular stance, as a sender of messages, and if he wishes that stance to produce desirable outcomes from his point of view, the first thing that he must be concerned about is his behavior as a receiver of messages. Regardless of how articulate the husband may be, how intelligent, how sophisticated, how smooth and polished as a sender of messages, his behavior in that context is not likely to be productive unless he tunes in on all that is implied by his wife's message, "If you really loved me." The extent to which the husband is capable of understanding and adjusting to his wife's "logic" is dependent upon his sensitivity, awareness, and empathic capacities as a receiver of messages. Similarly, if the wife wishes to avoid a catastrophe, she must understand the conditions that prompt her husband to exhibit what seems to her to be such apparent disinterest in her welfare or desires. If both parties concentrate on their behavior as senders of messages, that is, if they invest their time and energy into winning the argument, then the example is likely to have a very unhappy ending. The example will probably be repeated in some other form, and the cumulative effects of such repetitions are likely to have long-range and destructive consequences for the two-person system.

To pursue these basic perspectives in greater detail, let us consider a specific aspect of marital communication, the perception of communication patterns.

Perception of Communication Patterns

As part of a larger project, Larson (1965) gathered information on the perception of communication patterns by married couples. One hundred and four subjects participated in this study. They had been married for an average of three years, four months and had known each other for an average of two years, two months, before getting married. The mean number of years of full-time formal education were: husbands, 16.4; wives, 15.1. The subjects therefore must be considered young marrieds and do not represent the entire spectrum of ages.

The subjects were asked to describe their typical or characteristic patterns of interaction with each other. These descriptions were collected by having the subjects respond to an instrument developed by Ruesch, Block, and Bennet (1953) which taps a great many interaction dimensions untapped by other well-known assessment methods. Although these data were collected for other purposes, an interesting observation emerged when the descriptions of interaction patterns were compared: husbands with wives.

A. *How the Wives Perceived the Communication Context.*

From a wide range of alternatives, there emerged four consistent descriptions the wives gave to their husbands' behavior.

1. The pattern of interaction that the wives attributed most frequently to their husbands was one in which the husbands were apparently not really interested in the wives, were perceived as not really caring for the wives, were perceived as being relatively unresponsive and relatively unconcerned about the wives' interests and activities.

2. The second most frequently attributed communication pattern was one in which the husbands disciplined the wives, argued with them, controlled them, got annoyed at them, and tried to outdo them.

3. The third most typical communication pattern was one in which the husbands were careful not to upset the wives, were cautious in their presence, worried about the wives, and were perceived as having little confidence in the wives' maturity or stability.

4. The fourth most characteristic pattern was one in which the husbands were perceived as expecting a lot of their wives, getting impatient with the wives, inhibiting them, and embarrassing them.

If we were to pause here and summarize the most characteristic or typical patterns of interaction engaged in by the husbands, as perceived by their wives, we would have to conclude that the prospects for rewarding and satisfying communication in these marriages appear very bleak. From the wives' point of view, marital communication is about as far from the romantic, fulfilling, constantly rewarding pattern of interaction displayed in pulp magazines and on cinema screens as one could possibly get. However, our description of the perception of communication in marriage is not complete until we have examined the descriptions given to marital interaction by the husband.

B. *How the Husbands Perceived the Communication Context.*

From an equally wide range of alternatives, there emerged four consistent descriptions the husbands gave to their own behavior.

1. The husbands generally perceived themselves as understanding the wives, trusting them, being honest with them, acting in their interests, and being kind and reassuring to them.

2. The second most consistent pattern was one in which the husbands described themselves as having great attraction for their wives, liking them, not having mixed feelings about them, not getting impatient with them.

3. The third most consistent pattern was one in which the husbands described themselves as frequently agreeing with their wives, acting in their wives' interest, and giving in to their wives.

4. The fourth most consistent pattern of interaction as described by the husbands was one in which the husbands had conflicts with their wives, but tried to reassure the wives and tried to resolve the conflicts amicably.

When we compare the perceptions of marital communication, some obvious observations emerge. First, there seems to be quite a discrepancy between what the husbands are feeling and doing and what the wives are perceiving. In fact, if you go beyond the most characteristic interaction patterns, one of the interesting results is that the "understanding, trusting, honest concern for the other's interests" that the husbands say is most typical of their own behavior is the same pattern their wives say is least typical of the husband's behavior. (Individual mean rating equals 5.50 or "almost always"—Partner mean rating equals 2.11 or "almost never.")

There is another observation which appears equally obvious. If it is reasonable to assume that the discrepancies in the perception of interaction patterns do not reflect deliberate differences in the behavior of the individuals, that is, if the husbands are not deliberately acting in ways contrary to their wives' desires, then we may make the following argument: First, in order to overcome whatever problems are posed by the discrepancies, the differing perceptions must be recognized. As we suggested earlier in this chapter, this implies a focus on the communication behavior of the parties acting as receivers of messages. If the differing perceptions are identified and understood, then the individuals must work to overcome whatever constraints have been imposed or conditioned upon them. The wives may have to adjust their expectations for the amount of intimacy and affection their husbands display, and the husbands may have to overcome whatever restraints they feel toward outward displays of affection, concern, and reassurance.

This is really an awkward point, but it is an important one. In order to reinforce it, let us examine some data that have been derived from an investigation of interaction themes in disrupted marriages. DeBurger (1966) conducted a content analysis of 1,422 themes that occurred in letters to marriage counselors. The major problem themes described in these letters have been coded into a relatively comprehensive set of categories. In the marriages represented by these letters some basic findings emerge that reinforce the observations made above. One result indicates that of all the major problem themes, the most recurrent ones identified by the wives fall within the area of affectional relations. That is, a disproportionate number of major problem themes perceived by the wives involve situations in which the wives do not feel as if they receive adequate affection from their husbands. On the other hand, the themes that emerge from the husbands' descriptions of major problems involve problems other than affectional relations. The major problems perceived by the husbands involve sexual relations, personality problems of the wives, and in-law troubles.

It appears that there may be some truth to the popular notion that certain prescribed sex rules in our culture mediate against a satisfactory and complementary balance of intimacy, affection, and "tenderness" on the part of husbands and wives. Indeed, we suspect that even the discussion of such concepts as intimacy and tenderness may evoke marked negative reactions on the part of some of our readers. Realistically, however, this discrepancy in the basic communication patterns related to affectional matters may well represent the most consistent "communication breakdown" in marriage. Some of the information to be considered later in this chapter will reinforce this position.

The Question of Disclosure

One of the central themes in interpersonal communication theory revolves around concepts such as "openness," "candidness," or "disclosure."

Culbert (1968) has suggested that the disclosure of personal information, feelings, attitudes, and beliefs is one of the characteristics of a qualitatively rich interpersonal relationship. Similarly, Jourard (1959) contends that one way of determining the "closeness of the relationship," and the love, affection, and trust which characterize the two-person system, is the amount of personal information that one person is willing to disclose to another. Perhaps, the furthest extension of this position is that of Baker (1955). Baker has argued that the unpremeditated goal of interpersonal communication is silence. That is, individuals communicate until they have enough information about each other so that they can tolerate silence, or the absence of talk when they are in each other's presence. It may seem reasonable to conclude on the basis of our own experience that the extent to which we can tolerate silence, or the absence of talk, when we are alone with another is partially a function of the extent to which we really "know that other."

You are probably familiar with the observation that frequently strangers meeting on a train or in a bar will disclose personal information to each other that they would not disclose to some of their better known acquaintances. We would suggest that this is not typical of most disclosure in interpersonal communication. Indeed, Rutledge (1966, p.55) has observed that disclosure is frequently a gradual process in which restraints tend to be released, manners forgotten, frankness employed, and perhaps, hostility expressed, until the two people approach a tolerance level beyond which further disclosures become uncomfortable. At this point, limits are frequently placed upon disclosure, until the discomfort has been overcome and the tolerance level raised.

Disclosure is a particularly important concept in our discussion of interpersonal communication in marriage. Much writing in the popular literature suggests that open communication on all aspects of marital life leads to greater understanding and adjustment. However, there are serious limitations that one should place on that generalization. We have all encountered situations in which individuals in particularly playful or rueful moods give in to momentary impulses to make intense personal disclosures. We sometimes regret these disclosures, even beyond the point where we can derive any comfort from the convenient cop-out, "I'm telling you this for your own good." From the marital situation, the effects of such intense disclosures are long-range and cumulative and may even be destructive. The intensity of the involvement and the commitment which characterize the marital situation are such that the married couple experimenting with "truth sessions" may discover that their momentary experimentation will have consequences that go far beyond their expectations. The critical questions which should be asked are "Is the disclosure necessary, or likely to have productive consequences?" "Can the other person handle it?" The second question implies an almost moralistic assertion. The assertion is that when we disclose personal information to another, we are in effect "messing with his mind." If what we say has deep personal implications for the other, then the responsibility for the consequences clearly lies with the person who is doing the disclosing. Having presented these observations, however, we must admit that the best basis for making generalizations about the relationship between disclosure and marital satisfaction is to discuss several empirical investigations.

That women tend to disclose more personal feelings and information than men is a conclusion in which we can have some confidence. This conclusion has consistently emerged from a number of investigations (Jourard, 1961; Jourard and Landsman, 1960; Jourard and Lasakow, 1958). Katz, Goldston, Cohen, and Stucker (1963) have identified one specific difference in the extent to which husbands and wives disclose personal feelings and information, that is, wives reveal personal anxieties more often than do their husbands. Cutler and Dyer (1965) found that wives more often than husbands respond openly and negatively to violations of their personal expectations. Levinger (1966) discovered that among divorce applicants, the wives tend to verbalize "complaints" about twice as frequently as do their husbands. These conclusions support the notion we advanced earlier that wives may have a greater tendency toward personal disclosure in marriage, and may have greater expectations for the disclosure of personal feelings and information than do their husbands.

One general conclusion which seems to have considerable empirical support is that marital satisfaction is positively related to disclosure on most but not all topics of discussion. Luckey (1960) discovered that satisfied couples agreed more on evaluations of self than did less satisfied couples. Levinger (1963) found that more satisfied couples discussed most marital topics more frequently than did less satisfied couples. And in a more recent investigation, Levinger and Senn (1967) confirmed three hypotheses: (1) that wives tended to reveal more feelings than did husbands, but only when the other partner was the judge of the amount disclosed; (2) that disclosure of feelings correlated positively with general marital satisfaction; (3) that spouses' independent reports of the amounts of disclosure yielded significant positive correlation which indicated mutuality of communication.

In one of the more comprehensive investigations of marital interaction, Komarovsky (1964) supported the conclusion that wives tended toward higher self-disclosure than did husbands, and that wives indicated a greater tendency and greater desire to share their experiences with their husbands. One interesting outcome from Komarovsky's investigations was that although disclosure was positively related to marital satisfaction, there were a considerable number of instances in which dissatisfied wives tended to be high disclosers. More frequently, however, dissatisfied husbands tended to be low disclosers. It would appear, therefore, that marital dissatisfaction intensifies prior tendencies of the wives to disclose and of the husbands to conceal personal feelings and information.

Although these conclusions may be accepted with some confidence, it should be obvious to us that the impact of disclosure on marital satisfaction and adjustment may vary considerably, depending on the content of the disclosures. In an attempt to refine some of these conclusions, Voss (1969) conducted a small exploratory study involving 26 couples. All 26 couples were middle class, married 2–5 years, ranging in age from 25–30 years, college graduates with the husbands in early years of professional careers, with all couples coming from an urban environment but living in suburban areas. On the basis of interviews conducted with other married couples of the same general characteristics as those employed in her study, Voss identified 69 topics on which some disclosure was likely. She then gathered information on the extent to which the 26 couples disclosed their true feelings and attitudes on these 69 topics. Employing Karlsson's marital satisfaction index (1963), she also gathered information on the extent to which each individual was "satisfied with the marriage." Using factor analysis, a statistical procedure that allows for a relatively comprehensive investigation of relationships among all of the variables, Voss arrived at the following conclusions. Two clusters of disclosure items were associated with marital satisfaction. One was a cluster which Voss labeled "Shared Activity." The strongest positive association between marital satisfaction and disclosure had to do with the extent to which the couple discussed the proportion of time they wished to spend together and the kind of activities they wished to engage in together. The second cluster was one labeled "Children and Careers." Marital satisfaction was associated with greater disclosure on child-rearing beliefs and specific approaches and on future plans and personal goals of the married couple.

Although disclosure must be viewed as a critical variable in marital communication, we ought not to assume that disclosure on all topics is necessary. Disclosures that lead to a satisfactory adjustment of the individuals to each other may enhance the satisfaction of the marriage. Karlsson (1963,

p. 38) has summarized the point adequately: "Communicating dissatisfactions, in order to enable the spouse to minimize them, is a prerequisite for all adjustment. However, communicating dissatisfactions which one has already accepted as inevitable, would create dissatisfactions also in the other spouse, without any compensating increase in satisfaction."

Communication Outcomes

We attempted to establish in the earlier sections of this book that communication effectiveness is multidimensional. If we are to talk sensibly about effective communication, we must identify the kind of outcomes of which we speak. The basic variables and interaction patterns which lead to interpersonal attraction are frequently quite different from the basic variables and interaction patterns associated with interpersonal influence. And these, in turn, are different from those associated with communication accuracy. In fact, those chapters which deal with the three basic systems, the attraction system, the influence system, and the symbol system, may lead one to conclude that variables which facilitate one outcome, may, in fact, impede another. An exploratory investigation of marital communication which focused upon all three of these outcomes may illustrate this point.

Assume that a husband and wife are attempting to arrive at some approach to handling a specific discipline problem with one of their children. If person A is interested in having his feelings or attitudes *understood* by person B, or if person A is interested in *understanding* the feelings and attitudes of person B, and if the encounter does, in fact, lead to either of these outcomes, then we may say that the communication has been "effective"—at least in one sense. Suppose that person A is interested in having person B *accept or agree* with his particular analysis or resolution of the problem, or suppose that person A is interested in *accepting or agreeing* with the analysis and solution offered by person B. If the encounter leads to either of these outcomes, then we may say that the communication has been "effective"—but in a different sense. But frequently we behave as if we were really more interested in another outcome. Suppose person A wants the other to leave the encounter saying to himself, "My, but you're an intelligent, perceptive, superior person." That is, suppose that we are more interested in impressing the other with our brilliance and insight than in actually arriving at an accurate understanding of positions, or even arriving at an acceptable resolution of the problem. If the encounter produces such an outcome, we may still say that the communication has been "effective"—but in a third and still different sense. Of course, these may not be the only outcomes that the interacting individuals are interested in. One or both of the parties may be employing the encounter as a means of relieving internal tensions or antagonisms deriving from other sources, or of preparing themselves for an intense sexual encounter, or of avoiding a confrontation on some other issue. But let us restrict our attention to the three basic outcomes on which we have focused in this book.

One relatively comprehensive investigation of the interaction patterns of 52 married couples attempted to determine what interaction patterns were associated with each of these three outcomes. The study has been reported in greater detail elsewhere (Larson, 1967). A summary of the results will suffice here.

The researcher obtained descriptions of the ways in which each of the married persons typically or characteristically interacted with his partner. These descriptions covered a wide range of alternatives and were based on a set of categories developed by Ruesch, Block, and Bennett (1953). Using a range of topics, the researcher obtained measures of the extent to which one person agreed with the other, the extent to which one person understood the other, and the extent to which one person evaluated the other favorably, in terms of general personality dimensions. Before reading the results, ask yourself the following questions: (1) What pattern of interaction initiated by person A was associated with the greatest amount of accuracy on the part of person B in perceiving A's attitudes correctly? (2) What pattern of interaction initiated by person A was associated with the greatest amount of agreement on the part of person B with A's attitudes? (3) What pattern of interaction initiated by person A was associated with the most favorable evaluation of person A by person B? Even though we are talking about an exploratory study, with a comparatively small sample, the answers to these questions may surprise you.

First, the accuracy with which person B understood person A's feelings and attitudes on the topics was related to patterns of interaction in which person A expected a lot of the other, overestimated the abilities of the other to understand, did not provide encouragement for the other, embarrassed and inhibited the other, tried to outdo the other, got annoyed at the other, and argued with the other. In other words, the accuracy outcome was positively related to the extent to which one or the other person provided threat of unfavorable reaction to inaccurate or inappropriate responses from his partner. Second, the extent to which person B evaluated A favorably was related to patterns of interaction in which A controlled, dominated, was critical of, inhibited, or engaged in interactions that embarrassed, exhibited impatience with, and held high expectations for the other. In other words, the evaluation outcome was positively related to the extent to which person A acted in superior ways toward the other, or engaged in behavior that would seem to downgrade the self-image of the other. Third, the extent to which person B agreed with person A's attitudes on the topics was related to patterns of interaction in which A was patient with the other, was interested in the other's feelings and attitudes, tended to be reassuring, tended to agree with the other's positions, and tended to argue less and allow the other person ample opportunity to present his position. The influence outcome was positively related to a "soft sell" pattern of interaction, in which person A provided support and reassurance for the other, and did not intensify his persuasive attempts to the point where alienation might occur.

Fortunately, we do not have to conclude from these results that these are the only patterns of interactions likely to produce desirable communication outcomes. We're simply describing a sample of married people, and we are saying that for this sample, these are the three patterns of interaction that produced the highest scores on the measures taken to assess understanding, influence, and evaluation. But in a very general sense, each of the three patterns of interaction is associated with "effective communication" in that the outcomes meet traditional definitions of effective communication. However, we are attempting to demonstrate how any analysis of interpersonal communication must take into account the social context in which that communication occurs, as well as the particular type of "effectiveness" in which we are interested.

As far as marital communication is concerned, the outcome to be desired and the pattern of interaction that is most likely to lead to productive outcomes is the pattern associated with attitudinal agreement. It is one in which the parties give fair consideration to the others' point of view, do not push their position so strenuously, emphasize points of agreement, raise questions that allow each of the parties to clarify their positions, and allow each other to amplify their positions and the premises underlying them. Unfortunately, this pattern of interaction does not sound like much fun. You will probably admit that most people would prefer to approach a confrontation involving different points of view in a somewhat different manner. We would probably invest most of our energy and enthusiasm into establishing the validity of our position and the inferiority of the other's position. We would probably do all we can to whip the other into verbal submission. It's more fun to win. But we are convinced that in marital communication the payoff does not come in winning, it comes in working out in gradual and pedestrian ways the constantly appearing differences that threaten to become major disruptions.

The establishment of patterns for resolving differences and arriving at agreements has long been regarded as a critical factor in marital satisfaction. Karlsson has claimed, "An agreement—not necessarily explicit—on procedures for settling disagreements is associated with marital satisfaction." (1963, p.55) Shipman's (1960) investigation of 270 couples in which 32 were categorized as "very happy" and 32 were categorized as very "unhappy" discovered a consistent characteristic of the 32 unhappy couples. Among other things, the 32 unhappy couples were characterized by one partner being "vigorous and successful in argument" and the other partner tending to submit without much resistance. Particularly disruptive was the pattern wherein the wife was dominant and the husband either felt defeated and frustrated or withdrew from the scene. So long as there is some evidence that husbands may be less communicative than wives, such a pattern may pave the way for the withdrawal of the husband into a "male passive aggressiveness." Such a pattern may even have impacts that go beyond the immediate two-person system. Long-range studies under the direction of Stachowiak (1968) indicate that marked differences in the communicative tendencies of married couples, especially as these behaviors relate to decision-making processes in the family, may have severe negative consequences for the children.

Some Theoretical Considerations

The perceptive person must be impressed by the many changes gradually taking shape in our social institutions. These are not drastic changes, complete reversals, or conversions. Widespread social change in short time periods is very rare. Indeed, Lomas (1968) has argued that massive resistance to change is a necessary prerequisite for the kind of social outcries, protest, and social action programs that have characterized recent years. But the changes that are contemplated, and talked about, that is, the rhetoric that accompanies social change parades before our vision like a kaleidoscope of constantly changing focal points and emphases. Some of the concern focuses upon marriage. In the action stage, it takes the form of trial marriages and living together in the absence of the legal contract. In the rhetoric stage it takes the form of discussion of marriage as an "unnatural state."

Young unmarrieds frequently defend their decision to live together without a legal marriage contract by saying, "We love each other, and we don't want to spoil it by getting married." This is not necessarily a rash or impetuous point of view. All those things we have said earlier about basic variables in a two-person communication system may have to be altered when we consider the impact of the legal marriage contract on the two-person system. The marriage contract may make an otherwise adaptive and productive system relatively unproductive and maladaptive. Of course, we are speaking in very general terms, but we feel justified in asserting that the marriage contract imposes restraints on a basic two-person system which are reasonably rare in other social contexts. The potentially destructive thing about a marriage contract is that it may lead one or both parties to conclude that they are justified in doing things and sayings things to the other person that they would never consider doing or saying to another in a less constrained two-person system. One or both parties may even arrive at the unstated conclusion that they "own the other" or that the other "belongs to them." This underlying feeling of ownership may have bizarre consequences. A husband feels like going for a drive. "Where are you going?" she says. "I thought I'd just go for a drive." "How long are you going to be gone?" "Not very long." "Where are you going to go?" "Probably just out to the country and back again." "Shall I come along?" From this point, the conversation might go in many different directions. Disruptive consequences are by no means rare. The same feeling of ownership may lead the husband to expect that certain chores will be performed routinely, that the wife will do many special things for him without compliment and without his even apparently noticing them, that she should be content to do these many things for days, weeks, months, and perhaps longer, without any thanks or verbal gratuities, and that if she falters in the performance of her duties, he is perfectly justified in mildly reprimanding her for her failures.

Please do not misconstrue the point. We are not suggesting that these things happen in a legal marriage, but would not happen in the absence of a marriage contract. We are suggesting only that those tendencies toward ownership and intrusion may be intensified with the legal marriage contract. Indeed, the tendencies toward ownership and intrusion may be present in any long-range dyadic relationship. But there is greater potential for these tendencies to manifest themselves whenever external sanctions are imposed upon a two-person system. To reinforce the point simply, let's look at one of Rod McKuen's poems:

Listen
I don't apologize for being hard to know
    I am what I am
sulking will not change that
but apple pies and warm hands help
and I have never known a cat
that couldn't calm me down
by walking slowly past my chair.
So I'll smile for you in winter
if you'll go easy
and fill your rooms with roses when I can
if you'll stop beating me with words
and if in bed
you never turn away . . .

From *Listen to the Warm*, by Rod McKuen.
Copyright © 1967 by Rod McKuen. Reprinted by
permission of Random House, Inc.

All the religious and civil liturgy through which we walk into a marriage implores us to become "one." You and I no longer exist. Now it is WE. But this very seductive notion runs counter to a central concept in much human communication theory, the concept of self. The early writing of Cooley (1922) and Mead (1934) posited the emergence of a self-concept from communicative encounters with others. More recently, Rokeach (1968) has argued that the self-concept, viewed as a primitive belief, emerges relatively early in life, and has considerable stability. Rokeach has warned that confusions or distortions in the primitive identity beliefs may have disintegrative effects on the human organism. We are extrapolating from Rokeach's work, but we would suggest that the merging of two identities into one and the failure to take into account and adjust to the distinguishing characteristics of the other is a marked potential danger in the marital context.

Laing, Phillippson, and Lee (1966), in a detailed investigation of a small sample of marriages they classified as either "disturbed" or "nondisturbed," came up with results illustrative of the complexity of the issues involved here. First, it appears that in the nondisturbed marriages, the two people's self-perceptions are more similar. Secondly, in the disturbed marriages, it appears that there is less accuracy in perceiving the other's self as he sees it. Initial agreement in self-perceptions may require less adjustment on the part of the two individuals. But the point we wish to pursue is that where there are differences in self-perceptions, accuracy in perceiving, understanding, or empathizing with the other is crucial to the marriage. Some research on social perception (Cline and Richards, 1960, 1961) supports the notion that such accuracy may be a general trait varying by greater or lesser degrees across individuals. If this is true, it may be particularly difficult for us to resolve to become more understanding or accurate in our perception of others. But we must make some attempt at it. The alternative is so unattractive.

If people have relatively stable perceptions of self, it is reasonable to assume that they would prefer that others accurately perceive the image of themselves which they project. Goffman (1959) has elaborated on the ends to which we will go to project an image of ourselves to others. There is a classic example of the man on the merry-go-round who takes his child for a ride, but attempts by his demeanor to convince onlookers that he is bored and not enjoying himself, and in fact sacrificing for the sake of the child. Indeed, he may be comfortable only if he feels he is successful in projecting this image to the onlookers. Most wives know that there are ways of projecting to their husbands the image of attractiveness to other males. Most husbands know that there are ways of projecting to their wives the image of being manly and quite capable of handling almost any crisis that presents itself. We do many things that project images consistent with our own self-perception. But, what happens when we receive from others cues that lead us to conclude that they are not accurately perceiving the images we are attempting to project? Communication theorists might say that when the message is not getting through, there are at least two immediately available alternatives: (1) increase the signal strength, (2) employ redundancy. The second alternative, that of employing redundancy, would imply that when we feel our images are not being correctly perceived, we do more of the same kinds of things that we were doing initially in our attempt to project the image. The first alternative, that of increasing the signal strength, might imply that when we feel our image is not being correctly perceived, we intensify our projection by acting more manly and competent, or more sexually attractive than we were acting in the first place. If we allow our speculations to continue, this might imply that the husband goes out of his way to place himself in situations or to encounter circumstances that will allow him to prove to his wife his manliness and competence, and that the wife might go out of her way to bring to the attention of the husband events or circumstances that will allow her to prove her attractiveness to members of the opposite sex. It is interesting to speculate on the consequences such intensification of projection might have, especially if the other person gives no signs of understanding or appreciating the image which we consider to be an accurate self-portrayal.

It seems that we have returned to the same theme, with perhaps minor variations, that has been consistent throughout our consideration of communication in marriage. The theme is that communication in marriage must be viewed in terms of the more critical variables involved with receiver behavior, and the receiver's capacities for understanding or identifying the basic feelings, sentiments, and attitudes that operate as premises for the other person's behavior. We may identify desirable communication outcomes for this as well as other social contexts. Facilitating these outcomes is extremely difficult. We have identified only several of the many variables that influence the extent to which desirable communication outcomes are facilitated. The complexity of the task frequently proves overwhelming, and we are not inclined to be unduly critical of those who fail. After all, by the time you read this. . . .

References

Baker, Sidney J., "The Theory of Silences," *Journal of General Psychology*, 53 (1955), 145–67.

Cline, Victor, and James M. Richards, "Accuracy of Interpersonal Perception—A General Trait?" *Journal of Abnormal and Social Psychology*, 60 (1960), 1–7.

————, "The Generality of Accuracy of Inter-Personal Perception," *Journal of Abnormal and Social Psychology*, 61 (1961), 446–49.

Cooley, Charles H., *Human Nature and The Social Order*. New York: Charles Scribner's Sons, 1922.

Culbert, Samuel A., *The Interpersonal Process of Self-Disclosure: It Takes Two To See One*. New York: Renaissance Editions, Inc., 1968.

Cutler, B. R., and W. Dyer, "Initial Adjustment Processes in Young Married Couples," *Social Forces*, 44 (1965), 195–201.

DeBurger, James E., "Husband-Wife Differences in The Revelation of Marital Problems: A Content Analysis." Ph.D. dissertation, Indiana University, 1966.

Goffman, Erving, *The Presentation of Self in Everyday Life*. Garden City, N.Y.: Doubleday & Company, Inc., 1959.

Jourard, S. M., "Self-Disclosure and Other Cathexis," *Journal of Abnormal and Social Psychology*, 59 (1959), 428–31.

———, "Age and Self-Disclosure," *Merrill-Palmer Quarterly*, 7 (1961), 191–97.

Jourard, S. M., and M. J. Landsman, "Cognition, Cathexis, and the 'Dyadic Effect' in Men's Self-Disclosing Behavior," *Merrill-Palmer Quarterly*, 6 (1960), 178–86.

Jourard, S. M., and P. Lasakow, "Some Factors in Self-Disclosure," *Journal of Abnormal and Social Psychology*, 56 (1958), 91–98.

Karlsson, George, *Adaptability and Communication in Marriage*. Totowa, N.J.: The Bedminster Press, Inc., 1963.

Katz, J., J. Goldston, M. Cohen, and S. Stucker, "Need Satisfaction, Perception, and Cooperative Interaction in Married Couples," *Marriage and Family Living*, 25 (1963), 209–14.

Komarovsky, Mirra, *Blue Collar Marriage*. New York: Random House, Inc., 1964.

Laing, R. D., H. Phillippson, and A. R. Lee. *Interpersonal Perception*. New York: Springer Publishing Co., Inc., 1966.

Larson, Carl E., "Interaction, Dogmatism, and Communication Effectiveness: An Exploratory Study." Ph.D. dissertation, University of Kansas, 1965.

———, "Interaction Patterns and Communication Effectiveness in The Marital Context: A Factor Analytic Study," *Journal of Communication*, 17 (1967), 342–53.

Levinger, George, "Instrumental and Expressive Functions in Marriage." Working Paper #1, January, 1963.

———, "Sources of Marital Dissatisfaction Among Applicants for Divorce," *American Journal of Orthopsychiatry*, 36 (1966), 803–7.

Levinger, George, and D. J. Senn, "Disclosure of Feelings in Marriage," *Merrill-Palmer Quarterly*, 13 (1967), 237–49.

Lomas, Charles W., *The Agitator in American Society*. Englewood Cliffs, N.J.: Prentice-Hall, Inc., 1968.

Luckey, E. B., "Marital Satisfaction and Its Association with Congruence of Perception," *Marriage and Family Living*, 22 (1960), 49–54.

Mead, George H., *Mind, Self, and Society*. Chicago: University of Chicago Press, 1934.

Rokeach, Milton, *Beliefs, Attitudes, and Values.* San Francisco: Jossey-Bass, Inc., Publishers, 1968.

Ruesch, Jurgen, Jack Block, and Lillian Bennet, "The Assessment of Communication: I. A Method for the Analysis of Social Interaction," *Journal of Psychology*, 40 (1953), 59–80.

Rutledge, Aaron L., *Pre-Marital Counseling.* London: Oxford University Press, 1966.

Shipman, Gordon, "Speech Thresholds and Voice Tolerance in Marital Interaction," *Marriage and Family Living*, 22 (1960), 203–9.

Stachowiak, J. G., "Decision-Making and Conflict Resolution in The Family Group," in Carl E. Larson and Frank E. X. Dance, eds., *Perspectives on Communication.* (Speech Communication Center, University of Wisconsin-Milwaukee, 1968, pp. 113–24.

Voss, Frances, "The Relationships of Disclosure to Marital Satisfaction: An Exploratory Study." Master's thesis, University of Wisconsin-Milwaukee, 1969.

Chapter 10

Interpersonal Communication
On the Job

As depressing as it may be to some of you, we can assume that at some time in your life you will be formally employed in some sort of work. You must be satisfied with that work. Your employer must be satisfied with that work. The achievement of these goals by both parties is intimately related to one's interpersonal behavior. The delineation of this relationship between interpersonal communication and the satisfaction of employee and organizational goals is the focus of this chapter. The first section discusses the organizational climates within which the interpersonal communication occurs; the second section reviews some research that should offer guidelines for interpersonal behavior in organizational settings; and the last section discusses the possibilities of incorporating productive interpersonal strategies into one's own behavior.

Three Working Climates

Redding (Redding and Sanborn, 1964) and others say that "a member of any organization is, in large measure, the kind of communicator that the organization compels him to be." One of these influential and compelling factors is the organizational climate—which is a reflection of the prevailing assumptions about human behavior. The influence of the working climate is substantiated by a long list of studies measuring on-the-job behavior following training in human relations. These studies will be treated later in more detail, but generally it can be said that a working climate that did not support the principles learned in the training course would cause employees to return to their pretraining behavioral pattern—adapted to the prevailing climate.

Management philosophy and industrial climate have undergone vast changes in the last 150 years and Scott (1967) provides an excellent historical review of these approaches from 1830 to date. Our concern, however, is primarily with the kind of behavior elicited under the various kinds of managerial philosophies. In other words, how does a particular philosophy or set of assumptions influence the interpersonal behavior of a member of an organization? For this reason we will discuss three very different organizational climates—resulting from three very different views of man and human behavior. We have called these: (1) the Dehumanized Climate, (2) the Happiness for Lunch Bunch, and (3) the Situational Climate. The first two will be pictured as extreme conditions and their supporters will be portrayed as believing in a universal application of their ideas—that all jobs, all people, all organizations are best fitted to a single set of beliefs. Naturally, this was not always the case. Moderates and proponents of a situational approach existed in both movements. However, the literature from the field of organizational behavior seems to illustrate that many scholars and practitioners did not perceive the moderation or variability in these movements and responded to the inflexible, extreme position. For this reason it is not uncommon to find the Dehumanized Climate or the Happiness for Lunch Bunch as prevalent climates in today's organizations.

The Dehumanized Climate

Historically, many business organizations in Europe and the United States have been founded on some assumptions based on attitudes toward work and the nature of man derived from the baron-serf and master-slave relationship. Some of these assumptions were certainly evident in the work of Frederick W. Taylor (1919) around the turn of the twentieth century. Taylor is credited with a number of significant contributions to the general field of management, but historically his case has become a classic example for examining the conditions of a Dehumanized Climate. Generally, he is associated with a managerial philosophy that neglects human relations concepts in work groups. His concern for the human dimension is aptly illustrated in his writing, which at various times suggested that the work of his employees could be accomplished by an ox or a trained gorilla. Taylor and his followers considered the problems of production from the standpoint of the isolated worker. They assumed that people worked to satisfy one need only—the economic need. Further, there seemed to be the assumption that workers will share the interests of the organization—that there is no conflict between individual and organization. The reasoning went something like this: The individual worker is a rational person; it is rational to want more money; you can get more money by working hard; by working hard you can increase the production level; the company wants a higher production level so they should appeal to the worker's desire for more money; this way there is a mutuality of interests between organization and worker. Taylor's critics are quick to point out that man often reacts nonrationally regarding the rewards he seeks from his work; there may be many influential motives for working; workers are not always anxious to see their objectives in the light of organizational objectives; and the organization is a social system—not a group of isolated workers.

What are the characteristics of the Dehumanized Climate in today's organizations? We can expect to find a set of assumptions about man all of which rarely give much analytic thought to the complexities of the human personality. We can expect to find an organization which tries to keep the human elements from interfering with what are thought to be the primary tasks—efficiency and production. We can expect to find widespread assumptions that the "average man" is by nature, indolent and will work as little as possible; is inherently self-centered and indifferent to organizational needs; is by nature resistant to change; lacks ambition; dislikes responsibility; prefers to be led; and is gullible, not very bright, and the ready dupe of the charlatan and demagogue (McGregor, 1960). We can expect to find tight controls on individual behavior, manipulation, and an undue emphasis on motivation through fear. Some college classrooms provide excellent examples of such a climate. For that matter, Gibb (1965) has suggested that by the time we are hired by a business organization, most of us have already been exposed to and conditioned by many of these practices—that is, management characterized by high fear and low trust. He cites numerous examples of such practices in homes, schools, and churches. Thus, a business organization may inherit employees who are all too familiar with a climate characterized by what Gibb calls "defensive management." Blake and Mouton (1964) have described this orientation with the familiar cliché, "Nice guys finish last." The following statement is exemplary of some of the assumptions discussed above:

> Since so many members of lower, middle, and even top management in the typical large business enterprise of today are dependent, insecure, and ineffective—productive only because they are bossed by one or two hard-driving strong autocrats—the outlook for the widespread introduction of a genuine humanistic, democratic-participative philosophy of leadership in the near future looks dim indeed . . . benevolent autocracy . . . recognizes particularly that most people prefer to be led. (McMurry, 1958)

Responses to Dehumanized Climates

Perhaps one of the earliest commentaries on how people might respond in a Dehumanized Climate is found in Upton Sinclair's (1946) novel, *The Jungle*:

> Here was Durham's, for instance, owned by a man who was trying to make as much money out of it as he could, and did not care in the least how he did it; and underneath him, ranged in ranks and grades like an army, were managers and superintendents and foremen, each one driving the man next below him and trying to squeeze out of him as much work as possible. And all the men of the same rank were pitted against each other; the accounts of each were kept separately, and every man lived in terror of losing his job, if another made a better record than he. So from top to bottom the place was simply a seething caldron of jealousies and hatreds; there was no loyalty or decency anywhere about it; there was no place where a man counted for anything against a dollar. (pp. 59–60)

More recently, Gibb (1965) has suggested a list of "typical and frequent" responses to some of the practices often found in the Dehumanized Climate. To illustrate a few of his beliefs, let us use an example from an educational institution—the Dehumanized Classroom. In this example the teacher engages in the following behavior: (1) He evidences his distrust of the students by making students sit far apart during exams and during the testing he monitors the students very closely—trying to determine the subtle methods of cheating which he "knows are taking place." (2) He makes it clear that grades are extremely important and constitute the highest reward he can give a student in his class. His grading of the first exam also makes it clear that the only way to get the high grade reward is to fill in the completion blanks with "exactly the same word I used in my lecture." (3) Finally, in order to be able to control the students' behavior even more he is punitive of such things as "coming to class dressed like a hippie" and "not sitting up straight in class." He also stipulates that "three absences will lower your grade by two letters." As a consequence of his actions, the following situations may occur: (1) This teacher can frequently expect (and receive) fear and cynicism on the part of the students and their general distrust of him. (2) Since grades are an *ex*trinsic motivation and they are also the prime motivation for classroom work, students may not have much *in*trinsic motivation. They may take the position "I'll play your game and get your grade, but you're going to have to sell me on the value of this course material." The instructor in turn complains that he never gets any students who are really "wrapped up in the material." Similarly, he may find his students regurgitating his lectures (to play his game) while he complains about their lack of creativity. (3) Since the teacher makes such good use of tight external controls over the student's behavior, he can expect dependency from some and outright rebellion from others. The start of the rebellion may be characterized by questions requesting identification of boundaries and specification of rules—for example, "At what point does one's dress become hippie?" or "If I can bring in a note from my doctor will my absence count toward my three absences?"

The previous example dealt almost exclusively with responses to various kinds of behaviors. The *assumptions* underlying these behaviors were implicit. To make the relationship between assumptions about the nature of man, one's overt behavior, and the ensuing "typical" responses clear, let us examine another example from a speech by John Paul Jones (1961) to the American Management Association. Although the example uses a business organization, the implications for other organizational settings are clear. Jones begins by asking us to pretend we are his subordinates. We work for him. He then makes the following assumptions about us:

1. You are lazy and fundamentally desire to work as little possible.

2. You avoid responsibility as you would the plague.

3. You do not wish to achieve anything significant.

4. You are incapable of directing your own behavior.

5. You are indifferent to organizational needs.

6. You prefer to be led and directed by others.

7. You avoid making decisions whenever possible.

My job therefore, says Jones, is to motivate you, to do something to you, to reward and punish you, to control your productive behavior by these means. These things are not true of me, the manager. They are only true of you. Oh, I don't say these things explicitly to you (except when I'm angry) nor are they conscious principles. I have learned them by osmosis and by not examining the incongruity between my view of myself and my view of you.

If I don't say these things to you, how do I transmit them to you? Generally by my behavior. What kind of behavior?

1. I withhold information from you. After all, I'm the boss and have integrity. Confidential information is perfectly safe with me, but not with you.

2. I not only tell you what to do, but I quite often tell you how and when to do it. If I'm smart I may use a little participation as a gimmick, but the end result is the same.

3. I write all the important letters or I have you write them for me and I sign them. In some cases I may even have all the incoming mail delivered to me so that in my superior wisdom I can screen it.

4. I'll do all the upward and lateral communicating. If I think your idea is good, I'll handle it myself. If I don't think it's any good, I'll kill it right now because there is no point in bothering other people with harebrained ideas.

5. I'll ask you to study a problem and give me a recommendation. If you haven't been able to guess what's acceptable to me, I'll tell you to change the recommendation. Again, of course, I am using participation as a gimmick.

6. What I do communicate within the department, I'll communicate with each of you individually to keep you all competing for my favor, and also to insure that I'll be the only one who has all the information.

7. If somebody is interested in having you work for him, I'll decide whether I want to let you go or not and I will cut the deal then and there. If I decide that you are my property, you'll never know anyone else was interested in you.

Many more such illustrations are available, but I think these are sufficient to demonstrate the unconscious principles at work through my behavior.

What effect does this have on your behavior?

1. Since I don't share information with you, you become quite ingenious at ferreting out secrets. Now, of course, a secret is of no status value unless you can use it to prove to someone that you are "in the know." This is how we get leaks, and this is how you, my subordinate, "prove" to me that you have no integrity.

2. Since I tell you what to do and quite often how and when to do it, you don't reach for new work. Thus, you "prove" your laziness and dislike for responsibility.

3. You learn to communicate as I do, but not as yourself. And since I do the communicating, you learn very little about the other parts of the business or even very much about your own sphere of endeavor. Thus, you "prove" your indifference to organizational needs.

4. Since I either kill your ideas when they come to me or carry them upstairs myself, you stop generating new ideas and thus "prove" your lack of desire to achieve.

5. You don't bother to study a problem—it's much more practical to study me and anticipate what I'll buy in the way of a recommendation or a solution. By this you "prove" that you prefer to be directed.

6. Since I don't communicate with you as a group, you and your fellow subordinates use woodshed communication and form an informal but very effective alliance to keep me off your backs. This simply "proves" you are incapable of controlling your own behavior.

7. Since you never have to make any career decisions—I make them all for you—you never develop the reliance on self

or the spirit of risk taking that comes only with the experience of making decisions, thus "proving" that you avoid decisions.

As a consequence, you will be frustrated, apathetic, and resistant to organizational needs. You will appear to be lazy, incapable of directing your own behavior, unwilling to assume responsibility, and not interested in making decisions nor in achieving anything. In short, my assumptions will have been "proved" by a self-proving mechanism.[1]

It is easy to see elements of this example in others, but harder to admit that perhaps we too are guilty of such assumptions and behaviors. The all too natural tendency is to treat our experiences in life as support for what we already believe—not as an opportunity to learn.

The Happinesss for Lunch Bunch

This climate is the antithesis of the Dehumanized Climate. In this climate human relationships come first. While the assumptions and behaviors girding this climate may seem at first to have more appeal to the reader or come closer to the ideal, it suffers from its extreme and inflexible application of the assumptions and behaviors.

Just as the Dehumanized Climate had its historical and industrial roots in the philosophy of Frederick Taylor, the development of an undue preoccupation with human relations had its roots in the famous studies carried out at the Hawthorne (Chicago) Works of the Western Electric Company beginning in 1927 (Roethlisberger and Dickson, 1956).

Briefly, this is what happened in the early Hawthorne experiments. The problem was to determine whether a number of environmental changes would have any effect on the amount of worker output or production. Improved factory lighting was one of the variables to be manipulated. Girls who were assembling telephone relays were selected for the experiment. The experimenters increased illumination by using higher intensity light bulbs in the work area, and production increased. Then the experimenters replaced these light bulbs with some of equal intensity so there was no change in lighting level. Production continued to increase. In other experiments it was found that manipulation of almost any environmental variable

---

[1]Gibb has also commented on such a self-fulfilling prophecy: "Low-trust, high-fear theories, when put into practice, actually generate distrusts and fears that not only confirm the assumptions underlying the theories, but also provide emotional support and strong motivation to continue the low-trust and high-fear behavior." Gibb, *ibid.*

would increase production. Naturally, the investigators were unable to state any relationship between illumination and production, but their findings were undoubtedly much more important—the fact that the workers were responding to someone who showed concern for their welfare. This shift to an interest in the human work variables was a drastic shift from the emphasis on physical plant conditions. From this time forward, other Hawthorne studies were conducted to examine further the behaviors and attitudes of the employees. At one point over 21,000 employees were interviewed. As a result of these studies the personnel counselor was introduced to industry and the rise of the human relations approach began. The advent of the human relations approach was essentially that of a changing perception of the worker—as a human being with wants, desires, attitudes, and feelings *which affect his productive usefulness*. These studies highlighted the importance of the social factor on work performance—the influence of the network of social relationships on the output of the individual worker.[2] Thus, the movement began in American industry to develop a working climate which gave special consideration to the human dimensions of the work situation. Scott (1967) called it "industrial humanism" and defined it this way: "Industrial humanism embraces all movements which are liberal in spirit and which seek to bring to man at work freedom from oppression and an opoprtunity for self-determination" (p.43). This newfound concern for the human dimensions was undeniably a milestone in the history of organizational behavior. For some, however, the concept of human relations had a steamroller effect until it became a cult of human relations and produced in some organizations the Happiness for Lunch Bunch climate.

What are the characteristics of the Happiness for Lunch Bunch in today's organizations? We can expect to find that effective human relations are regarded more as an end toward which the organization should strive than as a means of achieving other objectives. Production requirements are believed contrary to the needs of people. We can expect that elimination of conflict is a primary goal of the organization or department within the organization. Conflicts and tensions are glossed over by humor or the fa-

---

[2]The Hawthorne studies did not demonstrate the success of the human relations approach as some authors have suggested. Important problems in the research methodology existed, but the studies did focus attention on the human dimensions as never before, therefore they are still considered classic studies. For a critique of the research proceduces and interpretations, see: Alex Carey, "The Hawthorne Studies: A Radical Criticism," *Sociological Review*, 32 (1967), 403–16.

miliar, "Don't worry. Things are going to get better. . . . Why, I remember when. . . ." We can expect that any form of employee motivation that is not based upon intrinsic, self-directed drives will be viewed with scorn, but parties, picnics, and social dinners are plentiful. In this climate we can expect to find the ultimate in participation and involvement in decision making—as close to having everyone participate in everything all the time as possible. There is a high identification with the work group. This climate is characterized by people who are friendly and avoid being rejected by others by not rejecting anyone themselves. Blake and Mouton (1964) describe a member of the Happiness for Lunch Bunch as follows:

> The . . . person's anxiety and doubt about his own acceptance contribute to an *oversensitivity* to the desires and wishes of others. The anxiety connected with fear of rejection, then can produce a person whose attitudes are . . . solicitous, acquiescent to others, malleable, and easily subject to changing attitudes to conform to situations, even though they themselves may be contradictory. (p. 77)

Responses to the Happiness for Lunch Bunch

In some instances the assumptions underlying the Happiness for Lunch Bunch climate will produce positive and productive interpersonal responses (just as some instances may require elements of the dehumanized approach). However, this climate (like the Dehumanized Climate) insures a high frequency of undesirable responses due to its inflexibility. For instance:

1. Since an absence of conflict is at such a premium, there is a preponderance of conflict avoidance behavior. Attempts are made to create the appearance of harmony and warm human relationships—amid the normal flow of tensions and conflicts present in any group of people. The constant stress on "agreement" in the work environment may cause a person to relieve his tensions with particular intensity in other environments—such as with his wife or girl friend! Although this may make him feel better for the moment, it does not act in a positive way to deal with or relieve frustrations and conflicts on the job. If the pattern of avoiding and smoothing over differences is an unchanging pattern, it is unlikely that it will produce many lasting, meaningful, or close human relationships. Exploring alternatives for dealing with such differences is an important phase of building a productive relationship.

2. The constant and central concern for the needs and welfare of

individuals and work groups creates within these individuals an expectation that these are the prime—if not the only—considerations. These may be the basic ingredients for eventual liquidation of the organization in which they enjoy this emphasis on human needs if the members' goals grow more and more inconsistent with the organization's goals (Fox, 1966). This is particularly evident when the members gradually become less and less committed to the organizational goals of production and efficiency when the organization's survival is almost totally dependent on them. Socially satisfied workers are not always productive ones.

3. It is also possible that persons who behave consistent with the tenets of the Happiness for Lunch Bunch will not receive the social support they expect. For instance, Moment and Zaleznik (1963) found that the persons identified as "social specialists" were not generally judged to be the most attractive socially by groups of middle- and upper-level administrators in conferences and policy discussions. Social specialists were not necessarily those individuals whom other participants wanted to get to know better or whom they liked most on the basis of the contact in the conferences. These social specialists were identified as persons who generally tried to maintain a friendly and joking atmosphere—one in which tensions could be released. This lack of support may also be engendered if the person is frequently perceived as conforming and changing his attitude to avoid conflicts. While it might be considered "mature" to acquiesce occasionally, there is a point at which one is perceived as "wishy-washy." In addition, a person who is primarily concerned with the needs and wants of others is of necessity in frequent contact with them—trying to identify these needs. Further disconfirmation can occur when a colleague of the social specialist feels that he is being "bugged," or that he needs privacy, or that he doesn't want anyone to try to solve his problems. Thus, if you really want to take people into consideration, you will not always use the extreme human relations approach.

Situational Climate

The Situational Climate operates on the assumption that the climate most conducive to the achievement of individual and organizational goals will vary with the situation and the individual. Its major characteristics are flexibility and analysis. Schein (1965) calls this approach the complex man orientation and lists the following assumptions as characteristic of this climate:

1. Man is not only complex, but also highly variable; he has many motives which are arranged in some sort of hierarchy of importance to him, but this hierarchy is subject to change from time to time and situation to situation; furthermore, motives interact and combine into complex motive patterns (for example, since money can facilitate self-actualization, for some people economic strivings are equivalent to self-actualization).

2. Man is capable of learning new motives through his organizational experiences hence ultimately his pattern of motivation and the psychological contract which he establishes with the organization is the result of a complex interaction between initial needs and organizational experiences.

3. Man's motives in different organizations or different subparts of the same organization may be different; the person who is alienated in the formal organization may find fulfillment of his social and self-actualization needs in the union or in the informal organization; if the job itself is complex, such as that of a manager, some parts of the job may engage some motives while other parts engage other motives.

4. Man can become productively involved with organizations on the basis of many different kinds of motives; his ultimate satisfaction and the ultimate effectiveness of the organization depends only in part on the nature of his motivation. The nature of the task to be performed, the abilities and experience of the person on the job, and the nature of the other people in the organization all interact to produce a certain pattern of work and feelings. For example, a highly skilled but poorly motivated worker may be as effective *and satisfied* as a very unskilled but highly motivated worker.

5. Man can respond to many different kinds of managerial strategies, depending on his own motives and abilities and the nature of the task; in other words, there is no one correct managerial strategy that will work for all men at all times.

Evidence for such assumptions continues to mount, and Leavitt (1959) may be correct in his prediction that we will see a growth in management according to task—using what seems best adapted for the task at hand. A number of studies make it clear that individual motivation is an extremely complex concept to determine. For instance, a rate-buster and an underachiever may manifest the same kind of behavior—a deviate who is indifferent to group norms and sanctions—but the assumption that such behavior stems from a common motivation would be a high-risk assumption. Gellerman (1963) has noted that even economic rewards can and do have vastly different meanings to different people. Money may represent basic security and love, power, a measure of achievement in society, or a means to the end of comfortable living. Vroom (1964) notes that motivations vary depending on managerial level. Sales and personnel managers are more likely to have strong or affiliative needs, whereas production managers tend to have strong needs to work with mechanical things. The higher the managerial level, the more likely self-actualization and autonomy needs are to appear. Lieberman (1956) found that union stewards' attitudes became more pro-management upon promotion to foremen. Then when the company suffered economic losses and returned these foremen to their former positions, the attitudes began to change again—back to pro-union. Vroom and Mann (1960) found that the nature of the job influenced the desire for a particular type of supervision—for example, package handlers desired employee-centered supervision, whereas, truck drivers and dispatchers preferred a more authoritarian approach. Burns and Stalker (1962) support the situational approach when they suggest that managerial climates will vary depending on whether a company faces constant change or is relatively stable. An excellent example of the complexity of this approach is found in the work of Stanton (1960) which suggests that an organization may select a democratic, authoritarian, or a compromise approach to management and still be considerate of the feelings and desires of its employees. No significant differences were found in supervisory attitudes on consideration toward employees in a company determined to have a democratic climate and a company determined to have an authoritarian climate. Stanton concludes: "The type of approach that a company's management may find most effective for its particular organization appears to be closely related to situational factors." Fiedler's (1967, 1969) work on leadership style confirms this notion again. Based on studies of over 800 groups, Fiedler concludes that the appropriate leadership style is governed by three factors in this order of importance: (*a*) leader-member relations, (*b*) the task structure, and (*c*) position power. He further finds that a task-oriented leader performs best in situations in which he has a great deal of influence or power and in situations in which he has no influence or power over group members. Relationship-oriented leaders tend to perform best in situations where they have only moderate influence over the group. To illustrate one aspect of this situational nature of leadership style, look at a group in which the leader is liked, where he has a clearly defined task and a powerful position. In this situation attempts at nondirective, democratic leadership may be detrimental or superfluous. Thus, a person working under such a climate may expect to find elements of the Dehumanized Climate, the Happiness for Lunch Bunch, and probably a number of variations on these themes.

Perhaps the most noteworthy advocate of the situational approach was Douglas MacGregor (1960). MacGregor pleaded for the "appropriate" approach based on examination, not automatic or overgeneralized reactions. His now famous Theory Y was based on the following assumptions:

1. Management is responsible for organizing the elements of productive enterprise—money, materials, equipment, people—in the interest of economic ends.

2. People are *not* by nature passive or resistant to organizational needs. They have become so as a result of experience in organizations.

3. The motivation, the potential for development, the capacity for assuming responsibility, the readiness to direct behavior toward organizational goals are all present in people. Management does not put them there. It is a responsibility of management to make it possible for people to recognize and develop these human characteristics for themselves.

4. The essential task of management is to arrange organizational conditions and methods of operation so that people can achieve *their own* goals best by directing their own efforts toward organizational objectives. This is a process primarily of creating opportunities, releasing potential, removing obstacles, encouraging growth, providing guidance.

The climate, then, was one in which the supervisory personnel adapted to the subordinate's current level of maturity with the goal of helping him develop, or progressively require less external control and to gain more self-control. Theory Y recognizes that there are still people who want to satisfy basic needs such as eating, shelter, security, safety, and even many social needs. However, it also realizes that there are a large number of persons who need to be motivated by what Maslow (1954) calls "upper level" needs: being respected, gaining recognition, status, realizing one's fullest potential in whatever guise it may take. In fact, one study suggests that the most desirable combination of need satisfaction draws from different levels of Maslow's need hierarchy. This study found that self-actualization and security were seen as more important areas of need satisfaction than those of social esteem, and autonomy needs. This was true for individuals in both bottom- and middle-management positions (Porter, 1961).

In spite of MacGregor's seemingly flexible approach outlined in Theory Y, many scholars and practitioners interpreted it as a soft and extremely permissive approach. Some authors even called for a modification, which they called Theory Z (Rosenfeld and Smith, 1965). Theory Z called for the use of external controls with some people and various degrees of self-control with others. However, as Haney (1967) appropriately notes: "Theory Z is quite unnecessary. Theory Y permits access to the full range of management approaches from external to self-control. Where on the spectrum to peg one's approach depends on his judgment of the subordinate's current state of development." In addition, Theory Y recognizes that regardless of the current state of one's development, there may be what appear to be extreme deviations under given circumstances. For instance, it is not uncommon to find a normally high achiever who occasionally needs to be a bum, a follower, a low achiever or needs to decline opportunities for status and recognition.

Responses to the Situational Climate

By definition, the situational approach attempts to elicit the "appropriate" responses for a given situation. When it is necessary to use a strict uncompromising type of discipline, it is used; when it is necessary to spend time in structuring experiences for a person's self-development, it is done. Thus, in theory it is the most desirable climate. In spite of the desirability of this climate some may point to possible pitfalls or undesirable responses.

For instance, it is clear we are still dealing with human judgments. For some it may be tempting to apply to others the same standards for "actualizing one's potential" that were important in their own development. Such a climate also demands a constant awareness that there will be differences in such things as the amount of time, patience, skill, and commitment demonstrated by the workers in this climate. Chronic understanding may lead to apathy or even resentment in some situations; overtrusting can be equally damaging. In time of stress it is easy to label excessive concern as favoritism or to demand greater "consistency" in the treatment of human relationships. Such reactions tend to erode the assumptions about man, human behavior, and their relationship to organizational goals which unite the workers in this climate.

Another potential negative perception of responses exists when a company begins to change the nature of its climate. It is theorized by Likert (1967) that a change in management tactics to a more supportive, communicative, concerned, participative approach is likely to have the short-range effect of showing no change or possible negative change in organizational efficiency. A change in the direction of being more demanding and coercive may improve organizational efficiency on a short-range basis. However, on the long-range basis (two years or more), Likert feels the more supportive approach will show lasting and significant improvement on all indexes of efficiency. Non Linear Systems, Inc., is one company of several in which such responses actually occurred (Kuriloff, 1963). Immediately after the change to a Theory Y approach, the company experienced a tremendous rise in morale and a tremendous decrease in production. It took three months to get production above the previous level. Then it was found that production rose as much as 30 percent higher than the previous level.

It is also important that the situational climate be supported at all levels in the organization. It is difficult for middle and lower management to engage in practices that do not receive support from top management.

On the other hand, the assumptions of the Situational Climate are likely to produce the following positive responses:

Assumption 1—A flexible climate that can adapt to the complex and changeable nature of individual and organizational needs is superior to a climate characterized by inflexibility. It is assumed that others should be approached with an attempt to understand them and accept them for what they are—to recognize differences and still maintain an individual point of view.

Probable Response 1—This is likely to increase a person's feelings of respect for his own personal worth and increase his respect for others. It will probably increase two-way communication because he is receiving acceptance from others. It may also bring out expressions of disagreement, which can then be dealt with. There is an expectation that in interpersonal relations efforts will be made to be analytical, not reflexive. In other words, people will generalize from their previous experiences while continually watching for unique elements in a given situation.

Assumption 2—Man is *not* by nature passive or resistant to organizational needs or prone to reject responsibility. The readiness to direct his behavior toward organizational goals is present and is especially clear when he sees the achievement of his own goals included in the achievement of organizational goals.

Probable Response 2—The perception of similarity in personal and organizational goals may produce a commitment that will increase productivity. This, in turn, may increase the amount of intrinsic motivation which could manifest itself in a greater responsibility for one's work. The counterresponse from management may be to increase the amount of responsibility, and the cycle continues.

Assumption 3—Man is *not* fundamentally lazy. Work and the desire for achievement is only displeasing to the extent that his previous experiences have been in organizational climates that have made it seem displeasing.

Probable Response 3—Others will accept the responsibility to construct experiences that will change behaviors produced in other climates.

In summary, organizational climate does influence interpersonal behavior. It begins with a set of assumptions about man and his behavior; these assumptions manifest themselves in overt behaviors toward others; and these overt actions influence the range of possible interpersonal responses. In one sense the climate acts on interpersonal relations, and the nature of the interpersonal relations acts in developing the organizational climate. In what kind of climate do you wish to work? Our bias has supported the Situational Climate because it offers more variety, which we believe is necessary to cope with complex individuals in complex organizations. If a person adopts these assumptions about man, he will continually test his assumptions and seek a better diagnosis—hence, causing him to create the "appropriate" climate regardless of the situation. What kind of climate will be produced by the set of assumptions you hold about yourself and others?

Interpersonal Communication Research in Organizations

For the last twenty years there has been an increasing number of attempts by behavioral scientists to investigate interpersonal behavior in organizational settings. This section will present some representative studies concerning productive interpersonal behavior. This research was largely conducted in what Etzioni (1961) calls utilitarian organizations—commonly referred to as industries. Although it is possible to make generalizations to other types of organizations (churches, schools, voluntary organizations, military, prisons) with different goals and purposes, they should be made with caution.

Isolated Communication Attitudes

Since Barnard's (1938) classic statement that "the first function of the executive is to develop and maintain a system of communication," thousands of isolated attitudes and opinions concerning communication and organizational performance have been gathered from business executives. The term "isolated" refers to the absence of any attempt to relate the attitude to other measures of performance or behavior. Such statements are typically found in the numerous communication studies which compile the results of questionnaire surveys of industrial personnel. One such study concerned the attitudes of the presidents of America's largest corporations toward communication principles and practices (Lull *et al.*, 1955). A representative response came from William White, former president of the New York Central Railroad when he said,

> Effectiveness of management personnel of all grades is very dependent upon the ability to communicate orally not only the policy of the company but suggestions as to how work should be done, criticism of poor work, and the application of discipline, and of course the general field of human relationship.

In this same study 48 of the 50 presidents surveyed felt there was a definite relationship between effective communication and employee productivity. While such statements are interesting, it is difficult to make valid assumptions about the relationship of such an attitude and the kind of behavior it produced in the sender or the kind of response it elicited from the receiver. However, some researchers have gone further and attempted to relate communication attitudes to other measures of performance—chiefly effective supervision.

Effective Supervision

In a comparative study of two hospitals, the importance of communication attitudes was clear after the discovery that such attitudes influenced nurse turnover and *even patient recovery rates*. Gellerman (1968) concludes his analysis of Revans's study by noting:

> What *is* surprising in all this is that the effectiveness of communication should have so much to do with what is *unspoken*; with attitudes, with the openness or defensiveness of superiors, and with

whether reassurance and support can be communicated right along with facts and instructions.

In 1949, Meyer gave a battery of tests to the best and poorest foremen (rated by upper management) and found the most discriminating test was that of the foreman's attitudes toward his employees. Since then other researchers have tried to identify certain communication attitudes that were characteristic of effective supervisors in a variety of organizational settings. For instance, Mandell (1949) gave a test of supervisory attitudes to 278 foremen in different types of work and concluded that faith in people is the distinguishing factor. As Mandell says, ". . . the poorer supervisors revealed a lack of faith in human beings—they are pessimistic, and they are 'sour.'" Mann and Dent (1954) asked superiors to rate their foremen in three categories of effectiveness. The top-rated supervisors were described this way by their employees:

1. He's a man with whom employees feel free to discuss important things about their jobs.

2. He lets his employees know where they stand.

3. He is one with whom employees feel free to discuss personal problems.

4. He is not "bossy," "quick to criticize," "a driver," or "unreasonably strict."

5. He lets employees work pretty much on their own instead of supervising them too closely.

6. He is a "leader of men," "likable," "reasonable."

Funk (1956) tested communication attitudes as they were related to the rated productivity of 106 foremen. He found that those who were rated high in productivity had more favorable attitudes toward communicating and more self-confidence in their communication behavior. He was able to find some attitude items which discriminated between high- and low-productivity foremen. He reports the following as characteristic of high-productivity foremen.

1. He likes to talk more.

2. He likes to speak in front of a group more.

3. He believed that talking was the most important part of a foreman's job.

4. He reported speaking up more in conferences.

5. He believed it was fairly easy to explain company policy to the workers.

6. He didn't believe that talking to workers was a waste of time.

7. He believed in "kidding" and "shooting the breeze" with his workers.

8. He believed in taking time to listen to the workers' problems.

9. He believed more in the importance of the workers.

10. He did not believe in being "hard-boiled" or "stern" with workers.

11. He thought less of information obtained from the grapevine.

12. He felt he knew how he stood with his boss.

13. He felt he was informed of changes before they took place.

In a similar study, Simons (1962) attempted to identify communication attitudes which would distinguish "more successful" and "less successful" supervisors in a large urban convention hotel. He reports that the following are "definite or possible" distinguishing factors. They indicate that more high-rated supervisors:

1. Were judged by the researcher to be "permissive" based on "gestalt" evaluations of supervisory responses.

2. Considered a course in "Human Relations" most useful out of six courses in supervision presented to them.

3. Said that they consulted with their employees before rescheduling or reassigning work.

4. Said that, rather than offend employees who came to them with silly questions, they explained or discussed such suggestions with employees.

5. Said that they gave advance notice of impending layoffs to their employees.

6. Said that they would ask or persuade rather than tell or demand if confronted with the necessity of assigning unpleasant work.

7. Said that they would try to get action if employees came to them with just complaints against general company policy.

8. Said that new employees should be told both good and bad things about the hotel rather than just good things.

9. Said that they reprimanded employees in private, rather than in front of others.

In a most extensive review of research, Likert (1961) developed evidence to support the position that high-producing work groups and departments are characterized by people who have favorable and cooperative attitudes. He then presented research relevant to the attitudes and behaviors of supervisors who were engendering such favorable and cooperative attitudes—as perceived by the subordinates. The following generalizations about productive interpersonal attitudes and behaviors are based on the experimental and survey studies described by Likert.

Likert's work provides an effective transition from paper-and-pencil attitude tests to observations of actual, on-the-job behavior. Such observations are especially useful in making assumptions about the relationship of attitudes to behaviors. In addition, overt behavior seems to be important to workers and managers as well. Mann and Dent (1954) found that supervisors frequently made judgments about where they stood with their boss on overt behavior rather than on "the boss *tells* me where I stand."

A vast store of descriptive reports of actual on-the-job communication behavior is found in the work of Tacey (1960). He used the research technique called the critical incident method. Through interviews, diaries, and questionnaires, he gathered descriptions of actual incidents which had personally been observed by the respondents. From these incidents, Tacey developed a list of 676 behaviors which represented the practices of effective and ineffective foremen in his study. An analysis of Tacey's work suggests that some generalizations can be made concerning effective communication behavior for these foremen—regardless of whether it was directed upward, downward, or horizontally in the organization. An effective foreman's communicative behavior included the following characteristics:

1. He always tried to supplement one method of communication with another to ensure understanding—oral, written, visual, the actual object, etc.

Supervisors of High-Productivity Groups	*Supervisors of Low-Productivity Groups*
1. Inform employees as to current company conditions, expectations, and changes.	1. Tend to be critical of mistakes and punitive.
2. Keep employees posted on how they are doing.	2. Spend more time in short periods giving detailed instructions.
3. Frequently hear complaints and grievances.	3. Seldom solicit suggestions from employees.
4. Frequently recommend promotions, transfers, and pay increases.	4. Tend to exhort employees to be concerned about company goals to the exclusion of employees' goals.
5. Do not put "unreasonable" pressure on employees.	5. Tend to be hostile and threatening.
6. Spend less time directing supervising employees.	6. Tend to be suspicious of employee motivations and generally distrustful of employees.
7. Tend to be interested in the well-being of the employees as well as the company.	
8. Tend to be perceived as supportive, friendly, helpful, considerate, and fair.	
9. Show confidence in the integrity and motivations of their employees.	
10. Coach and assist employees whose performance is below standard.	
11. Develop work group loyalty— often through increased participation by employees.	

Table 10.1

2. He asked questions and repeated what was said to ensure understanding.

3. He kept people informed of changes, difficulties, progress, etc. He kept them up-to-date.

4. He was concerned about the welfare of his crew and demonstrated it by such things as: recommending promotions; taking time and being patient; rewarding them for good work and passing this information on to his supervisor; expressing confidence in his men and giving them initiative; adapting his communications to the level of the men and using examples with which they were familiar.

5. He was concerned with facts, evidence, details and generally communicated with specifics rather than generalities.

6. He sought information when he didn't have it and encouraged his men to do the same. He used information and suggestions passed up from his men.

7. He recognized his own shortcomings and mistakes, those of his men, and those of his supervisors. He discussed these freely and tried to arrive at corrective measures or solutions.

8. His communication showed an understanding of the job and company policies.

9. He took immediate action on communications to him. He did what he said he would do.

10. He anticipated problems.

11. He gave reasons behind orders.

12. His actions showed him to "be his own boss"; to take responsibility; to take initiative.

At this point we should make it very clear, as do the researchers, that such attitudinal and behavioral lists will not work well or have application in *all* situations involving supervisory behavior. This view is supported by communication theorists who tell us we must adapt our responses to the expectations, values, skills, and general background of the other person. It is also supported by two authors who constructed tests of supervisory attitudes which attempted to identify effective and ineffective supervisors in any organization. McCormick and Middaugh (1956) reported that the most effective key to answers on the famous *How Supervise?* test were found by developing the key, company by company. In the same manner, Pyron

(1965) found that he could not identify any cluster of items on his attitude scales which would consistently distinguish "good" and "poor" supervisors. However, his forced-choice scale could identify characteristics of such individuals in certain specified companies. Some generally recurring patterns characterizing effective foremen were:

1. He was quite knowledgeable of his job.
2. His work could be trusted.
3. He was fair.
4. He used an empathic response approach.
5. He encouraged suggestions and criticisms from his men.
6. He saw effective communication as an important part of his job.

Thus, while some broad principles or guidelines concerning the communication attitudes and behavior of effective supervisors may be derived, it is equally important that the supervisor exhibit a sensitivity to the special and unique characteristics of each situation and each person. After reviewing research from various academic disciplines and several different universities, Redding (Redding and Sanborn, 1964) also concludes that "there is *no* single, easily identifiable set of communication skills which reliably characterizes the good manager." However, he goes on to say that

> . . . it seems safe to conclude from them [research studies] that, by and large, the better supervisors (better in terms of getting the work done) are—in a very general sense—those who are more sensitive to their communication responsibilities. They tend to be those, for example, who give clear instructions, who listen empathically, who are accessible for questions or suggestions, and who keep their subordinates properly informed. (p. 60)

Empathy and Interpersonal Effectiveness

Although empathy has been defined in a variety of ways, it is frequently described as that process by which one person is sensitive to the thoughts, feelings, and actions of another. Some feel it is a process of identifying ourselves with the other person, or more familiarly, "putting ourselves in the shoes of the other person." The widespread application of this process would seem to be a desirable component for organizational success, and more specifically, Jarrard's (1956) review of the literature concludes, "empathy appears to be a necessary requirement for supervisory success." There have been numerous attempts to study the concept of empathy in industrial settings, but the results are still highly tentative. A discussion of some representative research follows.

Nagle (1954) investigated the relationship between productivity and employee attitudes toward their supervisor. As a corollary, he also studied supervisor sensitivity to employee attitudes and its relationship to both attitudes and productivity. He sampled 14 departments and 223 employees. Company executives supplied production ratings. Sensitivity was measured by having supervisors predict how employees answered a 22-item questionnaire. Nagle found that the more sensitive supervisors received more favorable attitudes and higher production from their employees. The author is quick to caution against making any causal connections from this study. Tobolski and Kerr (1952) administered an empathy test to automobile salesmen and found some predictive value of test scores for determining sales records and job success ratings. Another study (Van Zelst, 1952), involving union leaders, showed sensitivity and effectiveness to be highly correlated. Johnson's (1954) work suggests that employees with high morale can predict supervisors' responses better than those with low morale, but that supervisors cannot predict responses of employees with high morale with significantly greater accuracy than those with low morale.

These and other studies of empathy in organizational settings offer little more than hypotheses about the role of empathic ability. They all suffer from deficiencies in research methodology—particularly the tests for measuring empathy. After an extensive review of empathy tests, Smith (1967) felt that Hatch's (1962) forced-choice differential accuracy approach was the most sophisticated measure of interpersonal sensitivity available and used it in his research. Smith found that this approach did not evidence internal consistency reliability and thus did not provide an adequate measure of interpersonal sensitivity for the production supervisors in his study. The task of developing an adequate measure of empathy is a major obstacle in specifying the role of empathy in organizational behavior.

Any study in organizational settings should also consider the following contingencies: (1) The possibility that there may be greater rewards for vertical sensitivity (those above and below you in the organizational hierarchy) than for horizontal or peer sensitivity. The reverse may be true in educational institutions. Nevertheless, people often selectively choose those with whom they will exercise certain behaviors—for example, empathy. (2) In addition, the probability of selectivity with regard to message content. Nagle's work suggested, for instance, that supervisors found it harder to predict others' responses to statements that were ego-involving for them. (3) Empathy may only be a necessary part of some of the multiple success patterns in interpersonal behavior that are undoubtedly present.

Even though the measurement of empathic ability has been an elusive concept for researchers, the position taken earlier in this book would suggest that an accurate awareness of the ideas, feelings, and actions of others is a necessary prerequisite to understanding the effects of communication in an interpersonal situation. Unfortunately, there is no shortage of information to highlight distinct perceptual differences between communicating pairs in organizational contexts.

Perceptual Differences and Interpersonal Effectiveness

The underlying assumption in the following research is that gross perceptual differences between supervisor-subordinate pairs will reduce communication effectiveness and, ultimately, organizational effectiveness. Likert (1961) reports the following discrepancies between superior-subordinate judgments:

1. 90 percent of the top staff say foremen feel very free to discuss important things about the job with them; *but* only 67 percent of the foremen said they felt very free to discuss such problems with top staff. And—85 percent of the foremen said their subordinates felt very free to discuss important things about the job with them; *but* only 51 percent of the subordinates said they felt very free to discuss such problems with the foremen.

2. 95 percent of the foremen say they understand their men's work problems well; *but* only 34 percent of the men say their foreman understands their problems well. And—90 percent of the general foremen say they understand their foremen's problems well; but only 51 percent of the foremen say the general foremen understand their problems well.

3. 70 percent of the top staff say they always tell foremen in advance about changes which will affect them or their work; *but* only 27 percent of the foremen say that top staff tell them in advance about changes which will affect them or their work. And —40 percent of the foremen say they always tell their subordi-

nates about such changes; *but* only 22 percent of the subordinates say the foremen actually do tell them in advance about such changes.

4. 70 percent of the top staff say they always or almost always seek their foremen's ideas and opinions; *but* only 52 percent of the foremen say the top staff seek out their ideas and opinions with great frequency. And—73 percent of these foremen say they always or almost always seek their subordinate's ideas and opinions; *but* only 16 percent of the subordinates say their foremen actually do engage in such behavior. (pp. 47–53)

A study by Maier (1959) and his associates tends to dramatize these perceptual differences even more. In this case middle-level managers selected a subordinate with whom they would be paired in the study. The supervisor and the subordinate were both interviewed about various aspects of the subordinate's job—problems, duties, job requirements, and future changes. The expectation was that this method of pairing would reduce the disagreement on such items. Still, there were vast differences regarding particular obstacles and problems the subordinate faces. This was true even when the supervisor had previously occupied the subordinate's position! A final note on this study tends to emphasize the findings even more. After the study was completed and the results were made available to the company and to the subjects, a questionnaire was sent to those who had participated. The questionnaire asked if the supervisor-subordinate pairs had gotten together to discuss these differences. Seven out of the first twenty-two pairs responding *did not agree* on whether or not they had gotten together!

When executives of a large organization were asked to indicate how much time they spent with each other and what they talked about, one-third of the men disagreed about the topics of conversation (Burns, 1954). A study of selective perception (Dearborn and Simon, 1958) explains some of these perceptual differences. In this study executives representing sales, production, and public/industrial relations were asked to analyze a 10,000-word case study from a "companywide perspective." They were asked which company problem stated in the case they regarded as the major one. It was significant that sales executives chose a sales problem significantly more often than did other executives; that production executives selected production problems more often than did other executives; and that public/industrial relations executives consistently chose human-relations-oriented problems. Thus, departmental perceptions were highly influential in the probem analysis even though the subjects were explicitly told to put themselves in the president's position and analyze the problem from a broad, companywide perspective.

Kahn (1958) asked individuals from various levels of the organization what they thought were the most important aspects in a job. He then asked each person to estimate how their subordinates would rate them. Again important discrepancies existed between predicted ratings and actual ratings. One of the comparisons is listed below:

Variable	Foreman's Ranking for Themselves	General Foreman's Predicted Ranking for Foremen
Steady work and steady wages	1	1
High wages	7	2
Pensions and other benefits	8	3
Not having to work too hard	9	4
Good chance for a promotion	2	5
Getting along well with the people I work with	3	6
Getting along well with my supervisor	5	7
Good chance to do interesting work	4	8
Good chance to turn out quality work	6	9

Table 10.2

Reprinted from "Human Relations on the Shop Floor" by Robert L. Kahn in *Human Relations and Modern Management*, by permission of the North-Holland Publishing Company, Amsterdam.

Another approach in studying perceptual differences has been to examine semantic compatibility. Weaver (1958) used the semantic differential to measure the differences in the frames of reference for labor and management groups. He obtained responses of both groups to various concepts such as grievance, the labor movement, and the closed shop. Responses were marked on a seven-point scale that contained a list of polar adjectives like good-bad, fair-unfair, valuable-worthless, etc. For example:

The Labor Movement

good...........|............|............|............|............|............|............bad
fair...........|............|............|............|............|............|............unfair

From the responses to these semantic scales, Weaver was able to develop a comparative profile of labor and management frames of reference.

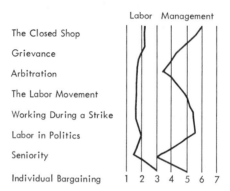

Figure 10.1

Reprinted from "The Quantification of the Frame of Reference in Labor-Management Communication" by Carl H. Weaver by permission of the author and the publisher, the American Psychological Association.

One of Weaver's conclusions was that for some concepts management seems to be holding less tenaciously to traditional frames of reference. Nevertheless, the profiles tell us that any of the concepts used in this study are likely to evoke vastly different meanings from labor groups and management groups. Korman (1960), using the same research technique, demonstrated that such semantic barriers are not limited to traditionally competitive groups like labor and management. He found significant semantic distance between top, middle, and lower management on such concepts as incentives, communication, quota, cooperation, and budget. Triandis (1959) used a similar technique in an effort to relate similarity in frames of reference with effectiveness of communication and liking for the other person. He found that his measures of frames of reference determined, at least in part, both liking and communication effectiveness—the more similarity in the "thought processes" of the communicating pair, the more communication effectiveness and liking.

The inescapable conclusion of such studies is that there are often vast perceptual differences between communicating pairs in organizations. Even though such differences may seem discouraging, they should provide useful expectations. An awareness of the probability of such differences should encourage efforts to identify these differences; this will increase the probabilities of communicative success by taking into account the criteria and values that characterize the thinking of the other person or group. Another factor that seems to affect the success of interpersonal communication is whether or not there is trust in the relationship.

Trust and Interpersonal Effectiveness

It is not an uncommon fear in a business organization that the expression of one's true feelings could be dangerous. Some laboratory studies in small group behavior stimulated Mellinger (1956) to conduct a field study of trust—a study which seemed to confirm the laboratory finding that low trust contributed to a distortion of information passed between subordinate and supervisor. In addition to pointing up the importance of trust to interpersonal behavior in organizations, Mellinger also found that simply increasing the amount of communication between the two parties will not necessarily create better understanding. It may even heighten the *mis*understanding depending on the mitigating factors in their relationship. Mellinger suggests an increase in communication may result in greater accuracy in perceiving the opinions of others, but only when trust and agreement are high initially. Other studies of conflict resolution also support this point.

Read (1962), in another field study of interpersonal trust, found that upward mobility of the subordinate had an important influence on the degree of accuracy or distortion in messages communicated from subordinate to supervisor. In fact, a high degree of upward mobility on the subordinate's part caused distortions in the message *even when there was a high degree of trust between the two parties.* Another factor that seems to condition the accuracy of communication is the degree of influence the subordinate perceives the supervisor as being able to exert (Pelz, 1952).

Thus, a lack of trust seems to act as a principal or codeterminant of communication distortion. Distrust can cause a reduction of the information shared and a suspicion of what little information is communicated.

Work Group Influence and Interpersonal Effectiveness

A person's response to any given interpersonal situation is not usually determined solely by the other person. Previously we discussed the influence of the organizational climate, but there are characteristics of one's work group which also influence interpersonal responses.

For instance, group cohesiveness may be an important factor. Numerous studies have reported how a normally high-producing worker has been pressured into conforming to a lower production level by his work group. If a work group member perceives group support he may feel freer to discuss, disagree, and make counterproposals. He is likely to respond to his supervisor with less defensive reactions and more problem-oriented behavior (Stotland, 1959). However, group cohesiveness can also act as a potent force in reducing levels of productivity—particularly when confidence in management is low (Seashore, 1954). Thus, perceived group support may have a significant impact on an individual's response to interpersonal stimuli—especially those which are potentially frustrating or threatening.

Another major area of study in recent years concerned the amount of work group participation in decision making. The results of these studies suggest several effects on work group members that will certainly affect their interpersonal relations. A good example of such influences is found in Morse and Reimer's (1956) study of workers in the home office of a nationally organized insurance company. The researchers chose a department employing about five hundred clerical workers with four levels of supervision. The department had four divisions. In two of them the researchers increased the amount of control by upper levels. This was labeled the Hierarchal Program. In the other two divisions they increased the worker's participation in decision making. This was labeled the Autonomy Program. At the end of the two-year study they found quite different social and psychological changes characterized the two groups. The implications for interpersonal behavior are obvious when the two programs are compared. Certainly this does not suggest that increasing participation will always be advantageous. In fact, some personality types actually become more uncomfortable under such conditions (Vroom, 1960). The reader should note, however, that the amount of perceived and actual participation by the work group will have an influence on interpersonal responses.

Change	Autonomy Program	Hierarchal Program
More willingness to see other people's point of view, more friendliness	28%	—
More cooperation, work better together	25%	—
More tension, nervousness, fighting, jumpiness, biting each other's heads off, harshness, less kindness	16%	35%
Greater dissatisfaction, disagreeableness, friction, less cooperation	31%	65%

Table 10.3

Reprinted from "The Experimental Change of a Major Organizational Variable" by Nancy Morse and E. Reimer, in *Journal of Abnormal Social Psychology* 52 (1956), 120–29, with permission from the American Psychological Association.

Argyris (1955), a well-known advocate of participative management, makes the following conclusions based on his studies of participation in decision making.

1. It [participation] will increase the degree of "we" feeling of cohesiveness that participants have with their organization.

2. It will provide the participants with an overall organizational point of view instead of the traditionally more narrow departmental point of view.

3. It will decrease the amount of conflict, hostility, and cutthroat competition among participants.

4. It will increase the individuals' understanding of each other, which leads to increased tolerance and patience toward others.

5. It increases the individual's free expression of his personality, which results in an employee who sticks with the organization because he needs the gratifying experiences he finds while working there.

6. It develops a "work climate," as a result of the other tendencies, in which the subordinates find opportunity to be more creative and to come up with ideas beneficial to the organization.

This review of research has focused on some of the factors influencing interpersonal responses in organizational settings. The degree of influence these factors exert varies with each interpersonal contact, but some general principles are available from the work of Jackson (1959).

1. In the pursuit of their work goals, people have forces acting upon them to communicate with those who will help them achieve their aims, and forces against communicating with those who will not assist, or may retard their accomplishment.

2. People have powerful forces acting upon them to direct their communication toward those who can make them feel more secure and gratify their needs and away from those who threaten them, make them feel anxious, and generally provide unrewarding experiences.

3. Persons in an organization are always communicating as if they were trying to improve their position.

Prescriptions for Effective Interpersonal Behavior

If you accept an underlying assumption permeating this entire chapter, it will be extremely clear that a list of rules or "steps to success" would be impractical if not impossible. The assumption is one of situationalism. The assumption is that the mixture of unique individuals, unique organizational systems, unique contexts, unique skills, and unique timing prohibits a "surefire package of rules" for effective interpersonal communication. More appropriate, it seems, is a formula composed of general guidelines which can accommodate specific prescriptions for a given situation. This general formula includes three main parts:

1. **A person must recognize the complexity and situational nature of the interpersonal process.** Effective communicators in organizations must be aware of the interaction of one's perceptions of himself, his perceptions of the other person, his perceptions of the organization, his

perceptions of his work group, and his perceptions of the general climate of the organization governing his interpersonal behavior. He must be wary of the simple explanation involving any analysis of interpersonal behavior. It should not surprise him, for instance, to learn that in one research study some of the most *inarticulate* foremen were associated with high-productivity work groups (Walker and Guest, 1952); it should not surprise him to learn that some people react negatively to increased participation in decision making; it should not surprise him that "giving honest and sincere recognition for a job well done" was a behavior associated with the supervisors of work groups with *low* morale (Pelz, 1952). The effective communicator should recognize that the effect of any particular communication depends upon prior feelings and attitudes of the parties concerned, pre-existing expectations and motives of the communicating persons, the amount of support each person receives from his membership in a group of peers, and many, many more.

2. **A person must behave according to the principle of supportive relationships.** Likert (1961) describes this as follows:

> The leadership and other processes of the organization must be such as to ensure a maximum probability that in all interactions and all relationships within the organization each member will, in the light of his background, values, and expectations, view the experience as supportive and one which builds and maintains his sense of personal worth and importance. (p. 103)

Generally, a supervisor with a "supportive orientation" would trust and respect his subordinates, have a sincere interest in their welfare, be sensitive to the needs and feelings of his men, be receptive to the ideas and suggestions of his men, be considerate rather than hostile, be fair and impartial. He acts in ways that will serve the best interests of his men as well as the organization. This does not mean he is totally concerned with human problems; he must also exercise his role as supervisor—otherwise he becomes just another member of the work group.

3. **A person's communication must demonstrate sensitivity and analytical skills.** This simply means that an underlying element of a person's approach to others must be an attempt to understand them and accept them for what they are. He must also be aware of and understand himself as a prerequisite to understanding others. He must be aware of differences in his outlook and those of another. He must be aware that *as the other person sees the situation*, he is probably right. He must be ana-

lytical in terms of predicting responses—that is, he should be able to predict the range of possible responses when the stimulus is an attack on the other person's personality or when he uses the word "always"—knowing that the receiver is aware of some exceptions.

Here it may be well for the authors to make an observation. For some, the preceding three points may be too vague. The question still looms, "Isn't it possible to list some guidelines generally found to be associated with effective interpersonal behavior in organizations—still recognizing the tentative nature of such a list?" If such a list were drawn from the research reviewed in this chapter, it might read as follows:

1. Information levels about jobs, organization, and other workers are not extremely low.

2. Subordinates feel free to discuss problems with supervisors.

3. Unreasonable pressures are not frequently perceived.

4. Communication is thought to be important. A concern for effective communication increases the frequency of such actions as: giving reasons behind orders, using repetition for increased understanding, employing multimedia methods, asking questions, seeking information when it is not known, using more facts and fewer assumptions, keeping people informed by actions and words, inviting participation in decision making.

5. A high degree of trust and faith in people is present.

6. There is general, rather than close supervision.

7. Action is taken on suggestions from others.

8. There is a supportive, rather than a threatening or hostile climate. People are not quick to criticize or "put others down." There is a willingness to answer even "silly" questions. Supervisors engage in coaching, promoting, and "sticking up" for their employees.

9. Members (particularly supervisors) generally do what they say they will do.

10. Good performance is recognized.

11. There is a high degree of interest in and awareness of feelings and thoughts of others—empathic ability is high.

12. Anticipating problems, looking for alternatives, and a general flexibility are present rather than adherence to rigid and unchanging patterns of response.

Improving Interpersonal Communication in Organizations

In previous sections we have outlined theory and research on effective interpersonal communication in organizations. The purpose of this section is to concentrate on what can be done to internalize behaviors and attitudes conducive to effective communication on the job. When one considers the investment in time and money and the results expected of business training programs in interpersonal communication and human relations, it is amazing how little scientific effort has been put into examining the results. Miraglia (1966) presented a thorough review of attempts to measure training effects and found the experimental and quasi-experimental research to be extremely limited.

One of the most consistent findings, however, in almost all the scientific studies focusing on the effects of training is the following: *The effects of training cannot be considered separate from the environs of the worker. You cannot create a behavior change which violates the culture in which the behavior is embedded.* The classic example generally used to support this conclusion is the work of Fleishman (1953). He found his trainees were unable to practice the human relations principles espoused in the course because their working climate did not always support such practices. This is why many have suggested training programs that begin with top management or programs that train two or more levels of supervision simultaneously.

In Fleishman's study the training program content and procedures were not clearly defined, but Miraglia (1963) provides another example of failure to implement training principles in actual on-the-job situations following training. Before any training in communication had taken place, Miraglia measured the following: (1) supervisors' on-the-job communication ability as perceived by their subordinates, (2) communication knowledge as determined by scores on a test, and (3) supervisors on-the-job supervision ability as perceived by their subordinates as well as by their superiors. Then the training program was given. It included lecturing on such subjects as listening, empathy, questioning, feedback, ego-defense, motivation, and the application of these things to the jobs of the supervisors. Then the supervisors role-played common communication situations applicable to their jobs with subsequent critiques from instructors and students. Following the training program, and again four months later, the same measures of supervisory abilities and communication knowledge were taken as before. In all cases measurements were taken for the group which had received the training and for another group which had not been given the training. The results showed no significant differences between the group with training and the group without training on measures of supervisory communication ability or general supervisory ability both before and after the training program. The group that had the training did, however, increase in communication knowledge over the control group following the training. It appears that the principles were learned, but not applied once the supervisors returned to their jobs—at least such changes were not perceived by the raters.

This shows that it is extremely important to consider the organizational climate in which these skills will be applied. There is also reason to believe that the more traditional training programs (patterned after traditional classroom approaches) will not provide the conditions necessary for making major behavioral changes. The work of Argyris (1962) gives us an example of the amount of work that may be involved in developing interpersonal competence in organization settings. Only the president and top executives of a large corporation were included in the training program— although Argyris used their immediate subordinates as a control group. His goal was to increase interpersonal competence for the ultimate effectiveness of the organization. He wanted to create more openness, trust, and confidence and reduce conformity, and management by detail, crises, fear and conflict. He reports success in achieving his objectives and proceeded as follows: (1) The first phase was one of diagnosis. He held personal interviews to determine the degree of interpersonal competence, adherence to organizational values, existence of defenses, conflicts, mistrust, etc. (2) Phase two consisted of observations of these executives in fifty-one meetings in which decision making was taking place. (3) Phase three was the feedback of results to the executives to help them see more clearly their system and its impact upon the organization. (4) Phase four was a laboratory training session (analogous to T-groups, or sensitivity groups). These sessions emphasized the behavioral modifications Argyris wanted to achieve. (5) Phase five included immediate posttraining evaluations. Three weeks after the training a meeting was held to discuss the experience, and postevaluations were again compiled by interviewing each man from six to nine months following the laboratory sessions. Although the effort expended in this program is the exception rather than the rule, it may be necessary to provide such extensive and intensive programs if we realistically expect behavioral changes.

Argyris (1966) was probably very close to being correct about efforts to change interpersonal behavior when he suggested that a "book can pose some issues and get thinking started, but—in this area, at least—it cannot change behavior."

References

Argyris, Chris, *Interpersonal Competence and Organizational Effectiveness.* Homewood, Ill.: Richard D. Irwin, Inc., 1962.

————, "Interpersonal Barriers to Decision Making," *Harvard Business Review*, March-April, 1966, p. 93.

————, "Organizational Leadership and Participative Management," *Journal of Business*, 28 (1955), 1. An illustrative case study is: Alfred J. Marrow, D. G. Bowers, and S. E. Seashore, *Management by Participation.* New York: Harper & Row, Publishers, 1967.

Barnard, Chester I., *The Functions of the Executive.* Cambridge: Harvard University Press, 1938, p. 226.

Blake, Robert R., and Jane S. Mouton, *The Managerial Grid.* Houston, Texas: Gulf Publishing Co., 1964, p. 48.

Burns, Tom, "The Directions of Activity and Communication in a Departmental Executive Group," *Human Relations*, 7 (1954), 73–79.

Burns, Tom, and G. M. Stalker, *The Management of Innovation.* Chicago: Quadrangle Books, Inc., 1962.

Dearborn, Dewitt C., and Herbert A. Simon, "Selective Perception: A Note on Departmental Identification of Executives," *Sociometry*, 21 (June, 1958), 140–44.

Etzioni, Amitai, *A Comparative Analysis of Complex Organizations.* New York: The Free Press, 1961, p. 31. "Utilitarian organizations are organizations in which remuneration is the major means of control over lower participants and calculative envolement (i.e., mild alienation to mild commitment) characterizes the orientation of the large majority of lower participants."

Fiedler, F. E., "Style or Circumstance: The Leadership Enigma," *Psychology Today*, 2 (1969), 38–43. See also: F. E. Fiedler, *A Theory of Leadership Effectiveness.* New York: McGraw-Hill Book Company, 1967.

Fleishman, E., "Leadership Climate, Human Relations Training, and Supervisory Behavior," *Personnel Psychology*, 6 (1953), 205–22.

Fox, William M., "When Human Relations May Succeed and the Company

Fail," *California Management Review*, 8 (Spring, 1966). Another general critique of the cult of human relations is found in: Malcolm P. McNair, "Thinking Ahead: What Price Human Relations?" *Harvard Business Review*, 35 (1957), 15–39.

Funk, Frank E., "Communication Attitudes of Industrial Foremen as Related to Their Rated Productivity." Unpublished Ph.D. dissertation, Purdue University, 1956.

Gellerman, S. W., *Motivation and Productivity*. New York: American Management Association, Inc., 1963.

———, *Management by Motivation*. New York: American Management Association, Inc., 1968, p. 44. Reprinted by permission of the publisher. © 1968 by the American Management Association, Inc.

Gibb, Jack R., "Fear and Facade: Defensive Management," in *Science and Human Affairs*, ed. Richard E. Farson. Palo Alto, Calif.: Science & Behavior Books, Inc., 1965.

Haney, William V., *Communication and Organizational Behavior: Text and Cases*. Homewood, Ill.: Richard D. Irwin, Inc., 1967, p. 20.

Hatch, Richard S., *An Evaluation of a Forced-Choice Differential Accuracy Approach to the Measurement of Supervisory Empathy*. Englewood Cliffs, N. J.: Prentice-Hall, Inc., 1962.

Jackson, Jay M., "The Organization and Its Communication Problems," *Journal of Communication*, 9 (1959), 161–63.

Jarrard, L. E., "Empathy: The Concept and Industrial Applications," *Personnel Psychology*, 9 (1956), 157.

Johnson, R. L., "Relationship of Employee Morale to Ability to Predict Responses," *Journal of Applied Psychology*, 38 (1954), 320–23.

Jones, John Paul, "The Management of Human Effort—A New Concept in Action." Speech delivered to the American Management Association, Fall Personnel Conference, September 25, 1961, pp. 3–5.

Kahn, Robert L., "Human Relations On the Shop Floor," in E. M. Hugh-Jones, ed. *Human Relations and Modern Management*. Amsterdam: North-Holland Publishing Co., 1958.

Korman, A. K., "A Cause of Communication Failure," *Personnel Administration*, 23 (1960), 17–21.

Kuriloff, Arthur H., "An Experiment in Management—Putting Theory Y to the Test," *Personnel*, 42 (1963), 8–17. See also: "When Workers Manage Themselves," *Business Week*, March 20, 1965.

Leavitt, Harold H., "Management According to Task: Organizational Differentiation," in Keith Davis and William G. Scott, eds. *Readings in Human Relations*. New York: McGraw-Hill Book Company, 1959, pp. 3–15.

Lieberman, S., "The Effects of Changes in Roles on the Attitudes of Role Occupants," *Human Relations*, 9 (1956), 385–402.

Likert, Rensis, *New Patterns of Management*. New York: McGraw-Hill Book Company, 1961.

———, *The Human Organization: Its Management and Value*. New York: McGraw-Hill Book Company, 1967.

Lull, P. E., Frank E. Funk, and Darrell T. Piersol, "What Communications Means to the Corporation President," *Advanced Management*, 20 (1955), 17–20.

McCormick, E. J., and R. W. Middaugh, "The Development of a Tailor-Made Scoring Key for the *How Supervise?* Test," *Personnel Psychology*, 9 (1956), 27–37.

McGregor, Douglas M., *The Human Side of Enterprise*. New York: McGraw-Hill Book Company, 1960.

McMurry, Robert N., "The Case for Benevolent Autocracy." *Harvard Business Review*, 36 (1958), 82–90.

Maier, N. R. F., W. Read, and J. Hooven, "Breakdowns in Boss-Subordinate Communication," *Communication in Organizations: Some New Research Findings*. Ann Arbor Mich.: Foundation for Research on Human Behavior, 1959. See also: N. R. F. Maier, L. R. Hoffman, and W. H. Read, "Superior-subordinate Communication: The Relative Effectiveness of Managers Who Held Their Subordinates' Positions," *Personnel Psychology*, 16 (1963), 1–11.

Mandell, M. M., "Supervisors' Attitudes and Job Performance," *Personnel*, 26 (1949), 182–83.

Mann, F., and J. Dent, *Appraisals of Supervisors and Attitudes of Their Employees in an Electric Power Company*. Ann Arbor, Mich.: Survey Research Center, University of Michigan, Series I, Report 4, March, 1954.

Maslow, Abraham H., *Motivation and Personality*. New York: Harper and Brothers, 1954.

Mellinger, Glen D., "Interpersonal Trust as a Factor in Communication," *Journal of Abnormal and Social Psychology*, 52 (1956), 304–9.

Meyer, H. H., "A Study of Certain Factors Related to Quality of Work Group Leadership." Unpublished Ph.D. dissertation, University of Michigan, 1949.

Miraglia, Joseph F., "An Experimental Study of the Effects of Communication Training Upon Perceived Performance of Nursing Supervisors in Two Urban Hospitals." Unpublished Ph.D. dissertation, Purdue University, 1963.

————, "Human Relations Training: A Critical Examination of On-The-Job Effects," *Training and Development Journal*, 20 (1966), 18–27.

Moment, D., and A. Zaleznik, *Role Development and Interpersonal Competence.* Boston: Harvard Business School, 1963.

Morse, Nancy, and E. Reimer, "The Experimental Change of a Major Organizational Variable," *Journal of Abnormal and Social Psychology*, 52 (1956), 120–29.

Nagle, B. F., "Productivity, Employee Attitudes and Supervisory Sensitivity," *Personnel Psychology*, 7 (1954), 219–33.

Pelz, D. C., "The Influence of the Supervisor Within His Department as a Conditioner of the Way Supervisory Practices Affect Employee Attitudes." Unpublished Ph.D. dissertation, University of Michigan, 1951.

————, "Influence: A Key to Effective Leadership in the First-Line Supervisor," *Personnel*, 29 (1952), 209–17.

Porter, Lyman W., "A Study of Perceived Need Satisfactions in Bottom and Middle Management Jobs," *Journal of Applied Psychology*, 45, (1961), 1–10.

Pyron, H. Charles, "The Construction and Validation of a Forced Choice Scale for Measuring Oral Communication Attitudes of Industrial Foremen." Unpublished Ph.D. dissertation, Purdue University, 1965.

Read, William H., "Upward Communication in Industrial Hierarchies," *Human Relations*, 15 (1962), 3–15.

Redding, W. Charles, and George A. Sanborn, eds. *Business and Industrial Communication: A Sourcebook.* New York: Harper and Row, Publishers, 1964, p. 29.

Roethlisberger, F. J., and William J. Dickson, *Management and the Worker* (11th printing). Cambridge: Harvard University Press, 1956.

Rosenfeld, J. M., and M. J. Smith, "The Emergence of Management Theory Z," *Personnel Journal*, Part I (October, 1965), and Part II (November, 1965).

Schein, Edgar H., *Organizational Psychology*, Englewood Cliffs, N.J.: Prentice-Hall, Inc., 1965, p. 60.

Scott, William G., *Organization Theory: A Behavioral Analysis for Management*. Homewood, Ill.: Richard D. Irwin, Inc., 1967, pp. 21–60.

Seashore, S. F., *Group Cohesiveness in the Industrial Work Group*. Ann Arbor, Mich.: Survey Research Center, University of Michigan, 1954.

Simons, Herbert W., "A Comparison of Communication Attributes and Rated Job Performance of Supervisors in a Large Commercial Enterprise." Unpublished Ph.D. dissertation, Purdue University, 1962.

Sinclair, Upton, *The Jungle*. New York: The Viking Press, 1946, pp. 59–60. Original copyright, 1905.

Smith, R. L., "Communication Correlates of Interpersonal Sensitivity Among Industrial Supervisors." Unpublished Ph.D. dissertation, Purdue University, 1967.

Stanton, Erwin S., "Company Policies and Supervisor's Attitudes Toward Supervision," *Journal of Applied Psychology*, 44 (1960), 22–26.

Stotland, Ezra, "Peer Groups and Reactions to Power Figures," in *Studies in Social Power*, ed. Dorwin Cartwright. Ann Arbor, Mich.: Research Center for Group Dynamics, University of Michigan, 1959.

Tacey, William S., "Critical Requirements of the Oral Communication of Industrial Foremen." Unpublished D.Ed. dissertation, The Pennsylvania State University, 1960.

Taylor, Frederick W., *Principles of Scientific Management*, New York: Harper and Brothers, 1919.

Tobolski, F. P., and W. A. Kerr, "Predictive Value of the Empathy Test in Automobile Salesmanship," *Journal of Applied Psychology*, 36 (1952), 310–11.

Triandis, Harry C., "Similarity in Thought Processes and Boss-Employee Communication," *Communication in Organizations: Some New Research Findings*. Ann Arbor, Mich.: Foundation for Research on Human Behavior, 1959. See also: Harry C. Triandis, "Cognitive Similarity and Interpersonal Communication in Industry," *Journal of Applied Psychology*, 43 (1959), 321–26.

Van Zelst, R. H., "Empathy Test Scores for Union Leaders," *Journal of Applied Psychology*, 36 (1952), 293–95. A related study that shows leaders to score higher on "predictive abstracting" is: C. G. Browne and R. P. Shore, "Leadership and Predictive Abstracting," *Journal of Applied Psychology*, 40 (1956), 112–16.

Vroom, V. H., *Some Personality Determinants of the Effects of Participation*, Englewood Cliffs, N. J.: Prentice-Hall, Inc., 1960.

———, *Motivation in Management*. New York: American Foundation for Management Research, 1964.

Vroom, V. H., and F. C. Mann, "Leader Authoritarianism and Employee Attitudes," *Personnel Psychology*, 13 (1960), 125–40.

Walker, C. R., and R. H. Guest, *The Man on the Assembly Line*. Cambridge: Harvard University Press, 1952. See also: A. N. Turner, "What Makes a Good Foreman," *Personnel*, 33 (1955), 382–92, and C. R. Walker, R. H. Guest, and A. N. Turner, *The Foreman on the Assembly Line*. Cambridge: Harvard University Press, 1956, p. 17.

Weaver, Carl H., "The Quantification of the Frame of Reference in Labor-Management Communication," *Journal of Applied Psychology*, 42 (1958), 1–9.

Chapter 11

Interpersonal and
Mass Communication

We have told you that we may stop the communication process at any given point in time and arbitrarily designate one person as the source and another person as the receiver. This allows us to look at all communication within the framework of interpersonal communication. However, to do this tends in many cases to distort what is actually occurring in the communication process. Very often a source has to communicate with a great number of people. At other times, and this happens even more frequently, a source may be communicating with one receiver while others are present. And, as we already mentioned, when another person is present this complicates the total communication transaction.

A basic principle of communication theory is that the more people involved, the more difficult it is to describe the communication process, and the more difficult it is for the source to have his intended effect on all his receivers. This is true for two reasons. First, whenever more than two people are involved in a communication transaction, there is potential for multiplication of channels between the individuals involved. As a result, any given individual, whom we can arbitrarily identify as source, has less control over the total communication involved. The second reason for the increasing difficulty in communication as the number of people involved increases is that communication between two people may lead to communication among other people. For example, if person A is the source and he communicates with B, and if other people present are interested in the topic of communication, it is quite likely that B might then communicate with C, C with D, D with E, and so on. This phenomenon is sometimes referred to as the multistep flow of communication. The greater the number of people through which an idea "flows," the greater the likelihood that the idea will become distorted.

The purpose of this chapter is to examine interpersonal communication within the larger societal context. We shall discuss three circumstances in which communication commonly occurs in society and see what relevance interpersonal communication has in each. We shall conclude with a discussion of the role of interpersonal communication within the context of mass communication.

The Small Group

Communication in the small group (we sometimes call it group discussion or conference) is very closely related to interpersonal communication as we have defined it in this book. In fact, communcation in the small group has been considered interpersonal communication by many people, and we have no quarrel with this view. Communication in the small group possesses at least three characteristics common to interpersonal communication. First, it is face-to-face communication. All members of the group are present while any member of the group speaks. Second, communication in the small group is "discontinuous" discourse. By discontinuous discourse we mean that people speak alternately, no one person in the group does all the speaking nor does any one person normally speak very long at a given time. Third, this type of discourse makes it difficult to identify who is source and who is receiver, because basically all members of the group are both, with their roles constantly shifting.

Because of the interaction during small group communication it is difficult for any single individual to control the effects of the communication. No specific person is the "source" who can manipulate the effects on the "receivers." There is a multiplicity of channels among the various participants, and each of these channels permits influence of one person upon another; however, at the same time each channel potentially serves to inhibit the effect desired by other people. Nevertheless, by virtue of the nature of discontinuous discourse in small group communication, it is possible for an individual member to determine the needs of the other members of the group and to adapt to them in such a way as to achieve his intended effect more easily than in circumstances where the discourse is continuous. In short, the response of person C may cause A to have a different effect on B than intended, but C's response permits A to adapt to C's needs and possibly increase his influence on him. It is no accident that most business and professional organizations make extensive use of small group communication in the decision-making process. This type of communication encourages each participant to voice some potentially good ideas, thereby allowing him to bring his influence to bear on the final results.

Communication through Public Address

Public address is one-to-many communication. Although it has one characteristic essential to interpersonal communication, in that it is a face-to-face type of transaction, there are important differences between public address and interpersonal communication. Public address involves continuous discourse. In public address it is easy to distinguish between the source and the receiver—the source is the person doing the talking and all other people present are receivers. Consequently, interaction is severely limited, making it more important for the source to be able to recognize, interpret, and adapt to audience response or feedback. In person-to-person and in small group communication it is possible to begin the transaction without knowing much about the other people involved and still be successful, but in communication through public address much better a priori receiver analysis is required for success. Although some adaptations of the message while communication takes place is possible in public address, the basic message must be prepared before the communication transaction begins. As a result, if the source incorrectly analyzes his receivers, he is likely to develop an inappropriate, and thus ineffective, message.

Another important element in public address is the effect of one receiver on another. As we noted in our discussion of small group communication, there is a potential multiplicity of channels among receivers. The precise effects of one receiver on another in a public address situation are not well known, but the results of a study by Hylton (1968) are highly suggestive. Hylton had a speaker present the same speech to three different audiences. Two of them included people Hylton had planted there. Approximately one-third of each audience, then, consisted of his confederates. In one instance Hylton told them to respond positively to what the speaker was saying, to give him positive feedback. In the other instance, he instructed them to respond negatively. Hylton found that when the confederates gave positive feedback the other audience members perceived the speaker as more credible and they changed their attitudes to be more in line with his. On the other hand, when the feedback given was negative, the other audience members perceived the speaker to be less credible and their attitudes tended to conform less to his recommendations. These results suggest that the effect of one receiver on another receiver may indeed be greater than the effect of the source on the receiver in this kind of communication transaction.

Mediated Communication

Mediated communication is a communication transaction that involves the use of print or electronic media, such as newspapers, magazines, books, radio, television, and film. Mediated communication is distinguishable from normal interpersonal communication in several major respects. First it does not involve a face-to-face transaction. Second, it involves continuous rather than discontinuous discourse. Third, there is a clear-cut source-receiver distinction. Fourth, there is little or no opportunity for immediate observation of receiver response on the part of the source. Thus, mediated communication requires that the source know his receiver in advance in order to prepare an appropriate message for him. If the message is not properly developed, there is no opportunity for on-the-spot adaptation; and, therefore, the message will not have its desired effect.

In mediated communication there may or may not be an opportunity for one receiver to affect another. If I read an editorial in the newspaper and do not discuss it with anyone else, no one else will influence my response to the source's message. However, if I do discuss the source's material with a colleague or a family member, he may influence my response to that editorial. Similarly, if I listen to the radio or watch television or a film, I may do so alone or I may do so in the company of other people. If other people are present, their responses may influence my responses and vice versa. This is clearly recognized by the packagers of television situation comedies. These shows normally carry "canned laughter" on the assumption that if I perceive other people laughing I will find the comedy more humorous and am more likely to respond favorably to it.

As we have noted above, as communication moves from the one-to-one interpersonal transaction through the small group and public address type transactions to the mediated transaction, the complications of the communication process increase sharply. It should come as no surprise, then, that most people recommend that if you wish to influence someone you should talk to him alone. This indeed, from a source's point of view, would be the most efficient communication environment to exert influence. However, it is not always possible for us to talk with whom we wish in a one-to-one setting. In many instances it is important for a source to communicate with literally millions of receivers. This is particularly true when the source is a national political candidate or when the source is a collective entity such as a governmental agency. Any politician will tell you that he would rather talk with every potential voter on a personal level, but obviously this is usually impossible. Similarly, while any upper-level bureaucrat in the Department of Agriculture will tell you that he would prefer to be able to discuss new agricultural techniques with each individual farmer in the nation, he is fully aware that this couldn't possibly be done. It is important, therefore, that we understand how interpersonal communication may be influential in a mass communication environment.

Interpersonal Communication in Mass Communication

Effects of Mediated Communication

Most people assume that if we want to communicate with thousands or millions of people we should employ the mass media. Research on the effects of mass media provides some support for that assumption, but not completely. Briefly summarized, this research suggests that if we merely want to inform people, the mass media are our best bet. But if we wish to influence them, the effect the mass media have apparently is negligible.

Early research by Miller (1945) suggested that the mass media might have only minimal effect even at the informational level. He found that 99 percent of the population learned of the death of President Franklin D. Roosevelt within one and one-half hours after his passing, and that 87 percent of those informed had gotten their information in face-to-face contact with other people. (The same situation prevailed when President John F. Kennedy was assassinated.) Later research, however, suggests that this was an exceptional circumstance. Deutschmann and Danielson (1960), for example, found that 88 percent of the population learned of the flight of Explorer I, President Eisenhower's first stroke, and Alaska's admission to statehood through the mass media. This and similar research taken collectively suggests that, except in cases of extremely shocking news events, most people learn of news events through the mass media.

This is not to suggest, however, that we get all our information through the mass media. Obviously, much of the information we obtain is not even presented by the mass media because it is not considered sufficiently newsworthy for broadcast or print. But the research does suggest that if something does appear in the mass media, that is where most people are most likely to become informed about it. This of course applies to the United States and other fairly highly developed countries. Naturally, in a country which has a high illiteracy rate and which is less developed technologically—where there is no television or film, and where there are only a few radios—the mass media have a more limited effect.

The research on the effect of the mass media on attitude or behavioral change is more consistent. The researchers have been unable to find that the mass media had a great effect on people (Berelson, Lazarsfeld, and McPhee, 1954; Katz and Lazarsfeld, 1955). In each of these major studies the influence on people's attitudes and beliefs could best be attributed to their interaction on a face-to-face level with other people.

Diffusion of Innovations

A major conclusion that we can draw from the research on the effects of the mass media is that if we wish to influence large numbers of people we must be able to influence the interpersonal communication in which they are involved. An area of communication research, often referred to as the "diffusion of innovations" area, provides us with considerable information on how we can communicate effectively with large numbers of people through interpersonal communication (Rogers, 1962). Although most of this research has been with the diffusion and acceptance of new products or procedures, the results should apply equally well to the diffusion of new ideas.

The findings from this research indicate that where the mass media are involved at all their effect is attributable to the media's influence on person A, who then communicates with B, who in turn communicates with C, and so on. This multistep flow appears to be common in all societies. However, the mass media are often not even present in the process. Essential to diffusion of innovations is the concept of the "change agent," namely the person who is responsible for introducing change within a society. The change may be the adoption of something totally new, or it may be a change from present procedures to new procedures. Professional people normally are exchange agents, by definition. They are employed in their society to produce change. They are, therefore, innovators. This sets them apart, in many cases, from the rest of their society. This distance between the change agent as source and his prospective receivers is extremely crucial.

To better understand the implications of the social distance between change agent and receiver, it is important that we consider the principles of heterophily and homophily. Figure 11.1 illustrates these principles. Heterophily may be said to be the degree of difference on any attribute or group of attributes between a source and a receiver. Homophily is the reverse, the degree of similarity on any attribute or group of attributes. A change agent is normally heterophilous with his receivers. His educational level, social level, and economic level, are normally quite different from the receivers. The homophily principle suggests that, given a choice, we tend to interact with people most like ourselves and that heterophilous communication is normally ineffective. If we examine Fig. 11.1 we see that source A and receiver A are homophilous. We would expect these two individuals, when given free choice, to choose to interact with each other and that interaction should be quite successful. But when source A communicates with receiver

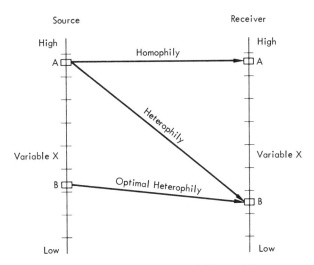

Figure 11.1 Heterophily and Homophily

B there is an heterophilous state. They would not normally seek to communicate with each other and, if such a communication transaction did take place, it would most likely be ineffective. An example of this type of heterophilous communication situation is the white Anglo-Saxon Protestant teacher in the black ghetto school. The source, the teacher, and the receivers, the students, have very little in common and we would expect that the communication between them would be difficult and probably ineffective. Similarly, the minister of agriculture in a developing country would be heterophilous with the native peasant farmers. If he would attempt to communicate with them, such communication would not only be difficult but ineffective as well.

On the surface, then, it would appear that homophilous communication is always to be preferred to heterophilous communication. This, however, is not quite correct. Purely homophilous communication is probably not possible because no source and receiver are ever perfectly alike. In addition, there must be some heterophily present for one person even to desire to change the behavior of another. The question thus becomes how much heterophily is desirable. There is no absolute scale for this, but the concept of "optimal" heterophily is important. Optimal heterophily is present when the source has only slightly more of attribute X than does his receiver, such as the case in Fig. 11.1 when source B communicates with receiver B. The implications of optimal herterophily for interpersonal communication in mass communication are large. To establish optimal heterophily, the major change agent normally will be unable to communicate with the ultimate receiver. Rather, he must employ intermediaries to conduct these communication transactions. These intermediaries will be more homophilous with the receivers than the change agent is with the receivers. The people most useful as intermediaries are those referred to as "opinion leaders." Opinion leaders tend to be much like their followers, but usually adopt new ideas somewhat more rapidly. Opinion leaders are often difficult to identify. But by definition they are the people to whom others turn for advice. For example, in a rural agricultural society the opinion leaders are normally the leaders of the village. At an even smaller level, a specific person may be the opinion leader because he happens to have his home or farm at a crossroad where he comes in contact with many passersby. In other circumstances, society creates its opinion leaders. For instance, nurses' aides and teachers' aides are "created" opinion leaders, employed as intermediaries between the hospital staff and the patient, or the teaching staff and the students. When utilized effectively, these intermediaries can greatly increase the impact of the professional change agents.

The change agent, then, must seek opinion leaders as intermediaries who will be influential on the ultimate receivers. Two common errors, however, are made by change agents. Since they, like others, seek to communicate with people who are homophilous with them, they may choose as an opinion leader a person much like themselves. This person may also be too heterophilous with the receiver to have much of an impact. But even when a suitable opinion leader has been chosen as intermediary, the change agent may inadvertently destroy the intermediary's effectiveness. When this occurs, it has been referred to as the "dhoti effect." We shall explain.

A certain project in Pakistan was producing substantial change in rural villages on the outskirts of a major city. Once a week the village leaders were being brought into the city for a discussion of new ideas. When they returned to their villages they communicated these ideas to the other villagers. In this particular part of Pakistan the weather is extremely warm, so naturally the wearing apparel of the natives is rather abbreviated; men wear a diaper-like piece of apparel called a dhoti. As a mark of status, people holding nonmenial jobs tend to wear their dhoties long; and the more elite members of the society wear them knee length. But the peasants wear theirs very short; otherwise the garments would get dirty in the fields.

After a while the people in the Pakistan project noted that fewer and fewer of the changes that they desired were being implemented. Later the reason for this became clear. The village leaders had unconsciously become more and more like the change agents with whom they worked. And they had gradually lowered their dhoties. This tended to set them apart from the other villagers and reduce their impact on them. This case has been facetiously referred to as the "case of the drooping dhoti." The important principle that we can draw from this example is that communication with a change agent may make an intermediary more like the change agent and therefore less effective in introducing change among the people who were his followers.

A review of the research on diffusion of innovations provides bases for several propositions concerning homophily-heterophily, all of which have an important bearing on the process of interpersonal communication (Rogers and Bhowmik, 1969; Rogers and Svenning, 1969). Some of these are enumerated below.

1. *Communication patterns are mostly homophilous.* People tend to communicate most with people with whom they share demographic and sociological characteristics. Young people communicate most with young people. Poor people communicate

most with poor people. Home owners communicate most with home owners.

2. *More effective communication occurs when source and receiver are homophilous.* The more nearly alike the people in a communication transaction, the more likely they will share meanings. Homophilous individuals will not only share a common language, but the words chosen will stimulate similar meanings in both source and receiver. Teenagers communicate best with teenagers. Mechanics communicate best with mechanics. Biology professors communicate best with biology professors.

3. *Effective communication between source and receiver leads to greater homophily in knowledge, beliefs, and overt behavior.* Homophily and effective communication are parts of a perpetual cycle. Homophily produces effective communication, and effective communication produces homophily. Asking which comes first is like asking which came first, the chicken or the egg. Each is dependent on the other.

4. *Desired change through communication is most easily achieved when source and receiver possess optimal heterophily in subject matter competence.* When two people believe that each is equally competent on a given subject, there is little likelihood of change in either person regarding that subject. Also, when two people are aware of a great difference in competence between them on a subject, little change in either individual should be expected. The more competent will feel he has little to learn from the other person and will tend to discount his opinions. The person who is less competent is usually suspicious of the more competent and, in addition, has difficulty comprehending what is said. Moderate differences in subject matter competence that are recognized by the communicators lead to the most efficient achievement of change. Such differences are optimal in that they are large enough for the receiver to accept the competence of the source and yet they are sufficiently similar so that suspicious reactions or difficulty in comprehension are not likely to intrude.

5. *Heterophilous communication is more likely to be effective if the source has a high degree of empathy with the receiver.* Empathy is the ability of an individual to visualize himself in the role of another person. When the source has empathy with the

receiver, he is better able to select messages that will have the desired effect on the receiver because he will have a better understanding of the receiver. As we have noted previously, the better adapted a message is for a receiver, the more likely it will have its desired effect.

6. *Heterophilous communication is more effective when the source has greater empathy than the receiver.* If the receiver has high empathy with the source, he may perceive the intent of the source and react accordingly. Since most communication transactions are influence-oriented, and since few receivers consciously desire to be influenced, this type of circumstance is not conducive to effective communication.

7. *If a source lacks information about his receivers, who are heterophilous from him, the source assumes they are homophilous, or should be, and thus communication is ineffective.* We all see the world through the eyes of our own beliefs, attitudes, and experiences. When we do not have information to the contrary, our tendency is to assume that these beliefs, attitudes, and experiences are shared by other people. When this is not the case, when heterophily is present, such assumptions lead to poor selection and adaptation of messages, hence ineffective communication.

8. *Heterophilous communication is more effective when the source attends to feedback from his receivers.* Feedback facilitates empathy. When feedback is unavailable or ignored, heterophilous communication proceeds along its normal, ineffective course unless empathy is present anyway. One of the most common causes of communication failure in business organizations is that feedback from lower-level employees is ignored or discouraged by upper-level employees. Heterophily exists in the first place, and a primary means by which it could be reduced is ignored.

You will realize that although we have tried to cover a large area in this chapter, we have barely scratched the surface. The essence of what we have said is that engaging in interpersonal communication is the primary means by which we can influence people. And even if we wish to influence many people we must continue to do so at the interpersonal communication level. Obviously, there is much more to mass communication and diffusions of innovations than what we have been able to include in this chapter. Our brief discussion was intended merely to serve as an introduction to interpersonal communication in these areas. As a student interested in this subject, you will undoubtedly take further course work and read other books that consider the material we have discussed here in much greater detail. We believe you will enjoy the experience and profit from it as well.

References

Berelson, B., P. L. Lazarsfeld, and W. N. McPhee, *Voting: A Study of Opinion Formation in a Presidential Campaign*. Chicago; University of Chicago Press, 1954.

Deutschmann, P. J., and W. A. Danielson, "Diffusion of Knowledge of the Major News Story," *Journalism Quarterly*, 37 (1960), 345–55.

Hylton, C. G., "The Effects of Observable Audience Response on Attitude Change and Source Credibility." Unpublished doctoral dissertation, Michigan State University, 1968.

Katz, E., and P. F. Lazarsfeld, *Personal Influence*. Glencoe, Ill.: Free Press of Glencoe, 1955.

Miller, D. C., "A Research Note on Mass Communication," *American Sociological Review*, 10 (1945), 691–94.

Rogers, E. M., *The Diffusion of Innovation*. New York: The Free Press, 1962.

Rogers, E. M., and D. K. Bhowmik, "Homophily-Heterophily: Relational Concepts for Communication Research." Paper presented at the Association for Education in Journalism, Berkeley, California, 1969.

Rogers, E. M., and Lynne Svenning, *Modernization Among Peasants: The Impact of Communication*. New York: Holt, Rinehart & Winston, Inc., 1969.

Author Index

Subject Index